The Christian
in an
Age of Terror

The Christian
in an
Age of Terror

Selected sermons of Dr Martyn Lloyd-Jones
1941–1950

edited by
Dr Michael Eaton

Kregel
Academic & Professional

The Christian in an Age of Terror:
Selected Sermons of Dr Martyn Lloyd-Jones 1941–1950

Copyright © Elizabeth Catherwood and Ann Beatt

Published by Kregel Publications, a division of Kregel, Inc.,
P.O. Box 2607
Grand Rapids
MI 49501

Published with permission of New Wine Ministries, West Sussex, United Kingdom.

Scripture quotations are taken from the King James version of the Bible.

ISBN 978-0-8254-2979-8

Printed in the United States of America

08 09 10 11 12 / 5 4 3 2 1

Contents

PART 4: *A Preview of History*

PART 5: *Paul's Order of the Day*

PART 6: *"Except the LORD Build the House..."*

Editor's Preface

The sermons of Dr Lloyd-Jones which I present here to a wider audience were preached at Westminster Chapel at a time when the nations of Europe were engaged in or were just recovering from very fierce conflicts. Dr Lloyd-Jones and George Campbell Morgan used to alternate their times for preaching. First Campbell Morgan would preach for a month in the morning and Lloyd-Jones in the evening. Then they would reverse the procedure. This is one reason why the sermon series of this time often consisted of four or five messages. In August 1941 Lloyd-Jones was very conscious of the dangers facing the church in Germany with the possibility that the same troubles might soon face England. He spent five Sunday mornings speaking on the danger of persecution and how it should be viewed. Four months later he was again preaching in the mornings and chose to preach a word of encouragement by way of bringing the people of Westminster to the great truths of the gospel. For a month he preached on Hebrews 1:1–3 on Sunday mornings.

The following August he was preaching during the morning services again and felt what was needed was to be found in Paul's exhortations in 1 Corinthians 16:13–14. Five sermons focused on each of the commands: *"Watch ye, stand fast in the faith, quit you like men, be strong. Let all your things be done with charity."*

By April 1944 the Second World War had been going on for more than four years. Raymond Swing – a popular American commentator on current affairs – had written a book entitled *A Preview of History* and many were wondering what would be the course of history in the next few years. As he often did, Lloyd-Jones chose to relate his preaching to this sense of anxiety about the future and the result was a short series of sermons on "A Preview of History" based on texts from Revelation 4 and 5.

By 1947 the war had come to an end and the "the doctor"[1] was embarking on the procedure of building up the congregation by a series of expository sermons. Campbell Morgan was no longer alive. One of the series of sermons at this time was entitled *What Is a Christian?* It was based on texts from Romans 8.

One other sermon from this period is of interest. The first Sunday in 1950 was the end of the first half of the twentieth century. Dr Lloyd-Jones used to encourage his people to take note of anniversaries and turning points in the years, and so a single sermon was preached on this theme at the beginning of the year and half-way through the century.

The five sets of sermons, plus one more from 1950, in many ways all belong together. They all show us "the doctor" at a time in his ministry when he was eager to build up the church at Westminster. Many members had been scattered during the war years and in 1945 Lloyd-Jones was conscious that he was virtually starting to build a church from small beginnings. Together these sermons give a picture of a preacher who is conscious that he is in the midst of a crucial time in history and he is speaking into that situation.

Since the rise of "terror" in the early twenty-first century, these sermons have become startlingly relevant, more than ever before, to what is happening in our own times. They should perhaps be read in a slightly different order from the one in which they were preached. *The Christian Facing Danger* is perhaps the new title that might be given to the sermons on Acts 12. What is the remedy for the Christian at such a time? First Dr Lloyd-Jones would have begun with our general knowledge and experience of the Christian faith. So *A Summary of the Gospel* comes in at this point. It leads to the question *What Is a Christian?* Then we might want to ask the question, *Where Is History Going?* The exhortation should surely come at the end. *A Word of Exhortation* from the apostle is what is needed after we have considered these great themes. But one more

---

1. Dr Lloyd-Jones was widely and affectionately known as "the doctor"; as a teenager I knew of no other way of referring to him. Even Mrs Lloyd-Jones used to refer to her husband as "the doctor".

message is strikingly relevant. We end with a word of soberness: *"Except the LORD build the house, they labour in vain that build it"* (Psalm 128:1).

The editorial work that has been done on these sermons is very minimal. I have left in the contemporary references and the preacher's style. The "improvements" I allowed myself were mainly matters of punctuation (as compared to the original printed versions of these sermons in the *Westminster Records*) and the removal of a few minor blemishes. The rest remains as close to Dr Lloyd-Jones' very words as possible. His introductions, in which he summarizes what he said on previous Sundays, are not needed in the printed version and so the opening remarks are abridged.

These messages of Dr Lloyd-Jones are not only very relevant for our times, they are also models of what preaching should be. They interpret and expound some passages of Scripture, but it will be noted they are not *mere* expositions. Even less are they simply Bible-survey or Bible-analysis. Dr Lloyd-Jones did not think that giving Bible surveys was "preaching" at all! These sermons are highly *applied* "expository sermons". They do not merely interpret the text; they also draw out its message. But they do not merely draw out the message; they press the message upon the people. This is what surely should be the case in all true preaching. Of course there is one other ingredient which cannot be captured on paper. When George Whitefield was asked whether permission could be given for his sermons to be printed he said, "I have no inherent objection ... but you will never be able to put on the printed page the lightning and the thunder."[2] There was "lightning and thunder" in Lloyd-Jones' own preaching at times. It cannot be captured in any medium at all. Even tape-recordings (of which there are thousands) and video-recordings (of which there are none of Dr Lloyd-Jones) cannot capture the sense of power which was often present when Dr Lloyd-Jones preached. The theologian J.I. Packer who went in 1948 as a young Christian to hear Lloyd-Jones said, "I went out full of awe and joy, with a more vivid sense of the greatness of God in my heart than I had known before."[3] I myself

2. D.M. Lloyd-Jones, *Preaching and Preachers* (Hodder & Stoughton, 1971), p. 58.
3. J.I. Packer, Foreword to D.M. Lloyd-Jones, *The Heart of the Gospel* (Crossway, 1991), p. 8.

as a teenage Londoner had much the same experience. I had heard stories about the preaching at Westminster Chapel and one day found my way there when Lloyd-Jones was preaching from Exodus 33 on praying for revival. I can scarcely put into words the impact it had on me. I tried to summarize it the following Sunday at a student prayer meeting on Pembroke Road in Bristol. Its main contents stayed with me for decades until one day I heard a recording of it and welcomed it as an old friend. The printed text cannot convey the power of Lloyd-Jones' preaching. But still the content of the messages will help us to see something of what such preaching should contain. The power must come in another way altogether!

PART 1

The Christian Facing Danger

CHAPTER 1

Religious Persecution

(Acts 12:1–3)

"Now about that time Herod the king stretched forth his hands to vex certain of the church. And he killed James the brother of John with the sword. And because he saw it pleased the Jews, he proceeded further to take Peter also. (Then were the days of unleavened bread.)"

I am planning to consider some of the great lessons that we find confronting us in the twelfth chapter of the Acts of the Apostles. Now it is very important, as we commence our consideration of this chapter, that we should realize that this particular book, the Acts of the Apostles as it is called, is not merely a book of history, but is something else in addition, and that that something else is the more important element of the two. That is, of course, something which we might say not only about this particular book, but about the whole Bible. There is in it that other element, the element of the supernatural, the element of the divine, the influence of the Holy Spirit pervading it. Because of that, this book is altogether different from all others. It is a human book, and yet it is something beyond that. It is a book of history, and yet there is a deeper meaning in its history. It is a book which contains a collection of facts, and yet it is not merely a collection of facts. Anything and everything we might say about any secular book of history is true of this book. But having said that, we must go further and add that in addition to all the lessons and all the advantages which we may derive and obtain from the perusal of any book of history, there is in the Bible that overplus, that something extra to be found which cannot be found anywhere else. This book is, of course, a record of the early Christian church. At the same time it is, in a sense, an epitome of the history of the Christian church throughout the ages.

A very interesting question which might be discussed in any place where men and women are concerned about the problems of life is, "What is the exact value of history? Does history repeat itself? Is it possible for you to study any one period of history, and as a result of your understanding of that period to forecast and prophesy what is likely to happen in any other period?" That is a question which has engaged the attention of the philosophers many a time, and is of interest also to the historians. There is a sense in which it is true to say that history does repeat itself. Human nature being what it is, there are certain qualities which persist and remain, and because of that men and women are likely to do certain things in similar conditions and circumstances. But at the same time it is obviously true that history does not repeat itself exactly. There are variations and changes and differences. But when you come to the history of the church there is a new factor, an entirely new principle, because the church is a spiritual association. The church is, in a sense, an unworldly, supernatural society and organization. It is true to say of the church that her history at any one period is indeed her history in any other period. I mean by that, that if you read this Book of the Acts, I think you will have a complete history the church. There is nothing that has happened in the subsequent history of the church that is not recorded in embryo in this book. There are people there who do the things that we do, and whose actions are more or less identical with our own. That is why I say that the Book of the Acts is not only a history of the early Christian church, but is a history of the church at all times and in all places. You get every one of the features of church life in this book. You get the dullness of the people, the quarrels and the mistakes, the persecutions and the rivalries. There is nothing which has happened since but that you get it in embryo here, because of the peculiar nature of the church. We have before us in miniature, as it were, in this amazing book what has been repeating itself ever since all down the running centuries. That is why it is true to say that any revival of religion is nothing but a return to this Book of the Acts. Any great religious awakening is just a return to this pattern and standard. You see here the constant change of emphasis, first upon doctrine, and then upon practice. There has always been this conflict between the emphasis on doctrine and on practice. In some ages it has all been a matter of doctrine, while in other ages doctrine has been almost ignored, and the whole emphasis has been placed upon practice. So the Book of Acts is not only a history of the early church; it is also a kind of epitome of the entire subsequent history of this great institution.

Now this twelfth chapter deals with just one great aspect of the life of the church, and that is, the church face to face with persecution, the church face to face with the world, the church combating and fighting the great enemy who is always set over against it. That is why I say that it is important that we should grasp the philosophy of this book. For what is given us in this chapter is a perfect representation of every era and period of persecution through which the church has ever passed. If you study the history of the church you will find that she has gone through periods of terrible trial and persecution. Suddenly persecution breaks out. Then it seems to expend itself, and the church has a period of comparative quiet and calm. Then again there is another outburst of violent persecution. Again it disappears, and there follows a period of rest. That has always been the characteristic history of the Christian church, exactly as you find it here. But what is of vital importance is that we should realize that the principles that govern this whole matter are laid down once and for all in this twelfth chapter of the Book of the Acts of the apostles. Here we find the various emphases. Here is the exact delineation of all the aspects of the warfare. Above all, here we are told in a very clear and explicit manner what the church has to do, and how she is to comport herself in order to emerge in a triumphant manner.

Now we are interested in this matter today, because there can be no doubt at all but that we are living at a time when we are witnessing one of those acute periods of this spirit of persecution of the church. We might, indeed, spend our whole time, by way of introduction, in studying the terrible facts concerning the religious persecution which is taking place on the continent of Europe at the present time [under the Nazi regime], and which has been proceeding now for a number of years. It is one of the disadvantages of Britain's insularity as a nation and people that we have not seen these things at first hand. We thank God for our liberty, and for the freedom that we enjoy of worshipping God, but I wonder whether at times it does not leave us in a state of complacency, and often of utter forgetfulness of those various lands elsewhere where people have endured things that match perfectly the account which is given us in this chapter of the persecution of the infant Christian church. You are aware of the terrible things that took place in Germany [in the 1930s and early 1940s], and formerly in Russia [in the days of Stalin]. I believe it is one of our duties as Christian people to acquaint ourselves with things like these, were it only that we might pray intelligently, and that we might play our part rightly as members of the Christian church who know something about the ministry of intercession and who feel for their brethren. Indeed, perhaps more urgently, we ought to consider this matter because we ourselves may one day be faced with the exact and selfsame thing. We do not attempt to prophesy, or to predict the future, but there are times when I believe we may have a period of religious persecution in our own land though not, perhaps, in the exact militant form in which they had it in Nazi Germany, and in other lands. But certainly there is a great danger that a spirit of materialism may sweep over this land of ours, and that Christian faith from being patronized and often ignored will be actively opposed. It is well therefore that we should prepare ourselves, and that we should acquaint ourselves with the nature of this spiritual warfare. But over and above all that, there is no greater tonic than to look objectively for a while at the conflict as it is depicted here. We see the enemy in his arrogance and the weak infant church. We follow the conflict through its various stages and see the ultimate triumph. This is a principle which applies not only in the life of the church, but equally in the life of the individual. What happens to the church collectively can happen to us individually and one by one. For we are all face to face with the same enemy, and we can emerge as triumphantly as the church did on this occasion which is recorded for us in this twelfth chapter of the Book of the Acts.

All I want at the moment is to look at the beginning of the story, and perhaps we can best do that by considering the two main characters, King Herod, and the apostle Peter.

Herod

Herod forever typifies antagonism to the church and the spirit of persecution. I wonder whether it has ever occurred to you that a perfect description is given in this chapter of certain contemporary personalities. Can you imagine a more perfect picture of a certain man – Hitler – than that which is given of Herod in this chapter? Does this not prove my contention that this is not only a story of the early church, but a story of the church at all times? Is Herod here not a perfect description of Hitler? Don't you see in his very appearance, and in all his characteristics and actions the selfsame man? And if we took the time this morning to go through the history of the church down the ages we would find that equally is it applicable to many another tyrant who has stretched forth his hand against the church. There is no originality about sin. These men all repeat the actions of one another; they all follow a pattern. They are all but the instruments used by the same fiendish, devilish power. There is a kind of mechanical sameness about their actions.

There are certain things which ought to engage our attention very specially. Observe **the arrogance of Herod**, the bombast, the pride. He "stretched forth his hands to vex certain of the church". The whole demeanour and attitude of the man are characterized by pride and arrogance. See him later on in the chapter, clothed in his gorgeous apparel, and delivering his oration to the admiring throng, who cried out in their stupidity and ignorance, "It is the voice of a god, and not of a man." What a typical picture of the power of evil, that worldly power that is ever raised against God, and against his church. I can never understand the attitude of those who say they do not believe in the inspiration of the Bible. Surely this very thing should convince us once and forever that this is no ordinary book. Here is a perfect description of contemporary history down to the very minutest detail. There is only one explanation for that. It is that we live in a spiritual universe where God is present. These factors work themselves out throughout the ages along certain definite lines. That is the first thing we notice here.

The next thing we notice is that **there seems to be no reason for this action of Herod**. He seems suddenly to have decided to persecute the church. We read that "because he saw it pleased the Jews, he proceeded further to take Peter also". He had already killed James, and finding that it was in accord with the whims of the people, he decided to go a step further. There is something quite irrational and unreasonable in his actions. We might well develop that as a principle. The sinful life is always an unreasonable life. Sin is always something that is based upon passion. Sin can give no explanation of what it does. That was seen on a large scale in the events which took place in Germany in the 1930s. It is just a desire to gratify a lust for power. Let us not imagine that this is something which is only true in the national and international spheres of life. It is the selfsame thing that explains sin in individuals. It is the desire to possess something that belongs to another, the desire for power. That is the explanation of some of the commonest sins of individuals at this present hour. It is always a characteristic of the anti-God spirit.

Another thing which characterized this man was this: **his supreme desire was to set himself up as God**. That was the objective in the last analysis. These people who came fawning to him, and who cried, "It is the voice of a god," knew exactly what pleased him. He desired that the people should regard him as a god, and should bow the knee to him. It always ends there when a man begins to travel along the road of self-glorification. That is something which has been evident in the modern world. The man who ceases to believe in God tries to deify himself. This is an age when we have believed in the endless possibilities of man.

Yet at the same time there is something ludicrous, and almost ridiculous in what we are told here about this arrogant, proud and boastful creature, who sets himself up as God, and who seems to be so independent of man. He feels he can govern the whole of mankind, yet observe **how sensitive he is to public approval and applause**. It was because "he saw that it pleased the Jews" that he proceeded to arrest Peter. Apply that again to the individual. It is still true of all men who seem to be governing everyone else. This apparent independence is merely on the surface. Those who ally themselves with the forces which are inimical to God are always the slaves of their own vanity and pride.

There, in mere outline, is a picture of the power that raised itself against the church. It is characterized by the worship of man, mighty power, arrogance and pride. It attacked the infant church which consisted of a mere handful of people. That is the background of the story.

Peter

Now look for a moment at the other character, the apostle Peter. There are one or two things that I want to say about him, and they are to be found in those words in brackets in verse 3: *"Then were the days of unleavened bread."* I do not know if you realize that those are very important words. Here again, we are given a reminder of the unique character of the nature of Scripture. There are two ways of interpreting Scripture. One is what you may call the exact method. The other is what you may call the imaginative method, and it is vitally important that we should employ both methods. Interpret these words by the exact method, and you will say that they mean this. Luke, the punctilious historian, must let us know that the precise time when this man was put into prison happened to be during "the days of unleavened bread". That is perfectly true. Or you may say that Luke, the very clever writer, gives you a little hint at the beginning of the story that had it not been during "the days of unleavened bread" King Herod would not only have taken Peter, but would immediately have killed him also. He could not do so because it was one of the laws of the Jews that no one should he put to death at that particular time. So here Luke, by writing these words, gives us the secret of how that which subsequently came to pass became possible at all. That is what you might call the exact interpretation, the statement of fact. But the moment you make use of the imaginative method other vistas open up immediately. Surely there is a very profound spiritual meaning in these words. Peter is arrested. He is placed in prison and we read, *"Then were the days of unleavened bread."* Does that convey nothing to us? Whatever it may mean to us, we can be very certain that it meant a great deal to the apostle Peter as he sat in that prison. Shall I read his mind? Shall I tell you what happened in that cell? "Oh, yes," says Peter to himself, "it was during the days of unleavened bread that Jesus of Nazareth was arrested" – Jesus, Peter's Saviour and Lord. These words in brackets, therefore, tell us three things.

The first is: **the servant is not greater than his Lord**. "If they have called the master of the house Beelzebub, how much more shall they call them of his household" (Matthew 10:25). "If they have persecuted me," said Christ, "they will also persecute you." Peter is arrested and placed in prison. Peter remembers that his blessed Lord had been arrested and put into prison at this very same time. In chapters 13 to 16 of John's Gospel, we see how our Lord seems to go out of his way to prepare his disciples for this very thing. He seems to lay down the principle that the extent to which we are persecuted is the measure of our discipleship. He says, "You cannot be my disciple without the world hating you. If they have hated me, they will hate you also." I commend to you the reading of those chapters of John's Gospel, keeping your eye on that very thing. You remember how the apostle Paul puts it: "All that will live godly in Christ Jesus shall suffer persecution" (2 Timothy 3:12). It does not mean that we have to be peculiar, or odd people. But the fact is that the saints of God have always been persecuted. Their lives have been a rebuke to the godless and their deportment has called forth enmity. The servant must reflect his Master.

The second principle is: **that we should always be careful to avoid sin**. Just sit there for a moment with Peter. Can you not imagine his feelings as he sat there, the prisoner of Herod, in the days of unleavened bread? His mind must have gone back to those other days when his blessed Lord had been arrested and he had denied Him. He had cursed; he had sworn. "I do not know Him," he had said. It all came back to him. Yes, sin reminds us of itself. But that does not mean that we are condemned. Surely every Christian looking back across his life feels the sin and the sorrow and the grief of certain things that he has done, even perhaps before he became a Christian. Do not blot the page! Believe in Christ. Be careful about your life and conduct. Something you may do now may cause you sorrow and misery in years to come. Those "days of unleavened bread" brought back to Peter the memory of his own failure and denial.

But we can go a step further. We must emphasize **the remarkable change in Peter**. On the former occasion, during "the days of un-leavened bread", he failed completely. He denied his Master and Lord.

He was so afraid of being arrested that he denied his Lord with oaths and cursing. But now what a marvellous change! What a different picture we find in this chapter! We find that he is himself arrested and in prison, and rejoices in it. There is a lesson that we can all take to ourselves. We may have failed Him, but He is prepared to forgive us. The twenty-first chapter of John's Gospel and Acts chapter 2 stand between the four-teenth chapter of Mark's Gospel, with the story of Peter's denial and weeping, and this twelfth chapter of the Book of the Acts. We may have failed, but if we repent we shall be forgiven and, still more wonderful, restored, and put again into the same position where we can vindicate our faith, and prove our loyalty.

There is the picture! The arrogant enemy, mighty and strong. The apostle of the Lord in his prison cell. But already we have seen another factor entering in, for the man in the prison who was once a failure and a weakling, is now a new man as the result of the grace of God.

CHAPTER 2

The Nature of the Conflict

(Acts 12:4 – 5)

"And when he had apprehended him, he put him in prison, and delivered him to four quaternions of soldiers to keep him; intending after Easter to bring him forth to the people. Peter therefore was kept in prison: but prayer was made without ceasing of the church unto God for him."

As we consider again Acts chapter 12, the first subject at which we must look again is this whole question of trials and tribulations.

Why persecution?

A question which must surely present itself to our minds is this. Why should the church ever be persecuted at all? Is there not something surprising and astonishing about the very fact of the persecution of Christians? If the church were a military or political power which might endanger the safety or the future of some such rival power we could understand the spirit of antagonism towards her. But the fact is that the church, apart from certain phases in the history of the Roman Catholic church, cannot be so described. She is a spiritual society which in no way competes directly with world authorities and powers.

These early Christians were law-abiding and peaceful citizens. They in no way threatened either the dynasty of King Herod or the Roman imperial power; and yet we find Herod at this point persecuting the church, and, later, the Roman Empire doing the same thing. What is the explanation? There can be but one true and satisfactory answer. The church, with its call to an ultimate and absolute allegiance to God,

23

challenges the totalitarian demands of the state. She points to a higher authority, and this always touches and offends the pride of rival rulers and governors.

Not only so, but the church by her life and her teaching **is the condemnation of everything that is worshipped and prized most highly by the world**. As the apostle Paul puts it, "The carnal mind is enmity against God." It manifests its enmity by hating those who are most loyal to God and who conform most closely to His dictates and commandments. No one called forth to such an extent the antagonism, the hatred, and the persecuting spirit of the world as our Lord and Saviour Jesus Christ Himself. The world, often unconsciously, recognizes in Him its greatest enemy. The accounts of the temptation in the wilderness show clearly that Satan realized that he was fighting for his life and for his whole dominion and power when he came face to face with Christ. It is because the church, when she is truly the church, continues thus to challenge the empire and power of darkness that she is persecuted by such powers.

In other words, the trials and tribulations and persecutions are **a sure proof that the church is really representing her Lord and Master**. That is why trials and tribulations come. As our Lord once said, "It must needs be that offences come" (Matthew 18:7).

With regard to the nature of such trials, we are reminded here that they may vary from slight personal insults and petty annoyances to an extreme and excess of wrath and violence. Persecution may be subtle and underhanded or it may express itself openly and without shame. There is no limit to what it may do or to the form which it may happen to take. In Germany in recent years [the period of the 1930s] we have seen it in its violent form, but any true Christian will be able to testify to its occurrence in the more concealed and subtle forms.

The character of the church

The next big subject which is dealt with in these two verses is that of the church itself. We are told here at least three things about the church. The first is **the nature of the church**. We find that Peter alone was put in prison, but it is made abundantly clear that Peter did not suffer alone; the whole church suffered with him. We find later on in the chapter that even in the middle of the night the members of the church were not only awake and thinking about him, but were engaged in prayer on his behalf. We are reminded thus of the essential unity of the church and further that the unity is an organic unity. When one suffers, all suffer.

This truth concerning the nature of the church is expounded perhaps most perfectly of all in 1 Corinthians, chapter 12, where Paul compares the church to the human body. Because of the organic nature of the union of the various parts of the body, because of their intimate vital connection in the matter of nerves and blood supply, it follows that no one unit can suffer without the whole suffering. "None of us liveth to himself, and no man dieth unto himself" (Romans 14:7).

Now this comes to us not only as a revelation of the truth concerning the nature of the church, but also as a question, and perhaps also as a rebuke. To what extent have we in the safety and seclusion of this country been aware of the suffering and the tribulation of our brethren in foreign lands on the continent of Europe [and elsewhere] during the past years? Have we made it our business to read about these things, to discover all we can about them, and have we felt that the suffering of our brethren is our suffering? The church, according to the New Testament, is not so much international as supranational. We all belong to the one same spiritual body and when we function truly as members of this body it becomes impossible for us to be content to enjoy our own Christian life within our own narrow circle without taking any thought for those outside that circle who are suffering. We need to be reminded of the exhortation which tells us, "Remember them that are in bonds, as bound with them; and which suffer adversity, as being yourselves also in the body" (Hebrews 13:3).

Secondly, **we are reminded of the weapons of the church**. The enemy, as we have seen, is mighty and strong. He commands soldiers and battalions, and has swords and weapons. But the picture presented by the church is entirely different. She knows nothing of such weapons; she cannot call upon any big battalions to defend her. She fights not with the sword but rather, as the apostle Paul put it, "the weapons of our warfare are not carnal, but mighty through God to the pulling down of strongholds" (2 Corinthians 10:4).

The only weapon which the church had on this occasion as she faced the threats and the power of King Herod was the weapon of prayer. Alas, far too often the church has tried to meet the world and its persecuting power with like weapons to those employed by the enemy. She has made alliances with the state and she has tried to strengthen herself in a material sense. She has been slow to discover what David discovered long ago in his fight with Goliath, that she cannot fight in the armour of Saul, but must ever use her own weapons with which she is familiar and which she is meant to use.

The third matter which is indicated with respect to the church is **the duty of the church**. We read here that "prayer was made without ceasing of the church unto God for him". An alternative translation has it "instant and earnest prayer was made of the church unto God for him". The duty of the church, therefore, is to use this her weapon with all her might and constantly. Here again we have to ask ourselves the question whether we have done so. To what extent have we been exercised in this ministry of intercession for those of our brethren who have experienced unspeakable suffering and tortures?

Glimpses of hope

The next matter which demands our attention in these two verses is what I would call glimpses of hope. The picture as we find it so far seems to represent the church as being in an utterly hopeless position. She is small in number, weak and without power. The enemy is mighty and powerful. Yet there are two things in these verses which not only hold out a gleam of hope but presage what ultimately came to pass.

The first is **the special precautions which were taken by Herod** to make sure of Peter's detention. We are told that he delivered him to four quarternions of soldiers to keep him. That means that he delivered him to sixteen soldiers. Later on we find that he took the further precaution of binding him to two soldiers, one on each hand, and in addition placed keepers before the door. If you read superficially you may think that this again is nothing but a mere statement of fact, another example of Luke, the meticulous historian, giving the minutest details in order to make his history perfect. But surely there is something infinitely bigger and deeper in this statement. Why does Herod take all these precautions with such a prisoner? Were Peter a king or some great political or military personage we could understand that, but he is nothing but a fisherman and belongs to a small group of lowly people lacking not only military power, but even social position and status. From the point of view of earthly power the prisoner is contemptible and yet Herod takes all these precautions. What is the explanation? It is to be found in what we read in the fifth chapter of this same Book of Acts. We are told that Peter and the other apostles were put into the common prison, but that during the night the angel of the Lord opened the prison doors and brought them forth. We are given an amusing picture of the high priest and the authorities sending officers to fetch the prisoners from the prison in the morning but returning and saying: "The prison truly found we shut with all safety and the keepers standing without before the doors, but when we had opened, we found no man within." Herod not only knew of that, he could not forget it. With all his power and his great pride and arrogance he pays this mighty tribute to the gospel. It is as if he turned to his subordinates and said, "We must take no risks with this man; he is dangerous. Remember what has happened already. We must make certain that he cannot escape." Thus unconsciously the persecuting tyrant admits that he is face to face with a power greater than himself.

The second gleam of hope is to be found in verse 5, in one word – the word "but". "Peter therefore," we read, "was kept in prison, **but** prayer was made without ceasing for the church unto God for him." Say what you will about the power of the enemy, describe his might and his strength with all your superlatives. But when you have done so, all seems to be cancelled by this phrase introduced by the word "but". Looked at in a purely material and carnal manner, the position seems desperate, indeed, hopeless. But through the darkness there gleams this hope. God is in this matter. God is concerned. God is on the side of the church and that makes all the difference.

CHAPTER 3

God Answering Prayer

(Acts 12:6–10)

*"And when Herod would have brought him forth, the same night
Peter was sleeping between two soldiers, bound with two chains: and
the keepers before the door kept the prison. And, behold, the angel
of the Lord came upon him, and a light shined in the prison: and he
smote Peter on the side, and raised him up, saying, 'Arise up
quickly.' And his chains fell off from his hands. And the angel said
unto him, 'Gird thyself, and bind on thy sandals.' And so he did. And
he saith unto him, 'Cast thy garment about thee, and follow me.'
And he went out, and followed him; and wist not that it was true
which was done by the angel; but thought he saw a vision. When they
were past the first and the second ward, they came unto the iron gate
that leadeth unto the city; which opened to them of his own accord:
and they went out, and passed on through one street; and forthwith
the angel departed from him."*

We have seen the might and power of Herod. We have seen the
weakness of Peter and the infant church. The contest seemed to be
hopelessly unequal. What could such a small body of helpless people do
against these great arrogant powers that were set against them, armed
with swords and every implement of war? But prayer was made unto
God for Peter. So though the picture looked hopeless, it was not really
so. God was there.

Here we find a great change. The whole situation has become entirely
different. Somehow or other, as I come across that word "and" at the
beginning of the sixth verse I feel that the atmosphere has changed. *"And
when Herod would have brought him forth..."* There is a suspicion

there that something is going to take place. At this point God enters in
and everything changes. Hitherto we have looked at men and what they
can, and what they cannot do. Now we are going to observe God in
action. That, after all, is the way of summarizing or epitomizing the
central message of the gospel – God in action. That is what we are going
to find in the verses that we are considering.

Perhaps the best way for us to consider this matter is for us to look at it
in this way. Let us put as a general heading "God answering prayer". We
left off before at that point where the infant church was praying to God.
Now we are going to see God answering prayer. We might divide this
general heading into two sections: (i) how God answers prayer; and
(ii) when God answers prayer.

How God answers prayer

What does this section of verses tell us about how God answers prayer?
First of all, God answered the prayer of this infant church **by giving the
apostle Peter the blessing of sleep**. When Herod was, no doubt, awake,
the same night Peter was sleeping between two soldiers, bound with two
chains. It is very important that we should stop at that point. Were we
asked the question suddenly as to how God answered prayer, we would
no doubt say that prayer was answered when the light shined in the
prison and the angel touched Peter, and the gates of the prison were
flung open. But there was something long before that. That selfsame
night Peter slept between the two soldiers. Let us try to catch the full
significance of that. It is such an important matter, but I can only touch
lightly on it in passing. Let us note some of the general points that are
clearly indicated in this word. Every single word in these verses, it seems
to me, is of great importance. "When Herod would have brought him
forth." When was that? Obviously it was at the end of "the days of
unleavened bread". He was anxious to please the people, but he could
not do it during those days. But now that period had come to an end.
Herod will take action. Peter knew all about it. Peter knew about "the
days of unleavened bread", as did King Herod. There is not the slightest
doubt that when Peter settled himself down to sleep he thought it was to

be his last night on earth, and that the next morning he knew not how early it might happen. King Herod would send his soldiers and Peter would be put to death. Nevertheless, Peter is found soundly asleep. That is how God answers prayer. That is the answer. By granting unto the apostle in prison, who knew that he would be put to death the next morning, the gift of sleep.

This is but one illustration of the many promises that are to be found both in the Old and in the New Testaments. Think of the third and fourth psalms. They are perfect introductions to the subject we are considering. Do you remember how the psalmist puts it? "I laid me down and slept; I awaked; for the LORD sustained me" (Psalm 3:5). "I will both lay me down in peace, and sleep: for thou, LORD, only makest me dwell in safety" (Psalm 4:8). The significance is obvious. It is one thing to lay yourself down, but what a different thing it is to sleep! And especially when, as the psalmist says, you are surrounded by enemies. In both psalms the writer says that enemies are risen up against him, these evil men who loved lying, and who are opposed to him and determined to destroy him. Yet he says, "I will both lay me down in peace and sleep." Why? Because the Lord sustained him. You find it everywhere. You remember that word in Psalm 127:2: "He giveth his beloved sleep", or "He gives to his beloved in sleep". Both are right. He also blesses His beloved when they are sleeping. You remember the promise of our Lord Himself: "My peace I give unto you. Not as the world giveth, give I unto you. Let not your heart be troubled neither let it be afraid." You remember how the apostle Paul puts it in the fourth chapter of the epistle to the Philippians, where he tells us to take our troubles to God in prayer, and the result will be that the peace of God shall garrison our hearts and minds through Christ Jesus. That, I say, is the first part of the answer to prayer.

I must just call attention to the amazing difference in this man Peter. You remember there was a time in his life when he was very much awake and afraid of death, and when in that hour of lying and cursing he denied his Lord. But here he is face to face with his own death, chained on the right hand and on the left to soldiers. But God giveth to His beloved sleep. This is a truth which is wondrously and amazingly true in the entire history of the Christian church during times of persecution and trial. There is nothing that stands out so gloriously in the life and conduct of the martyrs and the confessors. You read those stories and legends of the early Christians thrown into the arena to the lions, with a smile upon their faces, thanking God that they were counted worthy to suffer for His Name. You read the story of the martyrs and confessors all down the ages. It is but a repetition of this same thing: the ability to sleep even on the very last night of their life here on earth. They have to be roused the next morning to go to the place of execution. You come down to the Protestant Reformation and you think of Latimer, and Ridley[4] and others standing at the stake. You look at them. You do not feel sorry for them; rather you feel envious of them. You are sorry for the miserable people who put them to death. They stand there with a grandeur and greatness, with a poise and a balance and a composure, which makes men marvel. It is just God answering prayer. You come down to modern times and you think of Martin Niemöller[5] and the way that man, both in prison and concentration camp, seems to be shining out with the very glory of Christ in his face. And you think of others like him who have been put to death for the sake of their faith in Christ. It is all just a repetition of this selfsame thing. This is God answering prayer. It cannot be explained in any other way. God has promised that He will hearken unto the prayer of His people. He gives His saints who are loyal to Him, and to His cause, this something extra, so that in spite of the machinations of the enemy, they sleep calmly and peacefully the night before their execution. God is true to His promise. He remembers His own. God gives to His people a composure and a calmness which the world at its very worst can never destroy. That is the first answer.

Then we come to the second thing, and we may summarize it by using the very words that are to be found in verse 7. "**A light shined in the prison**." That is the second way in which God answers prayer. Here, again, is something which may well detain us for many sermons and yet I

4. During the reign of "bloody Queen Mary" (1553–1558) the Reformers, Cranmer, Latimer, and Ridley, were burnt to death in the market-place at Oxford, England.
5. Martin Niemöller (1892–1984), Lutheran pastor and political activist born in Lippstadt, Germany.

am anxious just to leave a composite picture in your mind. How full of suggestion it is! It is just another way of saying, "With God nothing is impossible." It does not matter what the situation is. "With God all things are possible." This truth is the very basis of our faith. Someone may say, "Do you believe that what is recorded here actually happened?" I reply, "If I did not believe this I should not believe the gospel, for there I see that God has entered in. I accept the miraculous; I accept the supernatural." The gospel is not a philosophy. It is not merely man's ideas or man's endeavours to reach a certain goal. It is God coming down. If I were to deny the historicity of this record I should have to refuse to accept the whole testimony of the epistles with regard to the person of our Lord and all that has been transmitted to us. Of course it happened! And it has happened many times since. I hope, however, to go a little further into this question of the miraculous element, but I leave it just at this point for the moment. Let us analyse this statement further: "the light shining in the prison". God acts, God comes in and brings deliverance to Peter. Let us look at it in this way.

Consider **the light shining** in the prison. Now light, of course, is ever that which represents God. We read in the first verses of Genesis that God, looking upon the darkness of the world said, "Let there be light." "God is light and in him no darkness at all." He is "the Father of lights, with whom is no variableness, neither shadow of turning". God manifested Himself as light in the burning bush that Moses saw. It is always the same. There was the light that Paul saw on the way to Damascus, that light which suddenly shone forth. What does it mean? It means the light as opposed to the darkness of sin and evil and iniquity, and that is why I find these words so instructive and interesting. We have been looking at the persecution of the infant church and at the power of Herod. We have been looking at those malign forces that were ever opposing the church in her witness. It is nothing but passion and lust let loose. It is nothing but the kingdom of darkness; it is hell. The opposite to all that is the light, the holiness, the purity of God, and the whiteness of eternity. In the hour of affliction we see the contrast between darkness and evil, and the light and holiness of God.

Here surely it also means something else. It means the light as opposed to the darkness of despair and hopelessness. There we see Peter in the cell and a mere handful of people praying for him. All seems to be hopeless; the contest is so unequal. Nothing can be done. We describe that condition as "being in the dark", and not being able to see the light. There was darkness and despair and hopelessness. Suddenly into that there shone the light, the light of God, the light of hope, the light which assures and encourages us. We realize that we are not left to ourselves. In exactly the same way the light denotes that which indicates the way out. There does not seem to be any way out for Peter. Then a light shines and it reveals the way out. It suddenly casts its beams over the dark road and we see a path. Light is that which shows us the way out of what seemed to be an impossible position. Light indicates the way that we must travel when we know not what to do. "A light shined in the prison."

Let us look at it also in this way: "A light shined **in the prison**." I wonder whether that emphasis has been brought out. I am perfectly certain that Luke was definitely led to use these words. Used as they are in this dramatic form they ought to fix the thing once and forever in our minds. "A light shined in the prison." In other words, I come to my original statement, "All things are possible with God." The picture seems utterly hopeless: Peter asleep, chained between two soldiers, other soldiers standing outside the door, which was probably also barred and bolted. The great iron gate shuts up the whole prison from the outside city. Nothing can be done. So we think – when we think only in human terms. But the whole glory of the gospel is that it tells us that God has come in, that nothing is impossible with Him. The whole message of this verse is just this: that it matters not what your situation may be, however dark, however black, however tight your bonds, however imprisoned and fettered you may be, if God wills your deliverance, it can be done, it will be done. Talk as much as you like about your chains and your guard of soldiers. Emphasize the strength of the bars and the bolts; tell me all about the first ward and the second ward, give me the weight of that massive iron gate which prevents your exit from your prison cell out into the city. Tell me all about the thick walls; be as eloquent as you can about the difficulties. It matters not at all! "With God all things are possible." In spite of the seeming hopelessness of the prison, Peter is brought forth. That is the second way in which God answers prayer. "A light shined in the prison." Peter is awakened. He follows the angel and he is left outside the prison gate.

In other words, the third answer which we give to the question, "How does God answer prayer?" is that **He does it in a way and in a manner that surpasses our every expectation and our highest hopes**. Now these words are very significant. Listen to them. "He went out, and followed him: and wist not that it was true which was done by the angel: but thought he saw a vision." The apostle thought he was having some marvellous vision; he did not believe it was a fact.

We read, too, of the reaction of the church when Peter came to them. When Peter knocked, a damsel came, named Rhoda. "And when she knew Peter's voice, she opened not the gate for gladness, but ran in, and told how Peter stood before the gate. And they said unto her, 'Thou art mad.'" This was the praying church. "But she constantly affirmed that it was even so. Then said they, 'It is his angel.'" We have already seen what fine people they were. They had spent the night in praying for Peter and when he comes out of the prison, he finds them still praying. They were men and women of prayer, yet when Peter knocked at the door, they could not believe that it was even he; they thought it was his angel. To them the thing is impossible.

How characteristic that is of God! How typical of God's method of answering prayer! We talk far too much about our faith and about our prayer. If we only concentrated on the power of God! He is much more ready to give than we are to receive. Get hold of that idea. There is a hymn which puts it perfectly:

> Thou art coming to a king
> Large petitions with thee bring.
>
> Come, my soul, thy suit prepare,
> Jesus loves to answer prayer.

Do not confine the possibilities of answers to your prayers. Remind yourself that you are praying to God and that with Him nothing is impossible. Prison cells and wards, chains and iron gates – they are nothing to the God who made the world and sustains everything by His power. He hearkens unto your plea. "Large petitions with thee bring"! You can never ask Him for too much. He is much more ready to give than we are to receive. That is how God answers prayer. He astonishes us; He overwhelms us by His munificence. There is no limit to His power to give.

When God answers prayer

Finally, a word on the second question: When does God answer prayer? We find our answer at the beginning of verse 6. "And when Herod would have brought him forth, the same night Peter was sleeping between two soldiers, bound with two chains." When does God answer prayer? God answers prayer sometimes at the very last moment. He could have delivered Peter on any one of the days of unleavened bread, but He deliberately leaves Peter in prison until the end of the days of unleavened bread. He leaves it until just an hour or so before Herod had intended to send his servants to fetch him out. Why does He do that? Surely we can answer the question. There are two reasons. One must be this. He leaves it until the last moment **in order to make the discomfiture and the defeat of the enemy still more obvious and complete**. I rather like this divine irony. I can fancy Herod turning to his courtiers and saying, "Tomorrow morning we will get hold of this Peter and we will bring him out and make a display of him before the people; and we will put him to death. And we will show these Christians who this Christ of theirs is." I can see it all. I can the jokes and the jeers that are made at spiritual things. I can hear the proud boasts of the enemies of the infant church. God allows them to do all that. And then, just they are, as they think, to produce the final end of the church, God delivers the prisoner and they are made a laughing stock before the people. He has always done that. I could give you numerous illustrations out of the Scriptures. And God still does it. My point is this. God will do it again. The Christian church has been passing through dark waters; the enemy has been proud and arrogant, not only in Germany but in our own land, with its materialism and rationalism. But as the psalmist tells us, "The Lord shall laugh at him: for he seeth that his day is coming." The discomfiture of the enemy will be made complete and obvious to the whole world.

The second reason why God leaves it until the last moment is this. **He tests our faith**. He proves us. He leaves us in the place of tension to discover whether we are really trusting Him. He does not deliver us at once. He does not answer the prayers of the church at once. He leaves it until the last moment in order that our faith may be tried. The wind is allowed to blow in order that the oak may become mighty and strong. God tests us in order that we may be made strong.

So we summarize all this by a word of exhortation at the close. My message is applicable to the church at large at the present time. It is equally applicable to any individual who may come across these words. Are you beset round about by difficulties? Do you feel that you are in an impossible position; that nothing can ever be done to solve your problem, or lighten your burden, or give you happiness and joy? Are you downcast and disconsolate? My message to you, on the basis of this word of God is, "Pray and take large petitions with you to God." Above all, I say, in the name of God, hold on. In His own good time, which we cannot always understand, He will answer; He will act. Pray on. Hold on and you will never be disappointed.

—

CHAPTER 4

Where Miracle Ends

(Acts 12:10–12)

"When they had passed the first and the second guard, they came to the iron gate leading into the city. It opened for them of its own accord, and they went out and went along one street, and immediately the angel left him. When Peter came to himself, he said, 'Now I am sure that the Lord has sent his angel and rescued me from the hand of Herod and from all that the Jewish people were expecting.' When he realized this, he went to the house of Mary, the mother of John whose other name was Mark, where many were gathered together and were praying."

What an amazing story we have here! Peter has been delivered. The angel has awakened him in his cell, has caused his chains and shackles to fall off, has brought him past the warders, past the guards who kept the door of the prison, past the first and second ward; the great iron gate that stood between the prison and the city has opened of its own accord and the angel has led Peter through the street. And then forthwith the angel suddenly departed from him.

I am very anxious that we should bear in mind that last sentence of verse 10. The angel so far has been doing everything, but now he suddenly leaves Peter to himself. And I am anxious that we should look at Peter as he stands there in the street. Two things are said about Peter, one in verse 11 and the other in verse 12. The first is that "When Peter was come to himself he said", and the second, in verse 12, is **And when he had considered the thing**. The words "the thing" are not in the original. The words are in italics in the Authorized or King James Bible to indicate that they have been added by the translators in order to make the sense complete. What is "the thing"? Some say that it means that Peter considered everything that had just taken place, that he began to meditate on all that had happened to him. Others say it is not that, because we read in the previous verse, "When he came to himself he said, 'Now I know of a truth, that the Lord hath sent forth his angel and delivered me out of the hand of Herod.'" So they would have us believe that Peter finding himself in the street and realizing that, after all, he was not so far away from the prison and the warders and gaolers and soldiers, began to say to himself, "I had better do something. Where are the leaders of the church most likely to be found praying at the moment?" and when he considered that thing he went to the house of Mary the mother of John.

It is quite immaterial for our purpose which of those two things is correct. I have not the slightest doubt that both are correct. But what I want to emphasize is this: that Peter came to himself and considered something – anything. I don't care what he considered. I am particularly anxious that we should look at these two statements about Peter in the light of what we have been told about him in the previous section. What we are told about him there is, that Peter went out and (in verse 9) "wist not that it was true which was done by the angel, but thought he saw a vision".

There is the contrast which I am anxious you should bear in mind. Peter, not knowing exactly what he was doing, following the angel mechanically, and then Peter coming to himself, considering, reasoning, arriving at a decision, and acting upon his decision. I think it is perfectly obvious that we are face to face here with two phases – or two aspects if you prefer it – of the Christian life. Previously we were emphasizing the miraculous and the supernatural. Here we are looking at what we may term the pedestrian, the arguable, the human. If you look at it in that way we may say that our subject at this point is the place of the miraculous and of the supernatural in the Christian life and in Christian experience. And when I put it like that I am anxious to include in that statement not only the miraculous as such, but also the whole question of supernatural guidance and direction in our Christian life. There is really no difference in principle between being guided by an actual angel and receiving within that miraculous supernatural guidance which is so definitely part of Christian experience. The general term will include all.

This is not only a very large subject, but also, I need scarcely remind you, a very thorny subject. It has been very hotly debated and contested throughout the centuries and has gained a great deal of prominence during the last few years. Clearly, in one discourse and one sermon, no man can possibly hope to deal exhaustively with such a vast question. All I am anxious to do is to gather what information we can from this particular passage. It seems to me to give us a great insight into this difficult question and it puts it in such a dramatic manner that we can none of us fail to remember it. We must ever hold in our minds the picture of Peter mechanically following the angel, not knowing exactly what he is doing, and, a moment later, the angel having left him, Peter thinking, considering, ruminating, working out a problem and acting on his own decisions.

General comments

Before I come to what seem to me the principles to be set forth in this passage I should like to make one or two general remarks. It does seem to me that the tragedy about the consideration of this question in the history of the church has been that **people have always gone from one extreme to the other**. Some emphasize the miraculous and the supernatural only, as if there were no other aspect of the Christian life. Others exclude the miraculous and the supernatural altogether, and regard the Christian life as nothing but a particular form of philosophy, a particular way of thinking. We have men basing their conduct and life, their outlook and activity upon one or the other of these propositions. That has led to a third element in the tragedy, which is the curious tendency on the part of people to play the one against the other, to exalt one against the other. It is a curious thing about the human mind, is it not, that we seem to find it very difficult always to hold two ideas at the same time in our minds?

Yet it does seem to me that there is no final way to understand the message of the gospel without realizing that **there are ultimately certain antinomies which simply cannot be resolved**. And there is no need to try to resolve them. Why need we say it is all miraculous or all not? If only we could get rid of this "either/or" in this bad sense, and substitute for it "both/and", most of our problems would be solved. There is no need to stress the one thing to the exclusion of the other. The two things are both valid.

Why is this important?

Why is it of such importance that we should consider this subject? I would like to adduce various answers to that question. In the first place, **because intellectual honesty, apart from anything else, insists on our doing so**. We have no right as Christian people to allow certain aspects of the Christian life to remain dark and vague and nebulous in our understanding. It is our business to think and reason and understand as far as we possibly can. Everyone should search for light and knowledge. The gospel places no premium whatsoever on ignorance and obscurantism. Surely there has been nothing in the history of the world that has so stimulated men to reason and think as the gospel of our Lord and Saviour Jesus Christ. It is our business to search the Scriptures and understand them as best we can, however upsetting to certain ideas and fancies we like to harbour, and however uncomfortable it may be to the flesh. We know perfectly well that there is nothing which is quite so easy as to shut oneself in a certain circle, repeating the same ideas, the same parrot phrases, and refusing to consider questions and problems beyond that particular circle. It is very comforting. You can live such a circumscribed and comfortable little life. Yet I suggest that the New Testament condemns such a life. It is our business to face the truth and explain the facts as best we can.

Another reason why we should face this question is, that **we must always be on guard to avoid doing or saying anything which can possibly bring the Christian religion into disrepute**. I put it in that form in order to make this statement. Nothing has antagonised so many people from the Christian life and faith as extravagant claims put forward on its behalf. People have claimed miraculous intervention when it is clearly and patently something that can be explained quite easily – in human terms. And because false and extravagant claims are made there are many intelligent people who are antagonised from the church and the whole of religion. It is our bounden duty in the interests of truth and the church and her Master to understand the position as far as we can lest we bring disgrace upon the institution to which we belong.

Another very practical reason for considering this matter is this: that **it is the one way of avoiding certain unpleasant and unhappy experiences which sooner or later always become the lot of those who refuse to think**. Any man who has been a minister for a number of years must have discovered in his people – if he does see people individually and privately, as every minister ought to do – that some of the most tragic cases with which he has to deal are those of people who have had the impression that the Christian life is nothing but a series of miracles, and who suddenly find themselves in a position where the miracle does not seem to take place. They think that God has left them and many of them think that they have sinned against the Holy Ghost. They become greatly depressed and sometimes actually go into a state of mental illness and imbalance. The way to avoid that is to try to understand New Testament teaching with regard to the interrelationship of the supernatural and the natural.

Finally, **this is the only way in which we can make certain beforehand that we will always know what to expect** and to do should we ever find ourselves in the kind of position that is described in this chapter. We know not what the future holds for us. There may be a dreadful time of persecution ahead of us. What are we to expect, what are we to do if we find ourselves in those circumstances in which Peter found himself? It is only as we have learned to understand something of the fine dividing line between these two elements that we shall be forearmed and prepared for any emergency that may arise.

Those are some reasons which make it our bounden duty to face this question. What is the teaching of this episode? All I can do is to give you the main headings.

The teaching

The first is a statement: **we have to recognize the definite fact of the miraculous in the Christian life**. Now, I put that in the form of a dogmatic assertion. This is not a matter to be argued about. We either accept the New Testament as the basis of our faith or we do not. Christianity is either based upon the revelation of God that we have here or it is a human invention. If the New Testament is not my supreme authority for matters of faith and conduct, then I cannot argue with a man who tells me that that is his supreme authority also. There must be a certain foundation before any discussion is possible. The position throughout the ages and centuries has been that men have accepted the essentials of Christianity as stated in this book. If that is done, does it not seem quite inevitable that the fact of the miraculous and the supernatural must not only be accepted, but accepted as being the first and the main element in the Christian life? I personally cannot see how anyone can believe in Jesus of Nazareth as Son of God and Saviour of the world unless he accepts the record of Him in the four Gospels, including the miracles. He is indeed the eternal Son of God made flesh. Not only do I believe that He worked miracles, but I find it impossible to believe that He did not work miracles. I expect Him to work miracles. Because He is unique and different, I expect certain signs and evidences.

Coming to the Acts of the Apostles, you find a repetition of the same thing. The miraculous element constantly enters into it. If you do not accept the credibility of those first witnesses, well, where is your Christianity? According to these men the early days of the Christian church were greatly marked by this evidence of miracles and super-natural power. God worked special miracles by the hands of Paul and Peter and thereby, it is said, led to a great increase in the church. The fact of the miracles is surely beyond dispute.

When you come down to the subsequent history of the Christian church you find exactly and precisely the same thing. I refer to the fact, not only of working miracles, but also of this miraculous guidance. Read the lives of the saints and you will find that God intervened in their lives. When they were not thinking about these things, God came in and spoke to them and did something or so manipulated their circumstances as to lead them to a certain place. I have no hesitation in saying that a man is not a Christian unless he can say with Paul, "I am what I am by the grace of God." A man looking back across his life asks himself this question: "Why am I where I am? Why am I sitting in this pew this morning, or preaching in this pulpit? Why am I this and not something else? Is it something I myself have done and decided?" Unless a person can say that the hand of God has come upon him, that there has been an intervention from the supernatural, it seems to me he denies the very basis of the New Testament representation of the Christian life. Being a Christian is not just being good and decent and moral. It means the intervention of God in one's life. It means the coming of the Eternal into human experience.

I put it into those general terms because perhaps in this connection it is the most convenient way of putting it. The fact of the miraculous is something that is made plain on the very surface of the New Testament writings.

Let us go on to another principle, that here we are given some light as to how this miraculous element works and operates in the Christian life. And here again I am only going to summarize. One thing I have to say under this heading is this: **the miraculous happens only in God's time**. That is very obvious in our story here. The angel came to Peter when he was asleep. Peter just follows the angel. God always makes the first move in these miracles and in this matter. If you read the account of the actual miracles worked by the apostles the same thing is quite obvious. You never find the apostles giving out an announcement that they are going to work a miracle the next day or some other day. Some people today put out posters announcing that miracles will be worked, say, next Thursday afternoon, and invite people to the meeting. There is nothing like that in the New Testament. Take an instance in the fourteenth chapter of the Acts. Paul at Lystra observes a man impotent from his birth. Probably he had never seen the man before and had no intention of working a miracle. God spoke to Paul and Paul spoke to the man. So you will find it in every instance and example throughout Scripture. It is always something that happens in God's good time.

When you look at the past history of the church you will find the same thing true of every revival and reawakening. There you have special, supernatural times in the history of the church. They come when least expected. The revival comes; it works its way and then passes, and the church goes through a period which may be quite ordinary. Then, following upon this, there comes another revival. Men and women cannot organize a revival. They may have meetings to attempt organization, but they never produce a revival in that way. They may take cognisance of the results, but the revival is God-made.

The second thing seems to be that **God always does what men cannot do for themselves**. The miraculous element comes in when man is face to face with something that he cannot do. Peter there in prison is just helpless, chained to a soldier on each hand, the doors shut and bolted, a soldier outside, and the great iron gates beyond. God works in a miraculous and exceptional manner when man is faced with a situation in which he can do nothing for himself. That is the principle which is equally applicable in all the other cases and examples found in this book and in all the subsequent history of the church.

That leads me to the next principle. **Miracles stop at the point when man's capacity is sufficient**. Man is then left to face the situation alone. That is why this text appeals to me so much: "And when Peter was come to himself", that is, after the angel had departed from him. Peter has reached the stage where he can use his own mind. He is left considering for himself which house he had better approach. The angel does not lead him to the house of the mother of John Mark. Peter does all that for himself. The miraculous stops just at that point when man's capacity is sufficient and there it leaves him to himself.

The lesson should be plain and clear, that we must not expect in our Christian experience a constant manifestation of the miraculous and the supernatural. That is where extravagance tends to come in. I read a book a few years ago bearing some such title as *Ten Thousand Miles of Miracles* – a total contradiction of New Testament teaching. The miraculous is the exception; it is not the ordinary. Once a thing is ordinary it is no longer miraculous. The poor man explained things as miracles which could be explained quite easily in terms of telepathy and psychology and even of ordinary coincidence. No, the miracle takes us to that point at which we can begin to act and reason for ourselves. The Christian life must not be represented as a continual manifestation of miracles. There were people in the church of Corinth who wanted to spend the whole of their time speaking in tongues. "Speaking in tongues is all right," said Paul in effect in 1 Corinthians 14, "but remember also the place of understanding and interpretation."

The miraculous and the ordinary

Shall we, finally, just ask what is the explanation or, if you like, the word, the philosophy of all this? Why is there the miraculous element and the ordinary? Why does the miraculous do so much for us after which we are left to ourselves? I would suggest the following answer. Under the miraculous a man is more or less in an automatic state. We have that in Peter, who did not know what was really happening to him. He thought he saw a vision. It is a mechanical state in which a man does not know quite what is taking place. He does it not knowing why or how. It is automatic. It is only when a man comes to himself, in the sense of this passage, and begins to reason that he truly grasps the significance of the miraculous.

I can put that in terms of the experience of conversion. There is a sense in which a man is aware of something happening and yet does not know what is taking place. He is in a charmed, rarefied atmosphere. It is only when he comes to think about it afterwards and reads his Bible and understands Christian truth and doctrine that he begins to understand the significance of it all. The actual experience of conversion does not in itself tell of the depth of eternal love that sent the Only-Begotten One to bear our sins. It is as we grow in grace and knowledge that we begin to appreciate something of the eternal heart. At first we are in the automatic state, which may be an enjoyable state; we do not truly grasp the profundities of this great salvation found in Christ. In other words, "considering" – that is the word in the text – has a distinct place in the Christian life. God does not want us to act as machines. God has made us and has given us a mind, a brain, the power to reason and to think. Are we to be asked to say that when we become Christians God suddenly jettisons His own creative work, the human mind and understanding? It would imply a contradiction in God's own work. God has so ordered it that there are some things that He only can do, and having done them He leaves us to ourselves that we may think about them and reason concerning them, that we may consider them and meditate upon them.

Thus it seems to me we have here a perfect blending of the action of God and the action of man. The impossible can only be done by God, but what a tragedy it is that people should wait and expect that God will do that which is possible for them to do for themselves. It is a tragedy that so many spend their Christian lives sitting, as it were, in an armchair and waiting for the heavens to open, when, if they considered the thing as Peter did it would be perfectly obvious that there were many things they could do for themselves. God grant us the grace and wisdom to do that for which we are competent, that which we are expected to do.

Shall I put it, finally, in a picture like this? Imagine for a moment that Peter, having been left by the angel, just went on waiting in the street where he was, believing that the angel would come back again to tell him where he should go. We do not need much imagination to see the result. The alarm would have been given in the prison, the soldiers would have been searching the streets, and Peter would very soon have found himself back again behind the iron gates. And that is exactly what ought to happen to such a man. When God has done the impossible for you and has placed you on your feet, He pays you the great compliment of expecting you to think and reason for yourself and to waste no time in getting to a place of safety. That is the only way to avoid backsliding; to avoid those wretched ups and downs in the Christian life. It is to recognize that the miraculous goes so far and then leaves us as beings endowed by God with qualities wonderful enough, capacious enough for us to work out our own salvation with fear and trembling.

CHAPTER 5

The Church Triumphant

(Acts 12:23 – 24)

"And immediately the angel of the Lord smote him, because he gave not God the glory: and he was eaten of worms, and gave up the ghost. But the word of God grew and multiplied."

Here again we see Herod in his arrogance and pride. We have a perfect description given of him in this twelfth chapter of the Book of Acts. He arrayed himself in his gorgeous apparel and sat on his throne, and made utterance to the people; and we are told that "the people gave a shout saying, 'It is the voice of a god, and not of a man.' " Then we read: "and immediately the angel of the Lord smote him because he gave not God the glory: and he was eaten of worms, and gave up the ghost. But the Word of God grew and multiplied." Now looking at these two verses, superficially we might, perhaps, be tempted to regard them as being nothing but an epilogue at the end of the chapter. We have looked at the story. We have seen this miraculous element comes into the Christian life, but that we are not to depend solely upon that. We must never be guilty of that of which the apostles themselves were guilty at the very commencement of their career. We find how, in the first chapter of the Acts, after their Lord had risen, and had ascended to heaven, they stood looking up into heaven; and the angel came and said to them, "Why stand ye here? That is not your business now. Go back to Jerusalem. Set yourselves to prepare to go on with the work." It is not that the miraculous and the natural are contradictory; rather are they complementary. We saw that if they were to be true to their Lord's teaching they must maintain the balance in their own personal lives and experience; that they must learn increasingly how to draw the line at that point when the miraculous ends, and they begin to use their own natural powers.

Now Acts 12:23–24 might appear to be nothing but an epilogue to all that, and we may be tempted to say that we have here nothing but Luke the historian, anxious to round off the picture. Yet, surely, the very terms of the text makes such an exposition quite inadequate. Admittedly it is a kind of historical footnote, but, surely the very way in which Luke puts it ought to make us see that he intended something more. It is regrettable, I think, that in the Authorized Version, a new paragraph starts with verse 24. How the good men who produced the Authorized Version ever allowed themselves to do such a thing passes my comprehension! The very word "But" ought to have been sufficient to show them that it was directly connected with what went before. It is clear that the writer meant us to see that there was a very direct sequence in the thought and meaning. "And immediately the angel of the Lord smote him because he gave not God the glory: and he was eaten of worms, and gave up the ghost. But the Word of God – in contrast to Herod – grew and multiplied." In other words, it means that Luke not only stated the fact, but also continued the theory, or, if you prefer it, put forward a philosophy. I like to think of these two verses as, in a sense, giving us a philosophical deduction which is drawn by the writer himself on the basis of the facts which took place, and which have been recorded in the chapter. If I were to paraphrase and amplify my text I would suggest that Luke intended to say something like this: "Now here we have got something which is not only a fact in and of itself, but which really gives us the key to the understanding of anything and everything that is likely to happen to the church along these lines at any time, or in any place. I have reported one case," says the writer, "but I am very anxious that you should realize that the one case is only just one specimen, which is a typical example of all the others. I have given you a report of one set of details and facts, but, in principle, they cover the entire history of the Christian church. As regards Herod," says Luke, "he was stricken and he died, but the Word of God, the church, grew and multiplied. There," says this man, "you really have the key to the understanding of some of the profoundest truths concerning the. Christian church." We need to analyse this statement in fuller detail. It will enable us to review everything we have been saying; at the same time it will enable us to grasp those principles which lie beneath the teaching, and, still more, it will prepare us and fortify us so that we shall be in a fit condition to face whatsoever may come to meet us in the days that lie ahead. Above everything else, it will give us a grand view of the whole sweep of the divine purpose going forward even until the end of time.

Principles

(1) The being of God

It is clear that there are certain principles enunciated here and I would put them for your consideration in the following form. The first is, **the persistence of the church is of itself a proof of the being of God**. Now that may sound a somewhat strange contention and proposal, and yet more and more as I consider this whole question, the more I am convinced that ultimately the soundest proof of the being of God is the persistence of the church. You are familiar with the various proofs that have been put forward from time to time of the existence of God; arguments from nature, arguments from design and order, moral arguments which tell us that as there are "good" and "better", so there must be "best" somewhere, and the purely philosophical argument which says that there is no effect without cause and, therefore, there must be an ultimate cause. All these arguments have been used and are being used, but the most powerful of all the arguments for the reality of God is the fact of the persistence of the Christian church. For myself, when I am confronted by anyone who doubts the truth of the Christian faith, I invariably start with the fact of the church, and I ask my opponent to explain, how it ever came into being in view of what we are told about the disciples at the end of the gospel. How can you explain the church at all? How did she ever come into being and how has she persisted since?

This is something which we can look at, perhaps, along two main lines. **How can we explain the persistence of the church in spite of persecution and opposition**, of which we are reminded so forcibly in this chapter? How is it that this body of ordinary, simple, unlettered, untutored men, without any might or battalions of armies to defend them, managed to escape from all this persecution which arose against them? They were persecuted by the Jews at first and then by the mighty Roman Empire. Think for a moment of this body of insignificant people, many of whom, especially in the gentile world, were nothing but slaves. How was it that that body of people managed to persist in spite of the terrible persecutions which took place in the first three centuries? For they were literally hounded from place to place and massacred in large numbers. An attempt was made to destroy the church the moment it was born by both Jews and gentiles. Consider too the attempt that was made to destroy the church from another direction, and, in many ways, a much more subtle one – the attempt to stifle the church and her message, on the part of philosophy. If you take the trouble to read history and an account of the Councils of the church in those first centuries, you will find that the church was fighting for her life quite as much in those Councils as she was when the Christians were being thrown into the arena, and when they were being hounded into caves and rocks. Greek philosophy and various mystery religions from the east came and made a deliberate attempt to so modify the teaching of the gospel as ultimately to neutralize it. To me there is nothing so astonishing and amazing as the fact that the gospel has come down in all its purity in spite of the onslaught of Greek philosophy and all those pagan cults and mystery religions. It is just another illustration of that miraculous deliverance of the church which we have been considering together in this chapter. And when you come still further down and consider the whole story of the persecuting zeal of the Roman Catholic church, the Papacy, a story which is familiar to all of us, is it not rather amazing that still we are able to meet together to consider the gospel of Christ in its simple evangelical form and pattern? The very persistence of the church, I suggest, is a proof of the being of God. How else can you explain it? How is it that this body of people, this institution, starting as it did, with such people, has persisted in spite of enemies of every type and in spite of their might and power and persecution? To me there is only one answer: it is the being and the power of God.

Then we can consider it also in this way. **How is it that the church has persisted and continued in spite of the weakness of her own members?** For the church has had to face trouble, not only from outside, but also from within. And it is very difficult to decide which of these two things, in the last analysis, is the more remarkable: that the church persists in spite of men like Herod, or that it persists in spite of people like you and me! In this chapter we find that the church really lacked faith. They thought, and said, that Rhoda was mad when she came in and told the disciples that Peter stood without. And Peter himself thought he saw a vision; he did not know what was happening. The whole story of the church, as it is recorded for us in the Book of the Acts and still more in subsequent church history, is full of the sins and failures and weaknesses on the part of Christian people. Yet, the astonishing thing is that the church is still here, the gospel is still being preached; there is this unbroken continuity in spite of the weaknesses of Christian people and believers. In spite of all that is so true of us, the church goes on. So that when the men of the world, who oppose the church, come forward with the hackneyed argument, "Look at the people who belong to the church," let us at once be ready with the retort, "How can you explain the fact that there is a church at all in view of what you say? No other institution has survived with such people. The church has persisted in spite of the failures and sins of her own members. That again is, surely, proof positive of the being of God."

When you come to look at the story of the church, you find that not only has she been brought into the furnace of affliction and persecution, and has been brought through miraculously by God, but that another great element in her story is that she has gone from periods of revival to periods of deadness. The revivals have never come from man; they have always come from God. Men and women became lethargic and weary and tired; they doubted and questioned. They became slack in their lives; and the church became a moribund institution. Then suddenly God intervenes and revives the church, and sends her on her way. I say that the very persistence of the church is ultimately the soundest and greatest proof of the being of God. "Herod was eaten of worms, and died – but the Word of God grew and multiplied."

(2) God's plan for history

My second principle is that **the persistence of the church is also a proof and demonstration that God has a plan, not only for the church, but for history, and for the ages**. The persistence of the church is indicative of a plan and purpose running right through to the very end. In other words, my text routs such an argument as that which was put forward by the deists of the eighteenth century. They said that God had made the world and had then turned His back upon it, like a man who makes a watch, winds it up, and leaves it to go on. There are many who think that God is not in control of the world; that having made it, He has left it to run on its own momentum. My text disproves any such contention. Surely it proves that God has His hand upon the church and upon the whole world. He not only deals with the church, but He deals also with Herod. There is evidence and indication here of a great scheme and plan for the ages and centuries.

This is a very important subject at the present time. Let us admit quite frankly that it is also a very difficult subject. As one looks out upon the world is it not difficult at times to believe in these things? Are there not many whose faith has wavered, whose love has become cold? They say, "If there is a God why does He allowed these wars and conflicts? Why is the enemy so proud and arrogant and the church so small and weak? Why is there but a mere handful of people to listen to the Word of God and crowds to listen to everything else?" The church is being neglected. As you look at things in the world, a superficial view would lead inevitably to profound pessimism. Appearances seem to be against us; and if you venture to look into the future there are indications that things are going to be still more difficult. Yet, we are shown very clearly certain principles of which we must take a firm grasp. We do not claim to understand everything, but there are certain things which are indicated plainly and clearly; things which we must accept.

The first is that **there is such a thing as the permissive will of God**. There is a classical illustration of that in this chapter. You remember that the first statement recorded here is that "Herod stretched forth his hand to vex certain of the church, and he killed James, the brother of John, with the sword." The rest of the chapter just unfolds the story that God did **not** allow Herod to kill Peter. There is your principle at once. God, in His own inscrutable wisdom, allowed Herod and the Jews to murder James, but he delivered Peter. If you go through the Bible you will find the same thing illustrated. Stephen is allowed by God to be made a martyr. Some of the finest people in the history of the church have died a martyr's death, while there are others who have been delivered and given their liberty. There is this permissive will of God. We may in our folly ask the question, "Why does God allow that person to suffer and why does He allow this person to live such a comparatively easy life?" We can, however, say that the permissive will of God does not, in the slightest degree, lessen God's sovereignty and lordship. The things that are allowed to happen are allowed by God for His own good and eternal purpose. God who delivered Peter could also have delivered James, but He did not choose to do so. The result is we have to recognize that evil is permitted by God in His own wisdom. God allows persecution to arise. He allows evil men to become arrogant. The rising up of Hitler and similar people is nothing but an illustration of the permissive will of God. The God who allowed Cyrus and Nebuchadnezzar to arise is the same God who allows similar men to arise today

We recognize this great principle of the permissive will of God. Then we go on to a second matter. **Behind, and over and above this permissive will, God's great purpose is, nevertheless, still being carried out**. You see that in this chapter. He allows James to be put to death and Peter to be thrown into prison. But the whole time God is there in the background. Just at the very moment when Herod was going to arrest Peter, God delivers Peter. Again, just as Herod was delivering his oration to the people, it was then that the angel of the Lord smote him and he died. That is a great principle which could be worked out at very great length. Work it out for yourselves as you study the Old and the New Testaments. And let us be careful to apply that philosophy to everything that is happening at this present time. Though God may seem to be away in the distance, we can be quite certain that through cloud and storm and hurricane God is surely bringing His own eternal purposes to pass.

(3) The destruction of God's enemies and the glorification of Christ

This brings me to my third principle: **the plan of the ages has as its ultimate purpose the destruction of God's enemies and the glorification of Christ**. I have said that God has a plan and a purpose, and that the persistence of the church demonstrates and proves that. The ultimate end of all is that God's enemies will be destroyed and God will be glorified over the whole earth. The fact is obvious in our text The end of this story, says Luke the historian, is this: "The angel of the Lord smote Herod, and he died." And that is going to be the inevitable end of all God's enemies. On the other hand, "the Word of God grew and multiplied". Take the case of this man Herod. Surely the miraculous deliverance of Peter should have opened his eyes. Surely he ought to have realized that he was fighting God, not man. But he raised himself up, he sat on his throne, he spoke like a god, and he accepted the worship of the people, and God struck him down. This may sound a harsh thing to do, but it is something implicit in the whole of biblical teaching; you will find it everywhere. Think of the Assyrian power. You would have thought that it was invincible and that it could never be defeated. But it came down like a pack of cards. Think of the might of Babylon and of Nebuchadnezzar. If you had lived at that time you would have said, "This empire will never be destroyed." Yet it vanished almost in a night. The same is true of the Medo-Persian and the Greek empires. It is always the same story. Turn to the New Testament. It is set out for us in the first chapter of the second epistle to the Thessalonians, where the apostle tells us quite clearly that when the Lord returns as conqueror His enemies will be destroyed. You find the same thing in the epistle to the Corinthians and in the second epistle of Peter; and in the Book of Revelation you see these evil powers ascending in their persecuting might and you see God working in the distance, with everything leading up to the great consummation when death and hell and Satan and the beasts, and all those evil powers, are flung into the lake that burns with fire and brimstone, and Christ reigns supreme over earth and heaven. It is very interesting to notice in regard to the final destruction of the enemy the element which comes out in Psalm 37:13: "The Lord shall laugh at him: for he seeth that his day is coming." Herod is seated on his throne, robed in his gorgeous apparel, delivering his grand oration. The next moment we see him eaten by worms. Oh, the glory and the wonder of it! To think that poor pygmy men should raise themselves against God and His might, and imagine that they can succeed. "The Lord will laugh." With a mere movement of His hand He will wipe His enemies off the face of the earth. The way in which He does it is a most fascinating theme. You will find it in the Bible.

Conclusions

Let me then say four things in conclusion: (1) We must never judge by appearances only. (2) We must always remember that the church is the church of God. (3) We need never worry about the future of the church and of Christianity. Let your pessimists say what they like. Let them publish their books and deliver their lectures. Let Christian people be full of foreboding as they think of the future. You need not worry. The church, being the church of God, is going on until her work is completed. (4) Our one business is to make certain that we truly belong to the church, that we live primarily to the glory of God, and play our part, however insignificant it may be, with all our might.

That is my reaction at the end of this chapter. If ever I have thanked God for the fact that I belong to the church it is as I read a text like this. If we are truly Christians, and truly members of the church, we are on the winning side. We are on the side of the church militant, the church triumphant. Our victory is certain and assured, come what may. There may be times of difficulty and distress; we are promised such things; but, and there is always that "but", the Word of God will grow and multiply, until the Lord, in His own good time, comes to wind this earth and all its affairs, and hands over the kingdom to God the Father. God grant that we all may know for certain that we belong as living members to the invincible church.

PART 2

A Summary of the Gospel

CHAPTER 6

Revelation

(Hebrews 1:1–3)

*"God, who at sundry times and in divers manners spake in time past
unto the fathers by the prophets, hath in these last days spoken unto
us by his Son, whom he hath appointed heir of all things, by whom
also he made the worlds; who being the brightness of his glory, and
the express image of his person, and upholding all things by the
word of his power, when he had by himself purged our sins, sat down
on the right hand of the Majesty on high."*

Why was Hebrews written?

I call your attention to these verses for precisely and exactly the same
reason which led the author of this epistle to write them. You remember
**he wrote this epistle to those Hebrew Christians because he was
anxious to strengthen them**; to establish them in the faith; to comfort
and console them, and to encourage them. Repeatedly, in the body of the
epistle, he makes it abundantly plain and clear that that was his avowed
object and intention. I propose not only to call your attention to these
verses, which constitute a kind of prologue or introduction to the entire
epistle, for that reason; but I propose also to do this very thing in exactly
and precisely the same way as it is done by the author of the letter. For
you will remember that there is nothing which is quite so characteristic
of this man's method as the fact that he is not content merely to give a
certain amount of general indiscriminate comfort and encouragement.
Being a wise and competent physician of the soul this man knew full well
that in order to comfort and encourage truly, one must first of all analyse

the condition and appreciate exactly and precisely the state of the people with whom one has to deal. So he administers his comfort and his consolation in terms of their actual, concrete situation. He takes the trouble not only to analyse their condition, but he is also very careful, at times, to reprimand them, and to administer to them some of the severest rebukes which are to be found anywhere in Holy Writ. Indeed, I remind you that from the strictly literary standpoint, nothing is quite so characteristic of the epistle as the way in which we find these alternating passages of grace and mercy on the one hand, and on the other hand passages minatory and threatening, and more terrible, as I have already suggested, than any passages which can be found anywhere else in the Bible.

That very fact, in and of itself, reminds us of this man's method. In order to encourage truly, he seems to say, I must first of all examine your condition and your case; and I must correct you on certain matters, and put you right on others; and then and then only can I really bring you to the place and position of blessing.

There is one general charge which he brings against them and that is that **all their troubles can ultimately be traced to the fact that they have failed to realize the greatness and uniqueness of the Christian gospel**. Many of these people had become fainthearted. Many of them were fearful. Large numbers of them were obviously complaining; but still more serious, many of them were beginning to look back with eyes of longing to Judaism – to that old economy, that old religion out of which they had been delivered and emancipated by their acceptance of the gospel of Jesus Christ.

Now, says this man, there can be ultimately only one explanation of all that, and that is that you have failed to realize this so great salvation. You remember that he elaborates the charge at the end of the fifth chapter where he suggests very strongly that they have failed to realize the greatness of the gospel, because they have not studied it sufficiently. He comes there to deal with the whole question of the priesthood of our Lord after the order of Melchizedek and he says: "Of whom we have many things to say, and hard to be uttered, seeing ye are dull of hearing. For when for the time ye ought to be teachers, ye have need that one teach you again which be the first principles of the oracles of God; and are such as have need of milk, and not of strong meat. For every one that useth milk is unskilful in the word of righteousness; for he is a babe. But strong meat belongeth to them that are of full age, even those who by reason of use have their senses exercised to discern both good and evil." That then is the essence of their trouble. They have not concentrated on this gospel. They have not studied it. They have not realized its absolute and utter uniqueness and greatness. And all their trouble arose from that. Therefore, of course, he goes on to say the only way to put them right is to remind them again of this mighty gospel; of its finality and its power, of its all-inclusiveness, and especially of its divine origin. That is what he does in this epistle. It is epitomized and summarized very perfectly in these first three verses.

The application today

Now, surely we can see that what is true of these Hebrew Christians so long ago can be said, alas, with all too much truth, about those of us who are Christian at this present time. Is not that description appropriate to our condition? Do we not present a state of affairs which is far too closely analogous to that? Is not that, in a sense, the essence of the modern problem? Surely that is the final charge to be brought against those representations of the gospel which have gained such currency and popularity in the past hundred years; which have presented the gospel as a vague moralizing concerning life and a declaration of high hopes and aspirations, or a mere appeal for ethics and conduct, and a good social outlook. Surely the final charge to be brought against such views of the gospel is not so much that they are erroneous and false, but that they are guilty, above all else, of failing to see the greatness of the gospel, its utter uniqueness and its essentially Divine origin. The ultimate charge to bring against such misrepresentations of the gospel is that they are guilty of reducing it to a mere view of life which can be put into series with other teachings. It is an insult to the gospel of Christ even to compare it with any other teaching. It is unique. It stands alone. There is nothing like it. The world has never known anything that is similar.

In exactly the same way, are not our problems and troubles and perplexities as Christian people to be traced ultimately to this selfsame origin? Is not our depression – if we are guilty of depression – ultimately to be traced to our failure to realize the greatness of the gospel? Is not our tendency to grumble and complain, our tendency to be faint-hearted and lose hope, our tendency at times to query even the goodness and the love of God because of things happening to us, to be traced to this origin? Are not all these things ultimately to be traced back to the fact that we have not realized the true nature of the gospel, that we have not grasped its essential uniqueness? In other words, we are guilty of that of which these Hebrews were guilty. We are in danger of letting things slip, of falling away from these eternal verities which are taught us so clearly and definitely in the pages of the New Testament. So I invite you to consider this great introduction to the essentials of the Christian gospel.

Introducing Hebrews 1:1–3

Here, as I have already suggested, is a very perfect summary of the claim which is made by the New Testament for this gospel, the claim which it puts forward for its utter, absolute uniqueness, the claim which it makes for it when it says that this, and this alone, is the gospel of God, and therefore the message which is needed by men.

We are struck in the very first word of the first verse by what is after all the very essence of the uniqueness of the gospel. It ever and always starts with God. The author, as it were, throws down the gauntlet at once. He starts with the name of God. He tells us, in other words, that the Christian gospel is a revelation. Here we are reminded of something which is ever the centre and very nerve and essence of the Christian religion. **It is a religion of revelation**. God is the Actor. It is God who does everything. That, of course, is characteristic of the whole Bible. You remember the first word of the first verse of Genesis, "In the beginning God..."! So often when men and women are discussing the problems of life and religion, whether in discussion or in books, they start with theories. The Bible always starts with God. "In the beginning, God created..."

You remember also the introduction or prologue of the Gospel according to John, "In the beginning was the Word, and the Word was with God, and the Word was God." Here, in exactly the same way, this man is anxious to bring these people back to the gospel. So he starts with these words, "God, who at sundry times and in divers manners spoke." The Bible is the record of the activity of God. God is the centre. Everything is of God, comes from God, and returns to God. In other words, we are faced at the very beginning with this category of revelation. It is God who speaks. It is God who acts. It is God who intervenes. It is God who originates, who plans everything everywhere. It is a revelation of what God is, and what God does. It is a record of God revealing and manifesting Himself. Therefore, of course, it is equally a record of God manifesting man to himself; and ultimately the purpose of this dual revelation of God and man is that man may be reconciled to God. That is something fundamental, something with which we must begin; for if we are wrong at this point we shall be wrong at all points. If we do not understand that the gospel is a matter of revelation, then we do not understand the gospel at all. Now I suggest again that perhaps the greatest need of all at the present time is that we should be brought face to face with that essential fact; and surely there is no time more appropriate for doing so than the season of Advent.[6] For this time which leads up to Christmas Day reminds us of the central fact of all history; it demonstrates the fact of revelation.

In these three verses the author tells us that God has manifested Himself in two main ways. There are two main revelations: the revelation in the old dispensation and the new revelation in Jesus Christ. There is his main division. At the moment I am concerned with the general aspects of revelation. You cannot look at this matter without being reminded at once of some of the fundamental principles and postulates of the Christian faith. They are all suggested by the very category of revelation. All I am anxious to do at the moment is to remind you of some of the implications of this whole idea of revelation.

6. This message was preached on 6th December 1942 when the "Season of Advent" was commencing for those familiar with "the church year".

Revelation

First of all we are reminded by the fact of revelation that **the ultimate object of religion is to enable men and women to know God**. Here again, surely, we must plead guilty to the fact that we are far too often content with things in the realm of religion which are subsidiary to and but corollaries of that. Is there not a tendency on our part to think of religion as but designed to make us good, or to make us happy, or to give us a certain high conception and noble view of life?

Now, obviously and clearly, true religion does lead to such results. It does make us good by the grace of God and it gives us an exalted and true view of life. But I would remind you that the first object of religion is not to do that. If we put any of these things first, we are doing violence to the teaching of the New Testament. Now this is vitally important for this reason. There are other religions and teachings which can accomplish all these things. The Christian religion is not the only religion. There have been modern systems inculcating morality and producing good people. By secular education and culture and dissemination of knowledge you can make people good to some extent. The Christian faith does not have any monopoly in that respect. That is not the difference between Christian faith and other religions. Nor is the Christian religion the only religion which can make men happy. Surely during the last twenty years that has been one of the commonest features of life – the search for happiness. People have found it in other systems and in various cults. So also psychology can, up to a point, give people happiness. But we are reminded by the very category of revelation that the first object of religion is to bring men to a knowledge of God. That I may be a good man is not enough. The question is, "Do I know God?" To be happy may be the most dangerous thing of all unless my happiness is based upon a knowledge of God. It may be the happiness of a person who has drugged himself, who has turned his back upon the problem or the situation. As our Lord put it once and for ever, "This is life eternal that they may know thee, the only true God, and Jesus Christ whom thou hast sent." I say it matters not at all what we may have, or what we may be, unless we have come to the position in which we know God. All the troubles of life, according to the biblical teaching, are to be traced back in the last analysis, to man's loss of the knowledge of God, man's alienation from God Himself, and the revelation of God. It is as man has lost the face of God that his troubles have multiplied; and the whole object of God's revelation is to bring man back to that knowledge. This is the first deduction which we draw from the contemplation of this principle of revelation.

Then the second, obviously, must be this, and it follows in a logical sequence, that **man in himself is incapable of finding God** or, in shorter terms, man's total incapacity to find God. Surely that is a matter that needs no demonstration or discussion. Does not the very idea of revelation imply this? If it is possible for man to find God then why is it necessary for God to reveal Himself, to manifest Himself? If man has the power and propensities which can enable him to arrive at a knowledge of God, then for God to reveal and manifest Himself is totally unnecessary.

But, going more deeply into the matter, **what is revealed to us by revelation shows how utterly impossible it is for man unaided ever or finally to know God.** For the God who has revealed Himself is a holy God, a God who is of such pure countenance that He cannot even look at sin. He is a God described as eternal light, "in whom there is no darkness at all". He is a God in whom there is "no variableness, nor shadow of turning". He is a God who in His very essence is the utter opposite and antithesis of everything that is represented by the word "sinner". Man, on the other hand, according to this revelation, is a creature who has sinned. He is one who is described as "darkness". He is one who is described as a child of the night. He is a creature of lust, of desire, one whose finest faculties and powers have been blunted and tarnished and soiled by the pollution of this foreign element that has come into life. That is the revelation that has been given concerning God and concerning man. Is it not obvious therefore that man by his own unaided efforts could not arrive at a knowledge of God?

In other words, there is the problem of sin. It is a moral problem. The tragedy is that many have regarded it as an intellectual problem. We have regarded religion as an intellectual matter and have struggled with the philosophies that have attempted to explain life. Yet here at the very beginning we might have saved ourselves all this useless trouble and agony and anguish, for the problem is essentially a moral problem. Let me grant readily that by means of knowledge we can discover certain things about God, as Paul argues in the first chapter of the epistle to the Romans. Through creation and other things we may be able to arrive at a certain knowledge about God and what God does; but the problem with which we are confronted is not that. What we desire is to know God, to be brought into intimate relationship with God; and that is essentially a moral problem. There can he no accord between light and darkness, between Christ and Belial. Before there can be true relationship and communion there must be likeness of nature. Revelation reveals that man as he is and of himself is incapable of knowing God.

Then there is another deduction and I think you will agree it is something that follows in logical and inevitable sequence. **That alone is true which is revealed**. Let me remind you of the steps. The ultimate goal of religion is to know God. Man by his own unaided efforts can never arrive at that knowledge. Therefore, thirdly, that alone is true which has been revealed. Now here again is a fundamental and vital principle. We are driven back, in other words, to the unique authority of this book which we call the Bible. Owing to our inability to discover God by our own effort, what right have we to set up our standards and canons and opinions, and determine what is true of God? All we know of God is that which in His infinite grace He has been pleased to reveal concerning Himself in the Scriptures. Yet I need not remind you that in most of the discussions which have taken place in recent years on Christianity we have forgotten this very vital principle. We have laid down certain opinions and have decided what God is to do and not to do; we have formed God according to our own image. Our opinions, the opinions of men, the statements of philosophers, have been allowed to usurp the position of the authority of this book. But how vain it all is, for we are tied down by revelation. God is there, in His utter holiness. I am here, a sinner. I can study, I can fast, I can pray, I can do good works, but I will never come to know God. Therefore what right have I to say or determine what is true about God? All I can know about God is what God has revealed concerning Himself. We must start with the Bible therefore. The only knowledge of God, the only true knowledge of God we can ever possess, is that which is contained in this book.

Therefore every sermon should start with a text from the Bible. Therefore every preaching of the Christian gospel should start with the Bible. We start with the open book, which is the only knowledge we can ever have of the being and nature of God. And the central sin of today is to substitute philosophy for revelation.

And that in turn brings us to another deduction. **What is revealed is sufficient**. The only revelation that we have is that which is contained here, and thank God it is enough. The very character of God, in and of itself, guarantees that. God would never mock us by giving us an insufficient revelation. The very fact of God giving us a revelation at all is enough, is sufficient; and God be praised, I say again, experience confirms the statement of the revelation. Go and discuss this matter with the saints of the ages and they will all tell you that what has been revealed is enough. In this book there is a sufficient revelation to enable me to find a way back to God. Here I am convinced and convicted of my sin. Here I see the uselessness of my own efforts. But here I also see Jesus Christ and Him crucified as an atonement for my sin and One who reconciles me to God. Here I am offered life, filled with power, might, and strength. Here I am given an everlasting hope that can never fade away. What is revealed is sufficient.

Of course there are many things which we still would like to know. There are many questions that we constantly ask; but the very category of revelation in and of itself tells us there are things we were not meant to know. It is for God to determine what we need to know and what we do not need. This was put once and for all in Deuteronomy 29:29. "The secret things belong unto the LORD, our God: but those things which are revealed belong unto us and to our children for ever, that we may do all the words of this law." The revelation, I say, is sufficient for salvation and for life, and with anything beyond that I must be content to say, "I do not know; I cannot understand." It is not the will of God that I should understand that, here in this world, but hereafter all things will be made plain. What is revealed is sufficient.

And that brings me to my last principle, namely, **that there is a**

revelation at all is entirely the result of grace. That in many ways is the most important principle of all. Oh, the amazing, wondrous grace of God! Man sinned. Man turned his back upon God. Man forfeited his right to communion with God. Man in that position is utterly helpless. He can do nothing. He cannot justify himself. He cannot reconcile himself to God. He cannot find God. Yet God, in spite of all, has deigned to reveal Himself, to manifest Himself, to draw back the veil from His face, and to give us these glimpses, this knowledge which is more than sufficient for us. The fact that there is a revelation at all is entirely the result of that amazing grace and love of God that give to us undeserving sinners such a knowledge, such wisdom, so great a salvation.

There are some of the first principles in connection with this doctrine of revelation. These are the fundamental postulates of the Christian faith. The ultimate object of true religion is to bring us to know God. It is a knowledge man cannot acquire in and of himself unaided. That alone is true which has been revealed. What is revealed is sufficient. That there is a revelation at all is the result of nothing but the amazing grace of God. Here then, as we approach the central fact of history, we are reminded of the basis of it all. God the Father in His infinite love has had mercy upon us and has granted us a revelation that means life, which is life eternal.

CHAPTER 7

The Value of the Old Testament

(Hebrews 1:1–3)

It is no part of the purpose and object of this author to derogate from the value of the old dispensation and the old revelation, as it is recorded, in what we call "the Old Testament". It is no part of his case in proving the superiority of the new to dismiss the old. Any understanding or reading of these three verses, which epitomize the whole of this epistle, which comes to that conclusion is entirely false. Indeed, there is one word in the second verse which precludes any such possibility. The writer says, "hath in these last days spoken unto **us** by his Son". He couples himself with those to whom he writes, from which we can fairly deduce the fact that he was himself a Hebrew, and a Hebrew in setting forth the excellence of the new would not permit himself to say that the old was valueless. The very terms of the first verse also make any such conclusion quite impossible. It is **God**, he says, "who at sundry times and in divers manners spake in time past unto the fathers by the prophets". **God** is the Actor. Everything that is done is done by God. This man, at great length in his epistle, compares the new and the old in order to manifest the superiority of the new. But at the very outset he reminds us of the fact that the old is as much a revelation of God as is the new. That the new is a fuller revelation does not mean that God was not the author of the old revelation. It is the same God, the one "who having spoken in times past unto the fathers by the prophets, now in these last days hath spoken unto us by his Son".

Now there is one sense in which, when we come to apply these verses and their message to ourselves, and to our own age, we find ourselves confronted by a slightly different problem from that with which this man was confronted. His great work was to show the superiority of the new over the old. Our task, in a sense, is to demonstrate the value of the old as well as the new! We have to do that for a number of reasons. The main reason is that we are living in a time when there are many who are prone and tempted to dismiss the old altogether. The Old Testament is no longer as popular as it once was. Some would even go so far as to say that it is a book almost unworthy of attention by Christian people and is certainly not a book for children. There has been a tendency to criticize or to despise the Old Testament. It may be that there are others who, while not taking that foolish and extreme position, may very well have a query in their mind which takes some such form as this. They say, "It is not that we want to dismiss the old, but we ask, is there any point in reading it? Now that we have the New Testament, is it not rather a waste of time to read the Old Testament and its revelation? When we have the sun in its full height and meridian in the New Testament, why do we need the lesser light in the Old Testament?"

Why did the church keep the Old Testament?

Now a very convenient way of dealing with such a position is to consider it in terms of another question, which is just another way of putting the same question. A better way of putting the question is this: Why was it that the early church decided to preserve the Old Testament and to use it, and to incorporate it with the New Testament, with the new literature, in one book which became known as the Bible? Why did the early church decide to do that in view of the treatment that was meted out to their Saviour and Lord by the Jews? How did it come about that Christian people who were so terribly persecuted by the Jews in the first thirty to forty years of their life as Christian people, decided to incorporate this ancient literature – these records which belonged to the Jewish race and people – with the new literature of a church that had become almost exclusively gentile? Why did they regard these ancient Scriptures as being of surpassing value and of the highest worth?

We can discover the answer to that question in the most convenient manner by considering the first of these three verses. "God, who at sundry times and in divers manners spake in time past unto the fathers by the prophets . . ." The reason why the early church preserved the Old Testament literature was because of what God had spoken in times past to the fathers by the prophets. We ask ourselves the question: what is the value of this ancient revelation to us? I suggest that nothing is so strengthening to faith and of such value to the life of the soul as that from time to time we should face a general question like that. We should, as it were, take a bird's eye view of the whole of the Old Testament. We can, perhaps, best do this by dividing up our subject under three main headings.

Preliminary facts

First, we must deal with **the pure mechanics of this subject**. Here the author at once provides us with a key by making his main sub-division. He says this was a revelation which was given "at sundry times and in divers manners". It is unnecessary, I am sure, for me to indicate that the word "prophet" in this passage must not be taken in the strict sense in which we regard it when we refer to certain books of the Old Testament as books of "the Prophets". The "prophet" in our text clearly means any man who stood in such a relationship to God that God could speak through him and could manifest Himself to the people by him. The prophets are those in and through whom God reveals and manifests Himself to the people.

The first thing that characterized this revelation was that **it took place in many parts**. It was a revelation which was given in successive portions; it was a fragmentary revelation. Nothing is more characteristic of the Old Testament than just that truth. The whole revelation was not given at once. The characteristic of the Old Testament was that a little was given here and another portion at another time. Perhaps the most convenient classification of these "many parts" is to adopt the historical classification. God revealed Himself first through the patriarchs. Then He revealed Himself in a very signal manner through Moses. He revealed Himself in the theocracy. He revealed Himself in the kingdom of Israel. He revealed Himself in the time of the Babylonian captivity. He revealed Himself in the period of the hierarchy that followed the captivity in Babylon. There is the rough and ready historical classification and sub-division of the revelation.

Coming to a little more detail in order to bring out these points we can show it in this way. Consider the different parts and portions of the one revelation which God gave at different times **through different persons**. Is it not clear that God revealed to Noah and through him the exact geographical portion of the world through which the final ultimate blessing should come? That man was allowed to choose his son, Shem, as the one through whom the blessing would ultimately be derived. That part of the revelation was given there. Then you remember that it was in and through Abraham that the revelation was given of the particular nation through whom this revelation should come. To Jacob, and through Jacob, was revealed the tribe. Through David and Isaiah the particular family. Through the prophet Micah there was given the very town of the nativity and birth of the Saviour. Through Daniel the time of his coming, the time of the Incarnation; and through Malachi, in a striking way, we read of the person and the work of the great forerunner, John the Baptist. I have merely selected certain examples in order to illustrate the general principle. Nothing is so clear and obvious, as you go through the Old Testament, as the fact that the revelation is given in successive portions and in a fragmentary manner.

Yet our account of it would be very inadequate if we failed to add another word. It was not only in many parts; **it was also progressive**. The initial promise is made after the Fall concerning the seed of the woman. Then further information is given to Noah and to Abraham, and as you put these portions together you see that there is a definite idea of progression. Each revelation adds to that which has gone before until the whole is made complete.

But I must say a word on this other term found in Hebrews 1:1. The author tells us that it was not only in many parts, but also **in many ways, or methods**. There is nothing more fascinating than to study this aspect of the matter in the Old Testament revelation, and of the ways in which God revealed Himself. You have that great fact of the theophanies. You read of them especially in the time of the patriarchs, how suddenly a person of surpassing beauty and excellence manifests himself. "The angel of the Lord" is a description which is often given to him. That is a theophany, a manifestation of God in a bodily form, not an incarnation, but a theophany. Then God manifested Himself in various other ways. He made a covenant with man; He revealed something concerning Himself and what He proposed to do. Then in a very striking manner God manifested Himself in action at the time of the exodus of the people of Israel from Egypt to be taken to Canaan. Then we have the "types", the revelations in the ordinances in connection with the Levitical law and what was revealed to man concerning the tabernacle, and the burnt offerings, and the sacrifices. All these things are "types" of what was going to happen in Christ in perfection later. But in every one of these ordinances God revealed some aspect and some portion of the truth.

Then we have those definite declarations of the Word of the Lord, and on the authority of the Lord, which enabled the prophets to stand and say, "Thus saith the LORD." You find it in the prophets especially, in the various interpretations that were given to the people of the circumstances in which they found themselves, sometimes in prosperity and at other times in misery and penury. In all these different ways "God spake in times past unto the fathers in the prophets".

Coming down to still greater technicalities, we read that sometimes God spoke to these men face to face. Sometimes He spoke to men in visions and sometimes in dreams. Sometimes men are transported into a kind of prophetic ecstasy and in that ecstatic condition they are able to pass on a revelation and a message of God. I can only give the headings in order to stimulate further study and thought. But this, clearly, is what this man has in mind when he says that "God in times past spake unto the fathers in the prophets, in many portions, and in many ways."

What is the result?

But I move to my second principle, which is a more practical one. I ask the question: What is the result of all this? What did God say to the fathers in times past? What has been revealed? And here again I can only summarize some of the most important things that stand out.

As one takes a general glance at the revelation of the Old Testament one sees that first and foremost **it is the revelation of God as the Creator**. We must put that first. Living in a world of time we must start with that. Here is a subject which merits our attention because it seems to me there is a tendency on the part of certain Christian people to be so absorbed in the idea of God as Saviour in Christ as to forget the idea of God as Creator. All the present vexed problems of the relationship of church and state, of the gospel and the material needs of man and so forth, are ultimately questions which can only truly be handled in the light of the doctrine of God as Creator. It is only as you remember that God is Creator that you begin to see any meaning in such terms as the various orders of society. It was God, after all, who made the family. It was God who established the nations, the kings, and the princes, and the rulers – a very important aspect of truth which we must never lose sight of. We have, in the Old Testament, God as the Creator, the Artificer of the world and of everything that exists. He is the One who sustains the universe and He rules over all.

Then, coming more specifically to the matter that concerns us directly as souls, we find **a revelation of the holiness of God**. Yes, God is the Creator of everything, but what is His character? That, of course, was the specific purpose of the giving of the law. In the giving of the law God, above everything else, states and proclaims His own holy nature. He declares that He is a holy God, a jealous God, one who demands our totalitarian allegiance and worship. He cannot abide any other god. His holiness was manifested supremely in the giving of the law.

Then, of course, as an essential part of that, there is **the demonstration of the sinfulness of man and the exceeding sinfulness of sin**. You remember Paul in Galatians, and again in Romans, argues that out. Why does the law come in at all? That is the question. The answer is: that the exceeding sinfulness of sin might be manifested and demonstrated. It is only in the light of the law, which reveals the holy nature of God, that man can see himself as a sinner; that man really begins to understand the nature of this foul canker that is inbred into his being, and that has marred the image of God, and brought chaos into the universe.

The exceeding sinfulness of sin! And that, of course, leads to another revelation, the revelation of **the problem of the reconciliation of man and God, and God and man; and the need of the atonement**. I am simply showing you the great pinnacles of the revelation, the glorious peaks that stand out above all the others as you look over the whole range. Holy God, sinful man! Consider the books of the Bible that really treat of nothing else but the problem of these two opposites – the exceeding sinfulness of sin, and the holiness of God, and the need of reconciliation. The great problem the whole time is the need of atonement; there is the whole problem of reconciliation. Then, lastly, the thing that towers up above everything else is the tremendous fact that **God Himself is dealing with the problem**. For, after all, the Old Testament is not an account of man trying to find God and seeking to be reconciled to Him. The whole glory of this old revelation is that it gives us the first intimation that God Himself – if I may use that anthropomorphism – takes up the task. God is busying Himself with it. It tells us that the Eternal, though He is holy, has, nevertheless, not turned His back upon man in his lost and sinful state, but initiates a process and prepares a way of salvation. Yet it does not provide us with salvation: it tells us of one to come, a Messiah. It looks forward to the fulfilment of the promise. It is something which prepares us and leads us on.

What is the value?

Now that, in turn, leads me to my third and last general principle. Again I ask a question: What is the value of all this to us? We have looked at the characteristic of the revelation. We have looked at the results of the revelation. Now I ask: What is the value of all this to us? The many parts and many ways of the revelation prove **the divine origin** of it all. For there is not only this progressive element, which I have mentioned, there is a further element of unity. All the parts indicate a definite scheme and plan. Cast your minds back to the origin, to the promise after the Fall. Run down the centuries and come to Noah. Go on again and come to Abraham. Think of all these gaps. Yet, in spite of the passage of the centuries, in spite of the differences in the men and in the instruments which God used, it is all part of the same mosaic, the same message, the same revelation, many parts and many ways demonstrating the divine origin of the whole. There could have been no collusion between these men; they were all divided and separated by centuries of time; they were so essentially different in their temperaments. The inestimable value of this old revelation is that it provides a wonderful proof of the truth of the New Testament. You remember Peter in his second epistle, speaking as an old man, says as his final message, "Moreover I will endeavour that ye may be able after my decease to have these things always in remembrance. For we have not followed cunningly devised fables" – and so on. Then he goes on to speak of what he and others had witnessed on the mount of transfiguration. But there is an even more striking proof than that. "We have also a more sure word of prophecy, whereunto ye do well that ye take heed." There is no fact which so strongly buttresses one's belief, especially in times and seasons when one is attacked by doubts and denials, as this perfect correspondence between the prophecy of the Old and the fulfilment of the New. Thank God for the old revelation.

But still more practical is the fact that we find in the Old the **proof of the absolute need of Christ**. We have to come under the law. Conviction is still the essential prelude to conversion. You will notice how in the third chapter of the epistle to the Galatians the apostle constantly plays on that theme. He says that the law was the schoolmaster to bring us to Christ; and if you do not come to him by that schoolmaster you will never come at all. The law is still essential. "The Scripture hath concluded all under sin," he says. Again he says that we have been shut up unto the faith by the law. In his epistle to the Romans he says that the law has stopped every mouth and made the whole world guilty before God. Too readily, perhaps, do we think of the love of God, this miracle and marvel of redeeming grace. Yet, if you read the lives of the saints and of the noblest souls that have inhabited the Christian church, you find they were all men and women who knew in their experience of the work of the law. The man who neglects the old revelation does so at his peril, for it is there we see the absolute need of the redeeming grace of God in the sacrifice of Jesus Christ.

There is something to be found in the Old Testament which, in a sense, is found nowhere else at all. I come back again to the idea of God as Creator. Here we are reminded that the world is God's. The world even of the unredeemed is God's world. God is not only interested in the redeemed; He is interested in the world which He Himself has made. And as you look at the Old Testament you will see that **God has got a plan for the world**. It is He who has introduced the orders of society. He has appointed for the nations the bounds of their habitation. It is He who has catered for man's every need. He has a plan for the world, and, still more important, it is a plan which can never be frustrated. There are these vast gaps between the different portions of the Old Testament. There are those intervening periods or centuries when nothing seems to be happening. Then the question is asked: Where is the promise of His coming? Remember it is God's world and He has a plan for it; and the world will go on inevitably to its final consummation. There we find the greatest source of comfort and encouragement, of consolation and hope that can be found anywhere on earth. You remember that the apostle Paul speaks of "the consolation of the Scriptures". He was thinking of the Old Testament Scriptures. There, he says, we see something that enables us to hold on. Therefore, in spite of men, in spite of circumstances, in spite of evil, let us be patient, let us be full of confidence. For God is behind all and the world is His, and His plan for it can never be frustrated. "God spoke in times past unto the fathers in the prophets", and He is still speaking. God grant that we may have ears to hear, and, above all, to hear the message that assures us that His hand is still upon the universe.

CHAPTER 8

From Glory – to Glory

(Hebrews 1:1–3)

As we approach this great statement again, there are two general principles which we must bear in mind and which are of fundamental importance. I emphasize them because I feel that it is very largely owing to the fact that they have been forgotten, or ignored, that we find ourselves in our present plight and position.

The gospel and history

The first principle of which we are here reminded is that **the Christian religion and the Christian gospel are based very definitely upon historical facts**. The Christian religion is a religion belonging to history. It takes its origin from history. I have mentioned that God's revelation of Himself in the old dispensation was also historical. God manifested Himself in and through the prophets, in human beings, and we saw how He did so at different times and in different places. That is why we are right, in a sense, in referring to the Old Testament revelation as being at the same time a history of the people of Israel. Part of the revelation was given through an historic people and through certain historic personages who belonged to that nation and arose out of it. The Old Testament revelation was **historical**; and precisely and exactly the same thing is true of the New Testament revelation. It is something of which we should never lose sight and never let go. The Christian religion is not, primarily, a philosophy. It is not, first of all, a view of life or ideas concerning life. The Christian religion, in the first instance, is a record of facts. It is an announcement of certain things which have taken place in the realm of history. The principles and the philosophy of the Christian faith are derived from, and based upon, those historic acts and facts. The gospel is "good news" in the sense that it is an announcement of something which God has done in time; something concrete, something definite, something that is as much part of the warp and woof of history as are the various facts which are normally recorded in our secular historical books. We are reminded of that by the very fact of Christmas. Everything of which we remind ourselves at Christmas arises out of those events which have come to pass. If anything which claims to be the Christian gospel is not intimately related to and definitely based upon those facts then it has no right to claim the name Christian, however good and excellent it may be of itself; however exalted a view of life it may offer, however noble, however tender, however beautiful, however wonderful. If the idea does not proceed immediately out of the historic facts it is not Christian, whatever else you may like to designate it. That is the first principle.

The second principle is that **the facts which are emphasized in this way by the Christian gospel are the essential and specific facts concerning the person of Jesus of Nazareth**. Or, to use a phrase which was once popular, we are showing that Christianity is Christ. He is the very centre of the Christian religion. He is essential to it; not in the sense that He is the one who first gave expression to the views and ideas which go by the name Christian; not simply that He is the one who first outlined this view of life. He is essential, rather, in His being, in His person, and in what He did as the God-man in addition to what He said. That is a distinction of which we sometimes lose sight, yet it is the very thing which makes the Christian religion utterly unique. Of no other teacher can it be said that He is essential to His teaching. If someone proved that Socrates had never written anything it would not, in any way, detract from the value which we can derive from his teaching. Socrates himself is not essential to his view of life; neither is Plato to Platonic philosophy. The same can be said of the other great exponents of the theories and views of life which have gained currency. In no case is the particular man essential. But this is not so in connection with the Christian religion. Here we are dealing with something in which the teacher is infinitely more important than the teaching. The most important thing is that we should realize the centrality, the absolute necessity of the person, Jesus of Nazareth. If you read the accounts which are given in the Acts of the Apostles of the preaching of the first Christian preachers, you will find that everywhere we are told that they preached Jesus. That was the characteristic method of the apostle Paul. According to the accounts in Scripture, when he was preaching in the synagogue to the Jews, he generally made two points. The first was that the Messiah must suffer and the second was that Jesus is the Messiah. The preaching was about the person and what was true and characteristic of Paul's method was equally true of the method of the various other early preachers of the gospel.

The background to Christmas

Now we must look at these facts in connection with Him as we are reminded of them by these first three verses of the first chapter of the epistle to the Hebrews. I am going to attempt to put it in another form, as a kind of prolegomena to Christmas. I am going to call attention to certain principles which must of necessity control our thinking about the birth of Christ if our thinking is to be of ultimate value to us. What has been the value of the Advent season to us in the past? Has it led to any permanent contribution to our spiritual experience? If it has not, why not? Perhaps we have not always approached it in the right way and manner. Here in this text I think we are shown the way in which all our thinking should he governed and controlled. I would put it to you in the form of three general principles or propositions.

1. The Person of Christ

First we must consider the Person of Christ. Who is this babe of Bethlehem? Who is that infant whom the shepherds went to see? Who is this babe who is held in the arms of the ancient Simeon and of whom the prophetess Anna spoke? Who is this Person? The author of this epistle to the Hebrews gives us the answer to that question in very striking terms. He does not argue. He makes a dogmatic pronouncement. The first

Christian preachers did not argue about Him; they just proclaimed Him. Perhaps we have a statement concerning Him here which is grander than that which is to be found anywhere else even in the Scriptures. Let me just remind you of the terms which the author employs. He says, "God, who at sundry times and in divers manners spake in time past unto the fathers by the prophets, hath in these last days spoken unto us by his Son." That is the Authorized Version, but in the original it reads, "hath in these last days spoken unto us by Son", not "the" Son and certainly not "a" Son. This is the emphasis which we find everywhere throughout the New Testament. It refers to him as the "only-begotten" Son. You remember the various occasions when the voice came from heaven and uttered those words, "This is my beloved Son in whom I am well pleased." That is the first statement that is made with respect to Him. He is the Son of God in an entirely unique and separate manner.

Then the author of this epistle goes on to amplify that in these most striking terms: "who being the brightness of his glory and the express image of his person, and upholding all things by the word of his power, when he had by himself purged our sins, sat down on the right hand of the Majesty on high". Here it is generally agreed that a better translation would be "the effulgence of his glory". What does that mean? Here is a statement which reminds us that the Son is not a reflection, not a refulgence, but the effulgence of His glory. By that is meant that Jesus, the Son of God, did not merely reflect the glory of the Father, but is the very glory of the Father in expression and in manifestation. Perhaps the best analogy, the best illustration to make clear this meaning, is that which has been employed throughout the centuries. The relationship between the Son and the Father has been compared to the relationship between the rays of the sun and the sun. The rays come out of the sun and yet they are part of the sun. At the same time then they are distinct from the sun. Now what the rays of the sun are to the sun, so Jesus the Son is to God the Father. He is the very glory of God and yet is distinct; is separate and has an identity of His own. What the beam of light is to the light so Jesus, the Son of God, is to the Father. He is the effulgence of His glory.

Then we are told that He is "the express image of his person", which you can translate if you like by saying that He is the very image of the

Person, or the substance of God. In other words, Jesus of Nazareth is an exact reproduction and manifestation of God. The authorities are all agreed here that the picture which the author has in mind is that of the image which is produced when we place a seal upon any soft substance, whether it be wax, or any substance which can receive an impression. When you place a seal upon it and then remove the seal you have impressed upon that substance an exact likeness, a perfect and complete representation of that which was on the seal. That is the idea which the author had in his mind when he referred to our Lord as the express image of the Person of God.

You remember our Lord Himself put it once and forever in those words of His recorded in the fourteenth chapter of John's Gospel, when turning to Philip He said, "He that hath seen Me hath seen the Father." He is the express image of the Person of God. To see Him is to see God. He is the exact likeness of what God is like.

Then we are told certain other things about Him. He is not only the effulgence of the eternal glory and the express image of God, He is also the one by whom God made the worlds. "By whom also he made the worlds." The same point is made in the prologue of John's Gospel where we are told that everything was made by Him "and without him was not any thing made that was made". You will find that same idea repeated constantly in other parts of the New Testament.

Finally, says this man who wrote the letter to the Hebrews, the Son of God is the one who has been appointed heir of all things. As everything was made through Him, as He was the instrument used by God in creation, so He has been made the heir of all things. There are the main terms in our text.

I would remind you of the significance of those words "being" and "upholding". It does not say that He **became** the brightness of His glory, but it says "**being** the brightness of his glory". It does not say that He was **made** the express image of His Person, but that He **is** the express image of His Person and that He does uphold all things by the word of His power. Perhaps I can best summarize it by reminding you of two words which have always traditionally been used in this connection. The Son of God is "consubstantial" and "co-eternal" with the Father. The babe in that manger is one who has **come** into this world. He does not start there. That is not His genesis, His origin, His beginning. He is consubstantial and co-eternal with the Father.

2. The actions of Christ

Now having looked in that brief way at the Person, we must consider for a moment the facts concerning what He has done. Here at once we cannot but be impressed by the very striking way in which the author of this epistle deals with that particular matter. You observe that he gives us three pictures. First of all he pictures the eternal Son **before He came into the world**. He gives us a vision of eternity. He shows us the trinity, Father, Son and Holy Spirit. The Son is of the very substance of the Father. There is the first picture, in eternity, in love.

Then I wonder whether you have observed the second picture. It is a picture of **the death on the cross**. Let me give you the exact words: "who being the brightness of his glory, and the express image of his person, and upholding all things by the word of his power, *when He had by himself purged our sins*, sat down on the right hand of the Majesty on high." From the eternal glory to the cross and the grave.

Then the last picture is another picture of **the Son of God in glory**: "sat down on the right hand of the Majesty on high". Now this is something, surely, which must arrest our attention. You observe that the author does not mention the birth of our Lord directly. He just gives us the three pictures: the beginning, the lowest point and the end. Surely it should fill us with wonder and amazement as we contemplate it. First there is the glory, then the shame and death of the cross, the burial and the grave. Then again we have the glory – Jesus seated at the right hand of the Majesty on high. In other words, the principle surely is that we must always regard the life of our Lord as a whole. There are details and incidents in it, and yet if we would grasp and appreciate the value even of those details and incidents, we must always view them in the whole context. The tendency on our part is to divide them. We are so earthly and so carnal in our outlook. We like to look at that crib in the manger. We like to sentimentalize over it. We paint our picture books; we concentrate on particular things. But not so the Scriptures. They view His life as a whole. Scripture gives a picture of the grand procession of the Son of God. It describes that majestic journey. Many details are included, but it concentrates attention upon the focal points.

Yet perhaps there is a sense in which the author of this epistle would have us also mention the details of the journey, so I would remind you of them. We are all so familiar with them that we tend to lose sight of their wondrous character. There He was in heaven, in eternity, in the bosom of the Father. Then He came to earth. He was born a babe at Bethlehem and we see Him lying in helplessness in the arms of people. Then a number of years pass and we see Him at the age of twelve astounding and amazing the doctors of the law in the Temple as He reasoned and argued with them concerning the Scriptures and the law. Then there follows a silence of eighteen years. We gather that He lived the life of an ordinary artisan, that He did His work as a carpenter. Then suddenly at the age of thirty He enters upon His public ministry. We see His miracles; we listen to the gracious teaching that comes from His lips; we observe His compassion and kindness. Then in rapid succession come the machinations of evil men, the conspiracy and the plotting, the condemnation, the trial, the cross, the mighty resurrection, the ascension, and there He is seated at the right hand of the Majesty on high. That is the journey.

3. The importance of Christ

Lastly, as my final principle, I would impress upon you **the importance of considering these things**. I have already suggested that it is important that we should study every detail, every incident in the light of the whole, that we should follow this author's example. I say again that the danger confronting us is the danger of sentimentalizing and of painting our beautiful pictures. While we weep over the details, I think I sometimes hear the voice of the Lord saying, "Daughters of Jerusalem, weep not for Me, but weep for yourselves, and for your children." Now we must not approach these facts sentimentally. You remember those striking words which we are told about His mother in the second chapter of Luke. We are told that "she pondered these things in her heart". She wondered what they were all about. In the third chapter of this epistle the author says, "Consider the apostle and high priest of our profession, Christ Jesus." Again in the twelfth chapter, "Consider him that endured such contradiction of sinners against himself." We must not merely note these facts; it is not enough that we just remind ourselves of them. Let us **consider** this amazing journey from glory to glory via Bethlehem and the cross. What do we find here? I give you just the headings, which I commend to you for your meditation.

First, there is **the humiliation** that was involved in it all. God "hath in these last days spoken unto us by his Son, whom he hath appointed heir of all things, by whom also he made the worlds". Yet that selfsame person was born as a babe in Bethlehem. We are told of Him that He grew and increased in knowledge and in wisdom. We read of Him that He has been appointed heir of all things. He is rightly the heir because all things were created through Him, and He has been given the universe. Yet He was rejected and despised. "He came unto his own, and his own received him not." Oh, the humiliation of it all! I read also in this epistle that he "upholdeth all things by the word of his power". Yet I see Him helpless in the hands of men and nailed to a tree. What a descent from the original glory of the Son of the eternal Father! Look at the helplessness of the babe at Bethlehem, the death on the cross, the burial in the grave.

Look for a moment at **the mystery**. Here is a mighty subject, but keep two things in mind. He emptied himself. That was involved in it. You remember the technical term – *kenosis*. The Scriptures tell us that "being in the form of God, he counted it not a prize to be on an equality with God, but emptied himself, taking the form of a servant, being made in the likeness of men". What does it mean? Towards the end of the nineteenth century there were those who argued that it meant He emptied Himself of His deity. But that is a misconception. He emptied Himself only of the insignia of His deity and glory. He is the express image of the glory of God, and that is something which can never be undone. While He was here upon earth He was still the Son of Cod. He was still the express image of the Person of God. He only divested Himself of the signs, the manifestation of His glory. That was the *kenosis*.

There was also the **incognito**. Have you observed how at one and the same time our Lord seemed to be revealing Himself and yet concealing Himself? You remember how He prohibits the demons to say who He is. You remember how He told those whom He had healed to go home and to say nothing about who had healed them. He revealed Himself and yet at the same time He concealed Himself. This is the divine incognito, the Son of God coming in the likeness of sinful flesh, taking upon Him the pattern of a man, revealing and yet concealing the mystery of godliness. Let us reflect upon that.

Then lastly consider **the purpose of it all**. Why did He come? That is the question. He came to reveal God in what He was and in what He did. Again I would remind you of His own words: "He that hath seen me hath seen the Father." Bethlehem leads on to Calvary. He came to this world in order to go to Calvary. It says, "when he had by himself purged our sins". This author tells us in the second chapter that Jesus was made "a little lower than the angels for the suffering of death". He came "to taste death for every man". That is why He came. He was born a baby in order that He might pass on to the cross. His birth is the essential prelude to His death on Calvary.

Yet there is another aspect of this matter from which we can derive consolation this morning. The point which is made at great length by the author of this epistle is that another result of His coming, of His incarnation, of His living amongst us, is that we have now a sympathetic High Priest. He has borne our nature. He has taken upon Him our flesh. He knew what it was to be tired, to be hungry. He knew what it was to feel grief and sorrow. He has been tried in all points like as we are, sin apart. The result is that there at the right hand of the Majesty on high we have a High Priest who can be touched with the feeling of our infirmities. He has shared our life; He has experienced our troubles. He has risen from the dead, but He is still the God-Man, bearing in His hands and feet and side the marks of His humiliation.

There, it seems to me, are some of the thoughts and principles which should guide our thinking. Why did He come? Remember, above all that He did all that for us. It is not a tableau; it is not a picture. The effulgence of the eternal glory, the express image of the Person of

God came down, was born in Bethlehem, lived a life, died a death, was buried in the tomb and rose again to rescue you, to redeem you from your sins, and to reconcile you unto God. "Thanks be unto God for his unspeakable gift."

CHAPTER 9

Supreme Revelation in Christ

(Hebrews 1:1–3)

The final Sunday of December in any year is always one which calls for a special message from the preachers of God's Word. It does so for two main reasons. One is that it is the first Sunday after Christmas Day and the other reason is that it is the last Sunday of a year. Now both those facts, in a sense, are such as to demand and to insist upon a special message. No one who is, in any sense of the term, a Christian can possibly face the fact of Christmas Day without asking certain questions. Above every other question which we must inevitably ask is the central question, "What is its meaning? What is the purpose of the Incarnation? Why did the Son of God come? What is the message to the world which came through the Babe who was born in Bethlehem?" Inevitably, I suggest, on the first Sunday after Christmas that question has to be faced.

"Stocktaking"

Then there is that other fact, that on the last Sunday of an old year it has been the custom for Christian people especially to regard such a day as a day in which one should indulge in the process of stocktaking, examination, and a review of the past. There are certain milestones in life. There are certain times, seasons and occasions when one is driven to such a process. I am well aware that in the last analysis these divisions according to almanacs and so on are, in a sense, irrelevant, when we realize that we are immortal and eternal souls and spirits. Yet we are in the flesh and we are frail, and it is a good and a right thing that we should be reminded by external circumstances, occasionally, of the vital importance of self-examination. That is something which one could illustrate very easily in many realms and departments. We are constantly being reminded that there is often a tendency to lag in our spiritual energy. As a result of fatigue or weariness we become so accustomed to things that we tend to lose a sense of vigour and exhilaration. It is right and important, therefore, that we should pause now and again, and remind ourselves of certain fundamental and primary principles. Exactly the same thing is true of men engaged in commercial and professional life. Most of the failures in life are due to the failure to assess the situation and oneself, to strike the proper balance, to discover exactly where we are and what we are doing.

Now as that is true in every realm and department of life, it is, above all, true of the Christian way of life. Nothing is so important therefore, I suggest, at a time like this, than that we should thus review our lives and examine again what are the fundamentals and essentials of this Christian faith. My contention is that the two things of which we are reminded on the final Sunday of a year really amount to precisely and exactly the same thing. Our thoughts concerning the coming of Christ, our review of life as a whole, and of its meaning and purpose, must drive us back to those first principles and essentials of our faith. Now I can think of no better way of doing this than by considering once more the great argument set forth by the author of this Epistle to the Hebrews in these three verses, in which he epitomizes the whole of the case that he unfolds in such a wonderful manner in the body of the epistle.

We have been trying to remind ourselves as we have considered this text, that the real thing which the author of this Epistle to the Hebrews would impress upon our minds is the superiority of this revelation which has come through the Son over all previous revelations that had been given. It is a unique revelation; it is altogether separate and distinct, and apart from all others in its superiority. Now the question arises, "What is it about this particular speech through the Son that made it so distinct and unique and entirely different from all else?" The best way of answering that general question is to consider the matter under some general headings.

How has God spoken?

Let us consider, in the first place how God has spoken in the Son or the manner of the speech. Now here we come at once to the answer in the very terms that are employed by the author in these three verses. **He tells us that God has spoken in the Son perfectly**. We can illustrate this by dividing it up according to these terms here suggested. The author of this epistle tells us that God at sundry times spoke unto the fathers by the prophets. And you remember in the Old Testament we are given the books and the writings and the works of these prophets. There was that mighty line and succession of prophets – those great men in Israel to whom God spoke and through whom God spoke, and who became the mouthpiece of God to the nation and people. We saw in our analysis of them that nothing was so characteristic of the revelation given through them as its partial nature. Not one of them was complete. It was a matter of a little here and a little there. To one was given this particular aspect of the revelation and to another something that was complementary and additional to it. We saw also how between them there was that marvellous unity, that composite picture. Yet each one of them, it has to be admitted, was incomplete. We are now given this striking contrast. At last a Prophet has come who is perfect, complete and enduring. You remember that that is, in a sense, the great theme of the whole of the Old Testament. They were looking forward to the coming of **the** Prophet. Now, says this man, He has come! God speaks now through one who is perfect: the Son. The revelation, therefore, in that respect is full, it is complete, it is perfect. The ancient prophets, good as they were, were fallible men and guilty of sin. Here is one who is sinless, spotless, perfect. He is, as we saw before, the express image of God; He is the effulgence of His everlasting and eternal glory. "He that hath seen Me hath seen the Father," said Christ. His words are perfect words. You read the Gospel and you find that even His enemies were amazed at the grace which poured forth from His lips; and they could not understand it. At last here is a perfect Teacher, a complete Prophet.

In the same way, **He is the perfect and complete Priest**. This man says in the third verse that "when he had by himself purged our sins, he

sat down on the right hand of the Majesty on high". Again, we go back to
the old dispensation and we see all the priestly order and ritual and
ceremony. The problem of sin had arisen and something had to be done
about it. Priests were appointed with the various gradations of their
office. They served in the tabernacle and at the altar. Yet not one of these
priests was perfect. That is the main argument in this epistle to the
Hebrews. You remember the author compares this perfect priesthood
with the imperfect Levitical and Aaronic priesthood that had gone
before. Here and here only is the perfect priest who can offer adequate
offerings unto God, a Priest after the order of Melchizedek, a priest who
is the Son of God. In exactly the same way the offering is a perfect
offering. "When he had himself purged our sins, he sat down at the right
hand of the Majesty on high." We observe the contrast in this epistle; it is
worked out in great detail. The shedding of the blood of bulls and goats
could never make anything perfect. That kind of thing could not purge
the conscience from dead works. It only covers sin in a ritualistic manner.
Men and women stand in need of a perfect offering. Before God's
holiness and righteousness can be satisfied there must be a perfect
offering, a perfect oblation, and it is only in Christ that that is found, for
He offered Himself as a lamb without spot or blemish and entirely
without sin. As the hymn puts it:

> "There was no other good enough
> To pay the price of sin.
> He only could unlock the gates
> Of heaven and let us in."

It is no longer the external sacrifices of bulls and goats, and the ashes
of an heifer, but the very body of the Son of God, broken for our
salvation.

Then **our Lord Jesus Christ is perfect also as King**. We are reminded
of this in our text: "When he had by himself purged our sins, he sat down
on the right hand of the Majesty on high." The world had been looking
and longing for a king. Mankind wanted to give its allegiance to one who
was worthy of it. There had been kings and rulers, judges and potentates

in the old dispensation, but not one of them was worthy of man's entire allegiance and obedience. There is only one who is worthy of that. He is the one who alone was found worthy to unlock the seals and to open the Book of Life, and to take His seat at the right hand of the Majesty on high. There are others in this world today, as there have been in the past, who have asked for, and made their claim to the totalitarian allegiance of men. But there is only one who is worthy of it – the Son of God, the effulgence of the eternal glory, the express image of the Father. He is King of kings; He is Lord of lords. He stands alone as worthy of our entire offering of ourselves.

So in Him, God has spoken perfectly – perfect Prophet, perfect Priest, a perfect offering and King.

It is also important that we should realize that **God has spoken finally** because He has spoken perfectly. That, again, is a great theme in this epistle. It keeps running through it like a kind of *leitmotif.* The author was concerned about these Hebrews. They were tending to drift away from Christianity. They thought they could go back. But his point is that if they once go back, there is no returning. This is the final, this is the last word. God has spoken finally in Christ. I say it with reverence, there is no more that even God can do. God came Himself in His Son. "God was in Christ reconciling the world unto himself." God has poured out His own heart on the cross. It is the last word of God. Nothing further can ever be done.

So that is the manner of the speech. God has spoken in His Son. It is perfect, and it is also final.

What has God spoken?

Now all this leads me to the second question. **What has God said in the Son?** What exactly is the point and the purport of it all? Here is the great theme of the New Testament gospel. Yet very resolutely and deliberately I would remind you of it. We can never repeat it too frequently. It is our duty to reiterate it lest we reduce this glorious gospel to a mere humanism, to a mere concern about social conditions, forgetting its eternal consequences. What has God said in the Son?

God has spoken to us in a final manner concerning Himself. That is the first thing. The first word of God to man is always a word about God, not about man. With all our self-centredness in recent years we have always been waiting for something which will make us happier or more comfortable. Yet the word of God is a word about God. It is because of this morbidity and introspection that we lose sight of the great authority of the Christian faith. In our concern about men, we have been forgetting God.

What has He told us about God? Christ has spoken concerning **the holiness of God** in a way that none of the prophets ever spoke. In our analysis of the Old Testament we found that "the prophets" told us of God as the Creator and of the giving of the law. But it is only in the Son that we begin to understand something of the holiness of God. You remember how when He prayed He addressed Him as "Holy Father". And you remember how, in the model prayer which He taught His disciples, having said, "Our Father which art in heaven," He hastened to add, "Hallowed be Thy Name." The holiness of God! Indeed, it is only as we look into the face of Jesus Christ that we begin to know anything about holiness. As we see His spotlessness and His perfection, and as we observe His hatred of sin and His abhorrence of evil, as we see something of the perfection of His life, we have a revelation of the holiness of God. It is in Christ, and especially upon the cross, that we see the holiness of God.

But, thank God, we see also **the love of God**. Only He has spoken fully and authoritatively to mankind about the love of God. There are gleams of it in the Psalms. "Like as a father pitieth his children, so the LORD pitieth them that fear him." But it is only in the Son that we can begin to know the meaning of God's love. We observe His compassion, how He never passed by suffering. Even when His disciples would have done so, He tarried. He showed His compassion, His sympathy, His tenderness. It is expressed for us once and for all in those memorable words, "A bruised reed will he not break, and the smoking flax he will not quench." There we see the love of God as it is revealed in Christ.

He has also given us a revelation of **the terrible nature of sin**. It is only in Jesus Christ that we can realize the meaning and nature of sin.

We think of the terrible problem of sin. That leads me to ask the simple question, "Why did the Son of God ever come into this world? What is the explanation of the Incarnation?" There is only one who is adequate to deal with the problem of sin. There was no other way of dealing with it. Had the mere word of God been enough his fiat would have gone forth. If the prophets, the priests and the Levitical ceremony and ritual had been adequate to deal with it, the Son would never have come. Why did the eternal Son leave the courts of heaven? Why was He born as a baby in Bethlehem? Why did He take upon Him the garment of sinful flesh? Why did He endure the contradiction of sinners for thirty-three years? There is only one answer. The problem of sin is so terrible and so deep, that there was nothing less that could have been adequate. The Son came because the Son had to come. And in Him God has spoken unto us concerning the nature of sin.

But we thank God for this further knowledge. **He has spoken also concerning the way of salvation**. Salvation is in the Son, as we have already emphasized; it is in Him alone. That is why the author of this epistle was so concerned about emphasizing and reiterating this. Christ is the only way of salvation. He is God's way of salvation. There can be no other. So he says, "Hold on to it."

God has spoken to us in His Son. Jesus of Nazareth is the only Saviour and Redeemer. He is essential to our relationship with God.

To whom has God spoken?

We come then to my last question, "**To whom has God spoken in this way?**" We have looked at the manner of speech; we have looked at the content. To whom has He spoken? The answer of this man is, He has spoken to us. To whom does that refer? Here, surely, is the most important thing of all. He has spoken thus not only to these Hebrew Christians, not only to the first apostles and martyrs and confessors. He has spoken thus to us – to you and to me. The most important thing, it seems to me, is that we realize God has spoken to us. There is a terrifying aspect to that statement. Here, again, is a great theme of this epistle to the Hebrews. Whether you and I have heard and realized the meaning of the speech, or not, the fact remains that God has spoken to us in Jesus of Nazareth, the Son of God. The greatest tragedy in the world today, even a greater tragedy than the tragedy of the wars that trouble the human race, is that the teeming masses of mankind have not realized that God has spoken to them in the Son of His love. But, my dear friend, with real urgency, I would remind you that He has spoken to you, and when the day comes for you to shake off this mortal coil and to stand in the presence of your Maker and Judge, you will not be able to plead ignorance, for God has spoken to you in His Son. Do you remember the words He Himself uttered in addressing the Pharisees? He said, "I am not going to judge you. The words that I have spoken unto you shall judge you." God has spoken to you and to me, and we are left without excuse. You remember how He said to the men of His day, "If I had not spoken unto you the words which I have spoken, then had ye not sin. But now ye have no cloke for your sin." Yes, He has spoken and we are all left without excuse.

But I would rather leave you with this statement in its positive form. If you have not realized until this moment that God has spoken, then realize it now. Do so for this reason, that you are an immortal soul, and that life is uncertain, and we are moving on. We are here today and gone tomorrow. Realize now that God has spoken to you. Though you may have sinned against Him, though you may never have thought of Him, though you may never have thanked Him for His goodness and kindness towards you, though you may have spurned the voice divine, though you may have dwelt in the gutters of sin, He, nevertheless, speaks to you. He has sent His Son into this world for you and the Son has borne your sins in His own body on the tree. He offers to forgive you, that you may make a new beginning, that you may receive new life, that ahead of you may shine the everlasting hope and the certainty beyond time of spending eternity in the presence of God.

PART 3

What Is a Christian?

CHAPTER 10

Having the Spirit of Christ

(Romans 8:9)

"But ye are not in the flesh, but in the Spirit, if so be that the Spirit of God dwell in you. Now if any man have not the Spirit of Christ, he is none of his."

Romans 8:4–17 is undoubtedly one of the most important passages not only in this mighty epistle to the Romans, but one of the most important passages in the whole of Holy Scripture. Nowhere, perhaps, is the balance of the Scriptures more perfectly illustrated and demonstrated than in this particular section. Now there is a sense in which it is almost impossible to consider any one verse or any one statement in this section, because the entire paragraph constitutes an argument as a whole. The apostle, as you know, has in the previous chapters been working out his argument for that central, essential principle of justification by faith. He has been proving and demonstrating it in theory and by example from the Old Testament, and by apt quotations from the Old Testament literature. He has been at great pains to show how the law could not save man from condemnation and that the law likewise was utterly incapable of enabling one to fulfil the commands of God. Up to the end of Romans chapter 5 he has been mainly concerned about the question of condemnation – how to deal with the guilt of sin and the condemnation of God upon sin; and he shows clearly that the law is quite incapable of doing that. Then he comes in chapter 6 to the more practical question of how we are to live; and here again in chapters 6 and 7 he shows how the law is quite incapable of enabling us to live the life we ought to be living. So, having worked out his argument, he ends with this thrilling declaration at the beginning of the eighth chapter, "There is, therefore, now no condemnation to them that are in Christ Jesus." But still he cannot leave it. Paul was never tired of repeating himself when he was dealing with great subjects like this. He again has to repeat it all by saying, "For what the law could not do, in that it was weak through the flesh, God sending his own Son in the likeness of sinful flesh, and for sin, condemned sin in the flesh; that the righteousness of the law might be fulfilled in us, who walk not after the flesh, but after the Spirit." Thank God, says the apostle in effect, we are delivered from all the condemnation that is associated with the law. The law, he says, was never meant to save us; that was not its function. It was meant to show us our utter inability by ourselves to get right in the sight of God. Thank God, he says, the law of the Spirit of life hath made me free from that.

The perfect balance

Here is the great central affirmation. Our salvation is altogether in Christ and we are saved not by our own efforts, but by His death on our behalf on Calvary's Hill. There, says the apostle, liberty is proclaimed. "There is therefore now no condemnation." But just at that point a danger arises. It is here, I say, that we observe this perfect balance of the scriptural doctrines which we ignore only at extreme peril to ourselves. The danger at that point is, of course, that we are tempted to say, "Very well, there is nothing for us to do. We simply thank God for Jesus Christ. We are saved in Christ who has died for our sin, and all that is necessary is that we should say that we are in Christ and that is the end of it." "Not at all!" says the apostle. That is the error into which men have often fallen and it is furthermore the charge that is so constantly brought against the evangelical presentation of the gospel. The charge that was brought against the first Christians by those who had fallen into various heresies, especially the Judaists, was that Christianity was a form of antinomianism, teaching that so long as you believe in Christ you can do anything you like; your actions, your work, your life, your conduct, are utterly immaterial. The whole realm of ethics is dissolved and we need have no concern about it. Now that is an utter travesty of the gospel and a charge which is utterly unfounded. Nowhere, perhaps, is that shown quite so clearly as in this particular section which we are about to examine.

You notice how the apostle really introduces the subject at the end of that third verse and in verse 4. He says, "God, sending his own Son in the likeness of sinful flesh, and for sin, condemned sin in the flesh, [4]that the righteousness of the law might be fulfilled in us, who walk not after the flesh, but after the Spirit." In other words, why did Christ die? What is the object of Christian salvation? Is it merely to give us forgiveness of sins? Is it merely to save the people who believe from hell and all its punishment and all its consequences? No, says the apostle, the object of salvation is not a negative one, it is a positive one. God did not send His Son from the courts of heaven and ask Him to endure all He endured on the face of the earth merely to save us from the consequences of our sin. Oh, no! God's object was that "the righteousness of the law might be fulfilled in us, who walk not after the flesh, but after the Spirit", or, as he puts it in writing to Titus, "that he might redeem us from all iniquity, and purify unto himself a peculiar people, zealous of good works". The whole object of the atonement, therefore, is not negative; it is positive. Christ has come to make us positively righteous. Christ endured and suffered all He did and died in order that we might be made righteous in a positive and real sense in the sight of God.

So there is nothing which is quite so dangerous as for us to divorce these various Christian doctrines from one another. The whole object of salvation is to enable us to stand righteous in the presence of Almighty God. To believe that Christ has died for us and our sins is not enough in and of itself. We must go on beyond that and apply certain other tests. That is why I am directing your attention to the ninth verse especially. Indeed the whole passage from verse 4 to 17 is of extreme importance in this connection. But looking at verse 9 is a good way of considering the passage as a whole.

Who is a Christian?

"Now if any man have not the Spirit of Christ, he is none of his." I regard that as one of the most serious and most solemn statements that is to be found anywhere in the Bible. It brings me face to face at once with this question: "Am I a Christian? What is a Christian? Who is a Christian?" Now this question is of tremendous importance, for this reason. According to the apostle here, if we are not Christian we are dead! Paul says here that the "carnal mind is enmity against God" (verse 7). "To be carnally minded is death" (verse 6); and "death", there, means to be outside the life of God. The man who dies in that carnally-minded state is lost. He goes into eternity outside the life of God. That is the terrible thing which we have to contemplate as we face this question. If we have not the Spirit of Christ we are dead; we are not Christian and we shall remain, if we are in that condition, eternally outside the life of God, in a state of spiritual death and of unhappiness and torment. But, on the other hand, says the apostle, if we are truly Christian we have life, and not only life, but also peace. "To be carnally minded is death; but to be spiritually minded is life and peace." Is not this the thing that people who really are awakened to their condition long for, to have life, to be in God, to know God, to share the life of God, to be at peace with God, to be at peace with external circumstances? What a wonderful and amazing offer – life and peace.

But I am concerned about this question not merely in terms of the subjective benefits that come to us, but for what I regard as a still more important reason. Never, it seems to me, has there been a time when it is essential for Christian people to be certain of themselves and of their standing so much as at this present hour. We cannot be indifferent to the state of the world around and about us. We see its sin and its unhappiness, its confusion and its uncertainties. Yet if we are truly Christian, if we really believe the message of this Book, we know that nothing can suffice for the world save this gospel. That, to me, is one of those things that really needs no proof or demonstration. The history of the recent decades surely proves without any doubt whatsoever that everything that man and the world attempt is a complete failure. What the world needs is the gospel and the gospel is something that can only be brought to the world as the result of the activity of Christian people. That is where, I say, the question comes down to us as a personal one and as an essentially practical one. It is for you and for me to tell men and women about this gospel. We are in an age when personal witness and testimony is of exceptional and unusual importance. It is for us, I say, as we talk to people and as we meet them in our business and professional engagements and in various other places, as they start talking about these things, about the general situation, about the international conferences, and as they ask what has gone wrong with the nations, what is the meaning of all this suspicion and hatred; it is for us to begin to talk at that point and to show that the gospel of Jesus Christ solves these problems personally and on the larger scale. But all that, of course, can only be done if we know exactly and precisely where we stand, if we ourselves are perfectly clear about this and are not hesitant and doubtful and are not ourselves querying and questioning as to whether we are really in the right position and whether we are Christian. There is no need to argue this point. If we are uncertain about ourselves we shall not be able to speak to others. We shall feel we have no right to do so. The man who speaks is the man who knows. It is "out of the abundance of the heart the mouth speaketh" (Matthew 12:34). Therefore, I say, that there is nothing so urgently and vitally important as that we should face this preliminary and first question, "What is a Christian? Am I a Christian? Am I one of those people who stand out "holding forth the word of life" (Philippians 2:16) at a time like this? What is it that makes one a Christian?

Some negatives

Let me point out certain negatives first. There are certain people, says Paul, who are "none of his". What is it that makes one a Christian? Obviously it is not an external attachment to a church. Paul does not say that mere attendance at a place of worship makes one a Christian. Paul does not say that living a good life alone makes one a Christian. Paul does not say that an interest in religion makes one a Christian. Paul does not say that reading many books on the subject and being interested in philosophies make one a Christian, or even being interested in the Word of God. The Pharisees knew their Scriptures and were very interested in them. It is a terrible thing to realize that we may have this Book as one of our main interests in life and yet not be Christian. What is it that makes one a Christian? "If any man have not the Spirit of Christ, he is none of his." To say that you believe in Christ is not enough in and of itself. To hold certain views about forgiveness is not of necessity adequate. Paul, the great preacher of justification by faith, here says, "If any man have not the Spirit of Christ, he is none of his."

Now here we behold this perfect balance of the Scriptures. But the immediate question for us is to interpret his words. What does he mean? What is it to have the Spirit of Christ? I am only Christian if I have the Spirit of Christ. There are many who would say that this means something like this: they regard it as having a code – as they put it – His code of life. There are others who say that to have the Spirit of Christ means we are to catch something of "the spirit of Christ". That has been the popular teaching in recent years. It means something like this: that the man who is truly Christian has what is known as the Christ-like spirit. He is a man who holds certain views. Some would say he must hold certain views on the question of war. The man who has the spirit of Christ, they say, is the man who is Christlike in his outlook and in his behaviour. He is, again, a person who never hurts anyone, never does anyone any harm, is always out to do good, is always out to be philanthropic. He is a man who in his general attitude and conduct and behaviour seems to have got something of the spirit of Christ. But surely that is an exposition of these words which we cannot accept for a moment, and for this good reason. There are people who use that language who – and I quote words that can actually be seen in print – would describe a man like Mahatma Gandhi [the political activist who resisted British rule in India] as being a Christian. They say, look at his life, has he not a Christlike spirit and attitude? Now the simple answer to that kind of argument is plainly this: that Mahatma Gandhi himself tells us specifically that he is not a Christian. What makes one a Christian is not what one does, but, essentially and primarily, one's attitude towards the Lord Jesus Christ. There are people who are very nice and kindly, who would not dream of hurting anyone and who believe in doing a lot of good, but who do not even believe in the Being of God, so that when Paul talks about having the Spirit of Christ he is not talking about a kind of temperament or mentality or outlook in general. He means something very much more specific than that; and indeed the context explains what exactly he does mean. He has already said, "Ye are not in the flesh, but in the Spirit, if so be that the Spirit of God dwell in you." He uses these terms interchangeably. At one moment he talks about the Spirit of God, the next the Spirit of Christ, and in all these cases the word "Spirit" is written with a capital "S". Actually, therefore, what the apostle is saying is that if any man does not have the Holy Spirit in him he is none of Christ's. So that what we have here is not an exhortation to look at the New Testament picture of Christ and to try to copy His spirit and live like Him, but rather a statement that if a man is not indwelt by the Holy Spirit of God he is none of Christ's and he is therefore not a Christian.

How do I know?

So that narrows down our investigation still further. The question we are now contemplating is this: how do I know whether I have the Holy Spirit or not? If the Spirit of Christ does not dwell in you, says Paul, you are not Christ's; you are none of His. Surely this is one of the questions that engages the attention of Christian people more frequently than any other. It is a difficult question and a question that leads to argument and discussion, not to say to a good deal of confusion. Who has the Holy Spirit? How may I know whether I have the Holy Spirit? What does it mean to receive the Holy Spirit? Do I receive the Holy Spirit the moment I become Christian or is it something that happens to me later on? We are all familiar with that verse that is so often misquoted in the nineteenth chapter of the Book of the Acts. You remember how Paul at Ephesus had met those disciples of John. The Authorized Version tells us that Paul said to these men, "Have ye received the Holy Spirit since ye believed?" On the basis of that translation it is suggested you become a Christian first and then there is a second blessing and you receive the Holy Spirit. You can be a Christian without receiving the Holy Spirit; you receive the Holy Spirit later on. There are stages in the Christian life. In the same way there are those who would differentiate between our justification in Christ and our sanctification and who hold meetings designed to give people the blessing of sanctification. They say that some people are not yet sanctified and that they must be led to this further blessing of sanctification, as if one could receive justification without at the same time being sanctified. Now these are some of the questions that the apostle faces in a very direct manner in this whole passage. Are these things separate? It seems to me that the apostle's answer is perfectly clear and plain. His whole argument, in a sense, is to show the foolishness of dividing and separating these things. That is where the fourth verse, I repeat, is of such importance: "... that the righteousness of the law might be fulfilled in us, who walk not after the flesh but after the Spirit." According to the apostle's teaching we are not in the Christian life at all apart from the action of the Holy Spirit. For the apostle argues that the man who has a carnal mind, the man who walks after the flesh, is not only not subject to the law of God, he is dead in trespasses and sin. No man can say that Jesus is Lord but by the Holy Spirit. There is no step in the Christian life at all apart from the Holy Spirit. Not only that, the apostle argues here that God in Christ does not merely give man forgiveness; God regards a man as righteous in Christ. A Christian is a man who must view himself altogether in Christ. Christ, says Paul in writing to the Corinthians, is "made unto us wisdom and righteousness and sanctification and redemption". You cannot divide Christ; you cannot say, "I have forgiveness from Christ, but I have not had sanctification from Christ." We either have Christ or we do not have Christ. We are either in Christ or else we are not in Christ. There is nothing that is so thoroughly unscriptural as to divide justification from sanctification and sanctification from justification. To say a man can be a Christian without having the Holy Spirit is to postulate the utterly impossible. The whole work is the work of the Holy Spirit, and if I am a Christian in any sense at all I have already received the Holy Spirit. Of course I am very ready to grant and admit that there are degrees in my **experience** of the doctrine. There are experiences of the Holy Spirit from time to time, and there are periods when one is more conscious of the action of the Spirit than at other times. But the doctrine is that if I have not received the Holy Spirit I am not a Christian in any sense, and I am altogether outside the life of God. Therefore these things must be taken together. We must regard the doctrine as a whole; we must preserve carefully the balance of the Scriptures and we must not put these things into almost antithetical positions.

How is the Spirit manifested?

So having established that, I go on to my last question: "How does my possession of the Holy Spirit reveal and manifest itself?" "If any man have not the Spirit of Christ, he is none of his." Here again, as I ask this question, I introduce you to a matter often debated during the long history of the church. How do I know whether I have the Holy Spirit or not? Here the trouble is generally due to the fact that men have become confused over what we may describe as the "special" gifts of the Spirit over against the ordinary normal working of the Spirit in the matter of Christian graces. The whole trouble in a sense is that people will persist in reading chapter twelve of the first epistle to the Corinthians to the exclusion of everything else. They say, "If you have not spoken with tongues you do not have the Spirit," forgetting that Paul in that very chapter says that not all Christians speak with tongues. Others say that if you haven't worked a miracle, if you haven't the gift of prophecy, if you cannot speak in an exceptional manner, or if you haven't had some outstanding experience, you are without the Spirit. The trouble often arises as the result of reading books about others. We read about men who had striking experiences, such as seeing a ball of light, and whose whole life was changed from that moment. Then we tend to say, "I have not seen a ball of light and therefore I have not received the Holy Spirit." It is the whole trouble of confusing exceptional manifestations with what I would describe as normal manifestations of the working of the Spirit. In other words, it is because we neglect a passage like this in the eighth chapter of Romans that we so often tend to think and to feel that we have never received the Spirit at all, and that therefore we are not in Christ. "If any man have not the Spirit of Christ, he is none of his." How do I know whether I have the Spirit of Christ? All I want to do is to read a list and I exhort you to study these phrases. Let me give you the list as the apostle gives it. Who are the people who have the Holy Spirit? How may I know whether I have the Holy Spirit? Here are the tests.

The tests

Look at verse 5. The people who have the Holy Spirit are those who "mind the things of the Spirit". That is one test.

Or consider verse 7. "The carnal mind is enmity against God." The person who has the Spirit, obviously, is the person who loves God, who is not at enmity against God.

But look again at verse 7. The person who has not the Spirit of Christ or the Spirit of God is the man who is "not subject to the law of God". Therefore the man who is the possessor of the Holy Spirit is the man who does not oppose God and loves the law of God.

Go to verse 13. I there see that the man who has the Spirit is the man who is concerned about "mortifying the deeds of the body".

What else? Look at verse 14. We find there the person who is "led by the Holy Spirit".

Then verse 15. Those who have the Spirit have "the Spirit of adoption, whereby we cry, Abba, Father".

Finally, in verse 16, "the Spirit itself beareth witness with our spirit that we are the children of God".

So then, how do I know whether I have the Holy Spirit? Have I spoken with tongues? That is not of necessity a test at all; it is not mentioned here. These are the tests. Who are the people who are justified? Who are the people who are in Christ? Who are the people who can look forward to heaven and all that it must mean to be with Christ? Here are the answers. You can take these separate points enumerated and you can group them into three main groups:

1. The first is **a general test**. What are my interests? What are the things I "mind"? On what does my mind turn and operate; that is the first test and it is a very general one. What are the things I am out for? Do they belong to the flesh or the Spirit?

2. Then the second test is: "**What is my attitude towards God?**" Do I love Him or is my attitude just one of fear? Can I say to God, "Abba, Father?" Does the Spirit bear witness with my spirit that I am a child of God?

3. And then lastly: "**How do I live?**" What is my conduct; what is the nature of my actions? Do I obey the laws of God? Am I concerned about pleasing Him?

Those are the tests. You need not have some ecstatic experience; you need see no ball of fire; you need not have anything astonishing or astounding. Do not covet these things, says Paul. The proof of the possession of the Spirit is something in a sense much more ordinary than that. What sort of a mind have you? What is the realm of your interests? What is your attitude to God and your feeling about Him, and what kind of life are you concerned about in your actual, ordinary daily life and living? "If any man have not the Spirit of Christ, he is none of his." Christian people, let us make certain of our standing, let us make certain of our position, let us take these verses and regard them as a mirror into which we look in order that, having looked at them, we may turn to God with thankfulness and praise, thanking Him for the gift of the Holy Spirit. Then, having done so, let us face men and women and say, "We are Christians, we are Christ's." This is our message; this is the word of God to you through us. "If any man have not the Spirit of Christ," whatever may be true of him in any other respect, "he is none of his."

CHAPTER 11

Having the Mind of the Spirit

(Romans 8:5)

"For they that are after the flesh do mind the things of the flesh; but they that are after the Spirit the things of the Spirit."

We are considering together this great passage of Scripture because it seems to me that the first duty of all who claim to be Christian in this modern world is to make certain of ourselves. Are we functioning truly as Christians? Are we like those New Testament Christians of whom we can read in these various epistles? They were letters that were written to gatherings of Christian people and in them accounts are given of the kind of life they lived and the sort of people they were. I say the question we must face is this: "Are we like these people?" Then we can go on and read about Christians in every period of revival and reawakening, when they really did affect society and when they produced results in society. Are we like these people? That is just another way of putting this question: "What is a Christian? What is he or she like? How can I know for certain whether I am a Christian or not?" That is the most pressing and the most urgent question that we can all face today. Before we begin to do anything else we must start with that. How can I know whether I am a Christian or whether I am not a Christian, in order that I may function as a Christian?

Two dangers

Now the argument of the apostle in this paragraph is that there are two main dangers that confront us whenever we face that question. The danger always is to go from one extreme to the other and to put the position as if it were either this or that. The two dangers, in other words, are these. The first is **the danger of those who say that all that is necessary in order to be a Christian is that one should live a certain kind of life**. That is what Paul means when he refers to "the law" in these various chapters. The Jews' idea was that if they kept the law as they understood it, then that would satisfy God and they would be righteous in His sight. And surely there are still large numbers of people who believe that that is what makes one a Christian today. You ask them, "What is a Christian?" and they say, "The Christian is a man who lives a good life." In other words, they are exactly in that Jewish position. Man by his own efforts, they believe, can make himself satisfactory to God. That is their whole conception of the Christian man – a man who is doing his best to live a good life. That is one extreme.

The second **danger is found in those who say that all that is necessary in order to be a Christian is that one should have a particular belief**. This is the other extreme view which says that the first view is altogether wrong. It says it must be wrong of necessity, because if that is what makes one a Christian, then why should we have the term "Christian" at all? Why not call it morality or humanism? And it is a perfectly sound argument. There can be no Christianity without Christ, and if Christ has made no difference then the term "Christian" is altogether unnecessary. So the second group of people say that what makes one Christian is one's attitude towards this truth. That it is just a matter of believing that Jesus of Nazareth is the Son of God and to accept the teaching concerning Him.

Now according to the apostle's argument here both these extremes are not only wrong, but they are dangerous and even fatal. To divide up belief and life, according to Paul, is a fatal and a tragic dichotomy. He says that to be truly Christian one must include these two things, belief and life. That is the great burden of his argument in these particular verses. Paul says that both these things are essential for the good reason that what makes us Christian is that the Holy Spirit dwells within us, and that is why I selected this particular ninth verse as my text. "But ye are not in the flesh, but in the Spirit, if so be that the Spirit of God dwell in you." In other words, the essence of being a Christian is that one receives a new life from God by the indwelling of the Holy Spirit. We have to get into a realm beyond conduct and belief and to realize that God gives us the gift of life by the Spirit. That is the key to the whole of this question of how we are to decide and determine whether we are Christian or whether we are not. The Christian, according to the apostle, is a man who has received a new nature. He has a new life in him; he has received a new spirit. Christianity, as a Scotsman of the seventeenth century, Henry Scougal, put it, is "the life of God in the souls of men".[7] It is nothing less than that. So that when I ask myself, do I know for certain whether I am a Christian or not? what I really ask myself in practice is this: is the life of God in me? Do I have the Spirit of Christ? Is the Spirit of God dwelling in me? Such a person is a Christian, and, thank God, in this passage the apostle gives us the tests which we can apply to ourselves. This is not a vague, mystical matter of feeling; it is not a matter of some indefinite, nebulous, sensibility.

Fortunately for us the apostle gives us some very plain, rigid and practical tests. You notice he puts it in this form. All mankind, according to the apostle, can be divided into two groups. He says that we are all either walking after the flesh or else we are walking after the Spirit so that "the righteousness of the law might be fulfilled in us who walk not after the flesh, but after the Spirit". Here are other terms he uses to describe the same thing: "to be carnally minded is death; but to be spiritually minded is life and peace".

Now there are two possible positions and only two possible positions. All men, according to Paul, are either living what he calls a natural life, a carnal life, a life in the flesh, or else they are living a spiritual life, that is a new life, this life in the Spirit, this life of God that has entered into their being. Now I think that this is something that in a sense needs no demonstration. Is it not perfectly obvious that if the life of God has entered into one's life, that life must be different? That is the great argument of the New Testament. It does not say that the Christian is only a little bit better than somebody else; it says he is different. He is a new man. "If any man be in Christ Jesus he is a new creature." The Spirit

7. See H. Scougal, *The Life of God in the Soul of Man* (Christian Focus), 1996.

of God has come to dwell in him and the Spirit of God cannot be in man without changing him essentially and vitally and in the depths. That is the New Testament claim. You see it, for example, as you look at the apostles before Pentecost and after. Similarly, as you read the lives of the saints you see this radical transformation, the life of God coming in.

The first test

Now the question is, how may I know if this life of God has entered my life? I reminded you before that there are some seven or eight tests which I grouped together under three main headings. Now I want now to deal more thoroughly with the first test. The first way in which a man can know whether he is truly Christian or not, whether the life of God is in his life or not, is by discovering what is his attitude as a whole. That is the message of the fifth verse. "For they," says Paul, "that are after the flesh do mind the things of the flesh, but they that are after the Spirit the things of the Spirit." The operative word is the word "mind". They that are after the flesh, the non-Christian group, do "mind" the things of the flesh. The apostle was very fond of that term. You will remember how in writing his epistle to the Philippians in the third chapter and the nineteenth verse he talks about those who are the enemies of Christ as those who "mind" earthly things. Then you remember in the twelfth chapter of this great epistle to the Romans he starts off like this: "I beseech you therefore, brethren, by the mercies of God, that ye present your bodies a living sacrifice, holy, acceptable unto God, which is your reasonable service. And be not conformed to this world; but be ye transformed by the renewing of your mind, that ye may prove what is that good, and acceptable, and perfect, will of God." That, according to Paul, is something which is always one of the first tests which we must apply to ourselves. The Christian is a man who has got a new mind. So Paul describes the non-Christians as those who are enemies and alienated in their minds by wicked works against God. Obviously this is something again that needs no demonstration. What he means by "mind" is not simply intellect; he means that which is deepest and most central in man; he means that which is at the root of personality and that which governs the whole of man's activity. It is the mind, the centre, the heart, the very core of man's life. The mind refers to the objects of thought, affection and desire. When Paul says therefore that the difference between the non-Christian and the Christian is that the non-Christian minds the things of the flesh and the Christian minds the things of the Spirit, what he is virtually saying is this: the non-Christian thinks about the things of the flesh, likes and desires the things of the flesh, is pleased by the things of the flesh; but the Christian, on the other hand, is a man who thinks about the things of the Spirit, lives and is pleased by the things of the Spirit and desires and covets the things of the Spirit. This inner "mind" governs the whole intellect and the emotions and the desires. Therefore we are face to face, I say, with a very practical test as we look at these words of the apostle.

Some negatives

Now he puts it to us in a negative and in a positive form, and I want to glance at both aspects of the matter.

The man who is not a Christian minds the things of the flesh. What does that mean? It means first of all and most obviously, that he is a person who is interested in the things that appertain and belong to the body. For instance, there is no need to ask about the position of a person who just lives for eating and drinking and dancing and to be amused, and who never rises beyond the level of the physical and animal part of his nature. That is clearly a non-spiritual person, one who minds the things of the flesh. It is terrible to contemplate the large number of people who are living on that level and on that plane. God made man, body, soul and spirit; but there are many who are living only in terms of the body and have not risen above it. They clearly are minding the things of the flesh. But the danger at this point is to think that Paul's description applies only to people like that. That is something which is quite false. The life of the flesh is more comprehensive than that. You notice that Paul's antithesis is between the life of the Spirit and the life of the flesh; the mind of the Spirit and the mind of the flesh. We must not think of this mind of the flesh only in terms of the grosser manifestations of sin. All are living this life which is purely in the flesh who are not definitely in the spiritual realm. In other words, we have to realize that the carnal mind, the non-Christian mind, includes people who are not guilty of these grosser and more obvious manifestations of sin. It includes a very much larger group. I can put it in this form. The apostle John says these are the people whose lives are governed by "the lust of the flesh and the lust of the eyes and the pride of life". This carnal life, this life after the flesh, is a life which is bounded only by this world and this life in time, and never at all gets beyond it. That is the essence of what he is describing. So we must not only think of those who are living in the very gutters of life; we must think of very good and very moral people, and perhaps very philan-thropic people. The test is, do they ever get beyond the realm of life in time and in this world and in this present existence? That is the test. If they never reach the spiritual level, then they have the mind of the flesh, and they mind the things of the flesh. In other words, we have to realize that a man can be full of political and social and economic interests and still only be minding the things of the flesh. A man can be most interested in culture; he can be fond of music and of painting and of art and still be minding the things of the flesh and living a carnal life. The test is, does he rise to the realm of the Spirit? This fleshly mind is one that never gets beyond life in time and in this world. Thus we have to remember that there are many who are living very good and very exemplary lives; there are many who are doing a great deal of good and who are very concerned about the state of the world, and who are working to relieve suffering, but who are still living the life of the flesh and minding the things of the flesh, because they never think in terms of the Spirit. Now that is the first test. Does our thinking get beyond the life which we are living here in time? Are we interested in anything beyond our comfort and our animal condition and the improvement of our minds while we are in this world? If we stop at that point we are in the flesh and we are minding the things of the flesh, and that, according to Paul, is to be spiritually dead. It is to be outside the life of God, it is to be in sin. So that culture and politics and the relief of suffering and the improvement of the world and moral uplift and all these things may still be purely in the realm of the flesh. That is the negative side of the subject.

The positive test

But let me emphasize that by turning to the positive. How may I know positively whether I mind the things of the Spirit or not? This is the vital test. "They that are of the Spirit do mind the things of the Spirit." How do I know whether the Holy Spirit is in me? The answer is: do I mind the things of the Spirit? What are they? Let me say again that it does not say the things of religion. We are living in critical days and in days when it is necessary for the preacher of the gospel to speak plainly. Merely to attend the house of God does not prove that a man has a spiritual mind. I may be interested in sermons, I may be interested in speaking and oratory. I may be interested in my own activities in the church, but these things do not prove I have a spiritual mind. Religion has often been the greatest and the most bitter enemy of spiritual truth. No, it is not merely to be religious and to have religious interests or to be surrounded by religious organizations and activities. Well, what does it mean? Obviously it means this, that I am concerned about the things to which the Holy Spirit draws attention. To mind the things of the Spirit is to be responsive to the things about which the Spirit Himself is concerned. What are they? Let me suggest some answers.

The first test, I think, that we can apply to ourselves to be sure on this point is this: "**Am I more concerned about the state of my soul than about anything else?**" That is the first simple question. I am concerned about the life of my body; of course I am. I ought to be. I am concerned about my life in this world, about food and clothing. I am concerned about political questions and social and economic questions – all quite right and perfectly legitimate! But how do I know whether I am spiritually minded? Here is the test: am I more concerned about the state of my soul than about all these other questions put together? Do I seek first the kingdom of God and His righteousness? Can I say that above all my concerns and interests and anxieties the one thing that is of greatest concern to me is my spirit, that unseen part of me that was put in me by God, my relationship to God? I say again that I can be very interested in sermons, in religion, in making a success of my life and yet not be concerned about my soul. I can have a purely intellectual interest even in the Bible, but that does not say I am spiritually minded. The spiritual mind is concerned about the inner relationship to God. We can put it like this. The man who minds spiritual things is as concerned, if not more concerned, about life in the next world as he is about life in this world. That is a very good test at a time like this. The carnal mind, I have tried to show you, at its best and highest never gets beyond this world and life. The spiritually minded man is the man who is concerned about life in eternity and the destiny of the soul and things ultimate.

The next thing which the Spirit calls attention to is **the Lord Jesus Christ**. You remember what our Lord Himself said about the work of the Spirit. He said, "He shall not speak of himself but shall glorify Me." Now there is no more sure test that anyone can apply to himself to determine whether he or she is Christian or not, than this: What is Christ **to me**? Is He essential to me? Do I know I am lost apart from Him? Do I believe that if He had not died for my sins I could never know God? Do I see in the Lord Jesus Christ the one and only Mediator between God and man? That is the essence of Christianity. The work of the Spirit is to glorify Christ. He makes us see our nature without Christ; He makes us see Christ as the Saviour who reconciles us to God. Where is Christ in my scheme of things? Is it not obvious again that I can be highly religious without Christ? But He is vitally and absolutely essential in the true Christian position.

Let me hurry on to some other tests. **Where does this Book come into my scheme of things?** Do I read it? It is the Holy Spirit who enabled men to write this Book. These writers were not philosophers; we are told that "holy men of God spake as they were moved by the Holy Ghost". It is the Spirit's work. If a man has a spiritual mind he will be attracted to it and will enjoy reading it. Do I find it as interesting as the newspaper or the novelette or the periodicals?

Then there is prayer. What is prayer? Prayer is not just rushing to God with a number of petitions. Prayer, clearly, is a desire to know God; a desire to commune with God, a desire to be in the presence of the Eternal, a thirst for God. You remember how the psalmist put it, "My soul thirsteth for God, for the living God." Any man who has the Spirit in him knows something about that.

What else? Obviously the new nature must lead to **a concern about the state of the world** as it is fallen away from God and opposed to God. The Holy Spirit is grieved because of the state of man. His work is "to convince the world of sin and of righteousness and judgment", and any person who has the Spirit dwelling within is bound to be concerned about these things. Let me again put a plain and simple question without apology. Christian friend, are you really concerned about the state of society today? I do not mean in a general sense. A man who is not a Christian can bemoan the immorality he sees in the streets; but as you see the way men are living today in their sin, is it a burden on your heart? Do you ever pray about it? Are you like your Saviour and Lord, a man of sorrows and acquainted with grief? Does it drive you to your knees? Are you pleading with God to visit the church with revival and reawakening? That is the test of the spiritual mind, a concern about God's honour and glory and about the things of God.

In other words, the person who has a spiritual mind is someone who spends much of his or her time in thinking about these things; who finds his greatest pleasure in this realm. He is the person who desires these things above everything else. Now I do not think that this is something that I need prove. There is a very simple way of putting it all. Who is the person who has the Spirit of Christ? Well, they are the people who are most like Christ. What was He like? Have I not been describing Him to you? Do you not remember how we read that a great while before dawn He went up into the mountain to pray to God? What did He say? Was it not His supreme concern that He might do the will of His Father? It was the things of His Father as a boy of twelve that He asked about – the business of His Father. Those were His first things and those are the things of the man or woman who has the mind of the Spirit. It is their relationship to God that counts most. It is the desire to know God better and more deeply. It is a concern about God's world. It is to glorify Christ and to be like Him.

Has not this also been the mark of the Christian man or woman at all times and in all places? Look at those people in the Acts of the Apostles and how they came together. They always wanted to be together; they wanted to pray together; they wanted to read God's Word together.

Come down the centuries and read about the great revivals. You will find that they spent their time in fellowship together and that they talked about these things and prayed to God concerning them. Are we doing so? Is this a hard doctrine? Does anyone feel that this is a harsh and a trying and a difficult doctrine? My dear friends, the apostle Paul wrote all this in order to comfort people and in order to strengthen them. Thank God, as I ask myself whether I am a Christian, the test is not, am I perfect? Thank God the test is not, am I sinless, am I never guilty of sin? Thank God it is not that! Otherwise I would be condemned. No, here is the test. Am I concerned about this immortal spirit that is in me? Am I concerned about my relationship to God? Do I desire to love Christ more deeply? Would I long to be more like Christ? Am I concerned about the world? If I am, well, then, the Spirit is in me, for by nature I am not concerned about these things. I suggest to you that this is the most comforting doctrine you can ever find. It is just to discover whether this activity of the Spirit is manifested in your life. Whenever He is present, those are the results to which He leads. Have we the Spirit of Christ in us? "If any man have not the Spirit of Christ, he is none of his." He is outside Him, he is dead. Have we the Spirit? If there is anyone who has not the Spirit, let me exhort you to get on your knees before God and acknowledge your deadness, and ask him to give you the gift of His Spirit. Christ put it like this. He said, If a son comes to his father and asks for a loaf, will he give him a stone? No! Well then, "If ye being evil know how to give good gifts to your children, how much more shall your heavenly Father give the Holy Spirit to them that ask him." If we are conscious of our need, let us acknowledge and confess it. Let us ask God for this priceless gift. He has pledged Himself to give it. If any man have not the Spirit of Christ, he is none of His. But if he has the Spirit of Christ and minds the things of the Spirit, he has "life and peace".

CHAPTER 12

Loving God

(Romans 8:7, 15–16)

"Because the carnal mind is enmity against God: for it is not subject to the law of God, neither indeed can be ... For ye have not received the spirit of bondage again to fear; but ye have received the Spirit of adoption, whereby we cry, Abba, Father. The Spirit itself beareth witness with our spirit, that we are the children of God."

We are considering together in the light of the teaching of the first half of this great eighth chapter of Paul's Epistle to the Romans, the marks and characteristics of the Christian and of the Christian life. The fundamental postulate which the apostle lays down is that the thing that marks out and differentiates the Christian is that he has received a new life. If we believe that the greatest thing in the world at this time is that men and women be made Christian, and may live their lives after the Christian way and manner, then our first business is to make certain that we are effective as witnesses and as ambassadors for the Lord Jesus Christ. The way to do that is to make evident and plain that we really are what, according to the New Testament, we ought to be. We do that by asking ourselves the following question: Are there in me these marks and signs and indications of the indwelling of the Spirit of God?

We have seen that one of the first tests is: Can I say I have a spiritual mind and that it is the things of the Spirit of God that really count and matter most with me? Are these the things on which and by which I live? That was the first test.

The second test

But I indicated that that was not the only test. Now I want to suggest that to leave it at that is not only not enough, but it may even, in a sense, be dangerous. The apostle supplements that by a second test. It is the test of our personal relationship to God. "The carnal mind," he says, "is enmity against God: for it is not subject to the law of God, neither indeed can be." Again, in the fifteenth verse, we read, "For ye have not received the spirit of bondage again to fear; but ye have received the Spirit of adoption, whereby we cry, Abba Father." Our relationship to God! This, then, is the second test of whether the Spirit of God dwells in us or not.

Now there are two or three general remarks which are of real significance in this connection. As one meditates upon this whole question of what the apostle says here about our relationship to God, and as one meditates upon what all the other writers of the New Testament say about the subject, there are certain things that strike one immediately. The first is this. **How prone we are to judge of ourselves in these matters by our own tests** and our own standards, rather than by the tests and the standards of the New Testament itself. In other words, when we ask ourselves the question, "What is a Christian?" and "Am I a Christian?" I wonder whether we would put as our first answer the fundamental test, "What is my relationship to God?" How prone we are to put it in terms of life or of morality or of general ideas. It is something which is almost incredible and astounding that, having our Bibles as we have them, and after having read them so often, nevertheless when we are suddenly questioned or question ourselves about these matters, how prone we are to apply tests that are never put in the forefront of the New Testament, but which are the tests put by the man in the street in order to determine what is a Christian or what is not a Christian.

Now the thing that is put first here is my relationship to God, not my life. The ultimate question is, "Where do I stand face to face with Him?" I remember reading a book some ten or twelve years ago which bore a very significant title and really told one everything that was in the book. It was called *Religion without God*. How true that can be of us. We have a religion, but it is without God; and we often have Christianity without Christ. How easy it is to be concerned about other things and forget the Person.

Then the second thing is **the remarkable way in which we tend to omit and forget the most central thing of all**. I am speaking specifically to Christian people. We are all very interested in our own inward states and feelings and moods and conditions. We are very much concerned about the blessings of salvation. We are interested in forgiveness and we regard Christianity as being a great thing because of its doctrine of forgiveness. "What is Christianity?" you ask. We reply, "It is that which gives me forgiveness of sins, that which gives me peace and happiness and joy and power in my life. It is something which gives me blessed and everlasting hope." These are the things we tend to talk about; and yet, according to the New Testament none of these things constitutes the *summum bonum*. None of these things is the ultimate of the Christian gospel. The ultimate is, "Blessed are the pure in heart, for they shall see God." That is the glorious thing at the centre here, that is the thing that really should be supreme in all our thinking and all our desiring and all our sense of gratitude. I do not desire to dismiss or to minimise any of the other things I have mentioned. They are all of great importance and of vital importance. Thank God for every one of them. Without forgiveness I am undone; without the blessings of the new life I am unhappy. Thank God for peace of conscience and for joy and happiness in Christian experience, but those things are merely the gifts, and the tremendous and amazing thing which the gospel of Jesus Christ offers is the Giver Himself. "Blessed are the pure in heart, for they shall see God." I ask again, is it not extraordinary and surprising that as we think on these things and talk about and meditate upon them, how infrequently we realize that this is the biggest thing of all? What if we were to catechise ourselves this morning and ask ourselves the question, "What would you say is the supreme blessing of the Christian life?" I wonder how many of us would almost automatically and immediately say, "The vision of God." To see Him, to know Him, to spend eternity in His holy presence. Now I say that that is clearly the thing that is emphasized everywhere in the Bible.

Take the life of our Lord Himself as it is described in the Gospels. Is it not made plain and clear that the thing that was always central with Him was His relationship to the Father and His knowledge of the Father? Beyond everything else He thanked God that He had known Him and that He was in communion with Him. Now the Spirit of Christ or the Spirit of God, dwelling in us, makes us like Christ so that evidently and obviously the big thing and the supreme thing for us should be this knowledge of God and this vision of God. You find the same thing exactly as you read the experience of the psalmist in the Old Testament and as you read the statements of the apostles in the New Testament. It is the knowledge of God, the desire to be in communion with Him, that they put in the supreme position.

My third general remark is that **all this is of particular importance and of particular urgency in our present peculiar situation today.** I suppose there was never an age in the history of the church when there was a greater danger of Christian people being content with believing too little, than at this hour. We are living in an age not only of scepticism and doubt, but of militant unbelief. We are living in an age when the vast majority of people are not concerned about these things at all. They are godless and irreligious; they do not think about these things. Now because of that we are beset by a very peculiar and subtle temptation, the danger of examining ourselves in the light of all these other people. When we are surrounded by people who believe nothing, the danger is to believe a little and to imagine that to believe a little is to be wonderful and to believe everything. Then there are others who occupy the so-called "modernist" position, who are clearly defective and wrong in their doctrine. Now the danger is to contrast ourselves with these people instead of comparing ourselves with the positive standard of the New Testament. The danger is to think that any belief in God is enough because the majority do not believe in God at all. I want to show you that that is a hopelessly inadequate standard which falls altogether short of that which is emphasized here by the apostle Paul. We must realize that a Christian is not just a man who believes in God. That is not what the apostle emphasizes. The Muslim believes in God; the Jews believe in God, and according to the apostle James, "the devils also believe in God and tremble". Belief in God is essential, but belief in God and the being of God does not make one Christian. To be Christian, according to the apostle, is something which goes deeper. The Christian is called into this peculiar relationship to God which is characterized by love.

Loving God

So let us consider what he says about it in terms of principles. The first principle is that **we are to love God**. "The carnal mind is enmity against God," says Paul. The spiritual mind, obviously, must be one of love towards God. Now what does this mean? Here is a term that is used in the New Testament and we use it ourselves. What exactly does it mean and imply? What does it mean to say, "We love God"? Perhaps we cannot do better than to look at Paul's negative. The carnal mind, he says, is enmity against God. In other words, there are large numbers of people who believe in God but that belief, far from leading them to love God, is nothing but the seat and breeding ground of enmity and of hatred and of antagonism to God. There are many in this world who believe in God, but they would be very glad indeed if someone could convince them and prove to them that there is no God. There are many who believe in God but who hate the very thought of God; and if they could but get out of His orbit how delighted and happy they would be! Now their feeling towards God is one of hatred; it is one of enmity. Their idea of God is of someone who is seated there in the heavens who is opposed to us and antagonistic to us, who is inimical to our truest interests and as it were just waiting to judge and to condemn and to punish us. They feel that God is someone who is altogether against us. A very sure way of discovering whether that is our attitude is this. When things go wrong in our life, when circumstances seem to be against us, when there is war and calamity, is our first thought, "Why does God allow this?" If that is our first impulse we are at enmity against God. If there is within us this feeling that God somehow is not a God of love and that God is not dealing fairly and squarely with us, that is indicative of an attitude that is fundamentally hostile to God. It is this carnal mind that the apostle describes here as being at enmity against God. Now we need not stay with this. It is an unpleasant subject, and yet, as at a time like this when it is vital that we examine ourselves, I put my simple question: What is my fundamental feeling with respect to God in the depths of my heart and of my being? What do I feel about Him? What is my ultimate attitude? Would I be glad if anyone could prove that there is no God? Would I be relieved if God somehow could be banished? To be in such a state or attitude of mind is the very opposite of everything that is taught in the Bible.

You remember the man who went and asked our Lord which is the first and great commandment, and this was the reply, "Thou shalt love the Lord thy God with all thy heart and with all thy soul, and with all thy strength and with all thy mind." You observe He does not say, you shall believe in God. "Thou shall love the Lord thy God"! That is what is to be in the first position. We are not simply called to believe in God. What we are called upon to do is to love God with all our heart and soul and mind and strength and our neighbour as ourselves. In other words, there must not only be an absence of any feeling of hostility to God, there must be a positive agreement with God's law. There must be a desire to please Him and to live for His glory and honour. In this matter we can never improve upon that famous first question and answer in the Westminster Shorter Catechism, "What is the chief end of man?" The answer is: "The chief end of man is to glorify God and to enjoy him forever." Not to believe on Him only, but to glorify Him, to love Him and live for His honour and glory.

Now that, as I have already reminded you, was obviously the chief thing in the life of our Lord. He said that He had not come to seek His own glory; the glory of the Father was ever His supreme concern. You cannot read these Gospels without seeing that that was the passion of His life. It was the guiding and controlling principle. He would suffer anything for the sake of God. That, therefore, is the test that applies to us when we consider whether the Holy Spirit, the Spirit of Christ, dwells within us.

But to us this comes in another way because you remember our Lord said very frequently that whoever did not honour Him, did not honour the Father. He showed the equality between Himself and the Father and how they were one. Listen to some of the terms He used. I read these words trusting that we shall examine ourselves as I read them. Listen to these words of Christ and see whether we can apply them to ourselves. "He that loveth father or mother more than me is not worthy of me." "He that loveth son or daughter more than me is not worthy of me." What is a Christian? A man who believes in God? That is not enough: "He that loveth father or mother more than me is not worthy of me; and he that loveth son or daughter more than me is not worthy of me"! Christ says He must be first and supreme; we must love Him more than anything or anybody. Then listen to these words of the apostle Peter in writing his letter to Christian people (how easy it is to skip over these things as we read them). "Whom having not seen ye love." Can I do better, I wonder, than just repeat the question? The test we are to apply to ourselves this morning is, do we love Him? Orthodoxy is vital and essential. Belief is absolutely essential; but the apostle goes beyond all that. The test is, do we love Him? Can I say honestly as I examine myself, "I love God; I love the Lord Jesus Christ? I have not seen Him, but I love Him." The carnal mind is enmity against God; the spiritual mind is love towards God.

This love also shows itself by **keeping His commandments**, by loving our neighbour as ourselves, by loving the brethren and by being consumed by a desire to be like Him and to place Him in all things above everything else. Do we love God? Do we love the Lord Jesus Christ? The Spirit is the Spirit of God and of Christ and He is the Spirit of love.

But let us consider the other verse for a moment, verse 15. The Christian, says Paul, has received "**the spirit of adoption**." This takes us a step further. What exactly does he mean by this? "Ye have not received the spirit of bondage again to fear; but ye have received the Spirit of adoption, whereby we cry, Abba Father." Again let us look at the apostle's negative, which is very helpful. The Spirit that we have received is not the spirit of bondage again to fear. What does he mean by that? Let me put it like this. We must not feel that all I have been saying is dependent upon us and that the gospel sets an impossibly high standard. That is the spirit of bondage, that is the spirit of fear. So the test at this moment is, how do I feel as I am confronted by these various statements? Do I feel it is asking rather a lot of me? Do I feel that it is compelling me to love God with tears and sweat and toil? Do I feel it is asking me somehow to forsake everything that is enjoyable and pleasant in life, and to scale some lonely height in this attempt to love God? Does all this come to me as a harsh and almost cruel demand? That, according to the apostle, is the spirit of bondage again to fear. But here we can do nothing better than read again those words from the first epistle of John: "There is no fear in love, but perfect love casteth out fear." "He that feareth is not made perfect in love."

But at this point there is often a problem in the minds of many people because in another epistle we are told that we are to approach God with reverence and godly fear because "our God is a consuming fire". How do we reconcile these two things? How can you delight in God on the one hand and approach God with godly fear on the other hand? You say "perfect love casteth out fear", and "there is no fear in love". How are these things to be brought together? The answer of the Bible itself is this. The fear of God which the New Testament inculcates is nothing but a reverent awe. It is not "the fear which hath torment"; it is not the fear that thinks of God as a tyrant and as someone who is set against us. It is not that fear which is craven; it is the fear that can only be known by love. It is a fear that is based upon respect; a fear that we shall wound or grieve or hurt the object of our love. So that there is really no contradiction whatsoever between these two things. The love that was inculcated in the Bible is not something sentimental or loose, or merely emotional. It is a love that is holy; it is a love that is constituted partly by awe and reverence. It is not that cringing attitude of love that is based upon antagonism and enmity to God. It is rather a love that is so conscious of God's holiness and of His glorious attributes that it is fearful of hurting and wounding. That is the force and value of the apostle's negative. The Christian, he says, is not one who has a spirit of bondage. He is one rather who has this Spirit of adoption whereby we cry Abba Father.

What does this mean? You see the sequence; the Christian does not merely love God. His love for God is a peculiar love; it is the love of a child for its parent; it is the love that a child feels towards his Father. In other words, says Paul, though God is so high and holy and absolute in all His power and majesty, the Christian, by the work of Christ and as the result of the operation of the Holy Spirit, is one who feels that he can approach that God and call him "Father". It is not a distant love; it is a love born of this peculiar relationship. This is how the psalmist puts it. "When my father and my mother forsake me, then the LORD will take me up." That is an Old Testament verse written by a man who spoke and lived before the days of Christ, before the Incarnation, before the miracles, before the death on the cross, before the day of Pentecost, before all these things we read of in the New Testament; and yet that man knew God in that sense. "When my father and my mother forsake me, then the LORD will take me up." Do we know God like that? Can we say something like that honestly out of the depths of our heart and from the very depth of our experience? Is our feeling towards God one of sonship and relationship? Do we know God in truth and in fact as our Father?

Consciousness of sin

I imagine someone wanting to ask a question like this at this point: "How can I possibly say that when I am so conscious of my sin? I believe in God but I know that I have sinned against God. How is it possible for me, conscious as I am of my sin, to address God as 'Abba, Father'?" Now the answer to that question is everything that the apostle has been saying in the previous verses. He puts it like this. We are conscious of sin because it is the Holy Spirit who convicts us of our sin. But thank God the Holy Spirit does not stop at that point. I have sinned against God, yet I believe by the Holy Spirit's instruction that God sent His Son into this world in the likeness of sinful flesh and for sin, and that He has condemned sin in the flesh by Christ and that thereby I am reconciled to God. I believe that God has adopted me into the position of a son. I could never make myself a son. I shall never be worthy to be called a son in terms of my own actions and conduct and behaviour, but this is the test. Do I believe that God in Christ by the Holy Spirit has made me a son, has adopted me into the family, and therefore though I have sinned and still sin I am nevertheless a son? "We have received the Spirit of adoption, whereby we cry, Abba, Father." In other words, I want to suggest that perhaps the best way in which we can test whether we love God or not is to test and examine our feelings when we have sinned against God. How do I feel when I have sinned against God? What are my feelings when, having sinned, I get down on my knees in the presence of God? Now I say that is the point of all points at which one can make certain whether one is a Christian or not. May I suggest some of the definite tests? As I get on my knees before God, is my feeling one of a criminal before a judge or is it a feeling of a sinning child in the presence of a loving and holy Father? Am I there like a criminal in the dock wondering what the sentence is going to be, or am I there as a child feeling that I have hurt and wounded one who has loved me with an everlasting love? Or take it like this, is my feeling at that point one of annoyance with myself because I have done this thing, or is it rather a feeling of grief that there is such a heart of sin in me as ever to give a desire to do that thing? That is the test of whether you are a child of God. If you are just annoyed with yourself for having been brought to your knees regarding this thing, you have the carnal mind. But if you are grieved because there is still in you a heart that loves sin, then I say it is an indication that you are a child of God.

Or let me put it like this: is the feeling on your knees one of annoyance with yourself because you have let yourself down and broken your own record and tarnished your own perfect copybook? Or is your feeling one of grief and sorrow because you have let Him down and because you are not a dutiful child and because you are a poor witness of such a Saviour and of such a Father there in heaven? Is the feeling that is uppermost one of ingratitude, a consciousness of base ingratitude to one who has done so much? I suggest to you that is ultimately the final test. There on my knees, conscious of my sin, am I looking at it in a legalistic way, a self-righteous and personal way, or am I overwhelmed by the thought of what this means to Him? The true child is concerned about the feeling of the parent and not about himself. The true child is not worrying about the punishment he may receive; what is worrying the child is that the relationship has been affected, that love has been grieved and wounded.

That is the test. Beyond doubt one of the best ways of testing whether we love God is to test our feelings and attitude towards Him when we have sinned against Him.

Perhaps I can put it best of all in the terms of a well-known and famous New Testament incident. Would you like to know for certain whether you are a child of God, whether you love God, whether you have got the Spirit of adoption which makes you cry Abba Father? Well, here it is: the story of Peter after the resurrection in the twenty-first chapter of John's Gospel. You remember how Peter had promised he would follow Christ through death and hell though everybody else might forsake Him, and how then he denied Him thrice with oaths and curses. Then you remember how that morning by the side of the lake when our Lord had cooked the breakfast for them, He turned to Peter and said, "Simon, son of Jonas, lovest thou Me more than these?" and he replied, "Lord, Thou knowest that I love Thee." Then the second time our Lord asked in effect, "Simon, son of Jonas, do you really love Me more than any of these? Then you remember what you said." Poor Peter! Again he replied, "Lord, Thou knowest that I love Thee." And then the third time, because he denied Him three times, "Simon, son of Jonas, lovest thou Me more than these? Do you really?" Peter was grieved that He asked him the third time, "Lovest thou Me more than these?" and with a breaking and bleeding heart he said, "Lord, Thou knowest all things, Thou knowest that I love Thee." That is the test! Can you say that, when you cannot defend yourself nor excuse yourself, when you feel there is nothing to be said in mitigation of your sin and failure, is there welling up from the depth of your being that broken cry to Him, "Lord, Thou knowest all things, Thou knowest that I love Thee"? Can you say that? That is the Spirit of adoption, and in spite of all sin and failure and all else it cries out "Abba Father." Not only to believe on Him, but to love Him.

CHAPTER 13

The Test of Conduct

(Romans 8:7–8, 12–14)

"Because the carnal mind is enmity against God: for it is not subject to the law of God, neither indeed can be. So then they that are in the flesh cannot please God ... Therefore, brethren, we are debtors, not to the flesh, to live after the flesh. For if ye live after the flesh, ye shall die: but if ye through the Spirit do mortify the deeds of the body, ye shall live. For as many as are led by the Spirit of God, they are the sons of God."

We are considering together the tests which we must apply to ourselves in order to discover whether we are truly Christian or not. That is in a sense the great theme of the first half of this chapter. We have been looking at verse 9 in which we read *"Now if any man have not the spirit of Christ, he is none of his"* – he is not a Christian. Here again we get the same thing in verse 14. *"For as many as are led by the Spirit of God, they are the sons of God."* That is the question – are we sons of God? How can we know for certain whether we are or whether we are not?

I have been pointing out that the apostle puts this whole doctrine in terms of the indwelling of the Holy Spirit. What makes us Christian, says Paul, is that the Spirit of God or the Spirit of Christ dwells within us. That is his central doctrine. Just to do certain things does not make us Christian. Merely to say we believe does not prove we are Christian. It is the receiving of the new nature, it is the indwelling of the Holy Spirit, that really proves we are children of God, and that shows itself in belief and actions. How then may I know whether the Holy Spirit is in me?

Now we must go forward to another test. It is none other than the test of conduct, the test of behaviour, the test of my actions and the quality of the life which I live. It is not only interesting, but remarkable to note how all these doctrines hang together, and how each one inevitably leads to the others. The Holy Spirit gives us a new mind. That immediately means we have a new way of looking at God and regarding God. Yet if I merely talk about loving God it can be quite unworthy, and the real test of loving God is to keep His commandments. "Who is he that loveth me?" said our Lord Himself to the disciples, and answered the question. "He it is who loveth me who keepeth my commandments." These things are inseparable, they all go together. Yet, of course, it is essential that we should look at them one by one. In other words, I am just indicating that this emphasis upon conduct and behaviour and life lived is something that follows inevitably and logically from our loving God. It does not come before it, but it follows it; it is an inevitable deduction from it.

Some difficulties

Now as we approach this whole subject of conduct and behaviour in the Christian life, perhaps the most helpful way to do so will be to indicate that this is a subject that has often caused a great deal of confusion. There is no aspect of the Christian life, perhaps, which has caused so much discussion and so much misunderstanding. There are at any rate three common difficulties which are expressed with regard to this matter. I am merely going to mention them in a few introductory words.

The first attitude is **the attitude of those who object altogether to the call to holiness**. Alas, there are many such! They dislike any sermons or addresses on the subject of holiness or sanctification. They say that the gospel is all right as long as it talks about forgiveness, and as long as it depicts in general a noble kind of life; but that when it begins to tell us what we ought to do and what we ought not to do, it becomes too narrow. If you preach holiness such people feel that it is intolerable and that it casts a reflection upon them. There is no need to argue with such friends. I would simply put it in a word like this. If we are at all to accept this Book as the revelation of God's mind, then there can be no argument on the question of holiness. "Be ye holy," says God, "for I am holy." It is impossible, logically, for anyone to believe in God and to desire to know

God without immediately seeing the utter absolute necessity of holiness. So if we object altogether to the teaching of the Bible on holiness and sanctification then it seems to me that there is no conclusion to draw except that we are strangers to the operations of the Holy Spirit. That is one difficulty.

The second is the case of **those who regard this question of holiness and of life and conduct as something in and of itself.** What I mean is this. They tend to isolate the doctrine of holiness from every other doctrine and to make of it something which is complete by itself. They would regard it, therefore, as a matter of law and as a matter of rules and regulations. I have in mind, for instance, that whole outlook upon the Christian life which is seen in the monastic idea. The whole idea of monasticism is that holiness is more or less a matter of rule and of law. As you know, the various "orders" among the Roman Catholics have their rules and regulations. Holiness is a set task and you are given daily instructions as to what you are to do, when you are to speak, and when you are not to speak. At other times you are to eat certain things and abstain from eating other things. Holiness becomes a set task, rules and regulations to be observed, something in and of itself. That is something which is not confined to Roman Catholics only. There are even those within the ranks of Protestantism who hold the same view. They have isolated it and made of it an object in and of itself, and when they preach holiness it generally means the denunciation of certain particular sins and an attack upon certain practices. It is a legalistic approach, a legalistic attitude. That is the second difficulty.

The third common difficulty about this whole subject is in a sense the exact antithesis and opposite of the second. It is **the view which believes in teaching holiness in terms of what we may describe as passivity.** Those who hold this view tell us that holiness and sanctification are something which the believer is to receive exactly as he receives his justification. They teach that you must make no effort about it at all, and they say the great trouble is that Christian people are trying to live a holy life and trying to practise sanctification, whereas all that is necessary is just to "let go and let God". "Do nothing but receive it; wait for it to come to you," they say. Holiness is something which comes just as a pure gift without any effort on our part, without any application of doctrine on our part. It is a matter of relaxing, of becoming passive and of receiving some additional gift.

I think it is good to hold these three positions in our mind as we now come to consider the positive teaching given here by the apostle on this whole subject.

The right setting

I think we will all agree that this eighth chapter of this epistle is in many ways a *locus classicus* with regard to the New Testament teaching on holiness and sanctification. According to the apostle this is not a subject to be argued about, but something which follows inevitably from the other doctrines. That, to me, is the first and most important thing of all. If only we put this doctrine of holiness into its right setting the difficulties to which I have been referring immediately disappear. One of the great difficulties has been the isolation of doctrines from one another and the tendency to form movements round particular doctrines, instead of seeing the inter-relationship of all the doctrines. That is the fundamental thing the apostle reveals here. Holiness is the inevitable outcome of our being Christian at all. Holiness to the Christian, to use our Lord's comparison, is what the fruit is to the tree. It is no use discussing the fruit apart from the tree; the tree must come first before you can come to the fruit. That is why it is so foolish to isolate this doctrine from the other doctrines. Now the apostle's doctrine can be put in this form: the Christian is one who is indwelt by the Holy Spirit. The Holy Spirit comes into him; the Holy Spirit gives him a new nature and the Holy Spirit leads him. The argument is, as I have already reminded you, "for as many as are led by the Spirit of God, they are the sons of God", and if we are not led by the Spirit of God, then we are not the sons of God. The Christian is a man, in other words, to whom something very vital has happened; he is a man upon whom God has acted. The Holy Spirit of God has dealt with him, has come into him. Christ is being formed in him. The object of the work of the Holy Spirit, ultimately, is to prepare us for God, so to deal with us as to enable us to stand in the presence of God in eternity. So it follows of necessity that if the Holy Spirit is in us that work must be going on in us. How does it manifest itself? How can I know whether that work is proceeding in me? Paul says the Holy Spirit does three things. He changes our minds and our outlook. He changes our desires and our affections, and therefore He changes and affects our wills. How does this work out in practice?

1. New attitudes

First and foremost, the Holy Spirit gives us a new attitude towards this question of conduct. He makes us approach it in an entirely new and different way. Perhaps we can best put that in the form of a number of negatives. The Holy Spirit makes us view this question of conduct **not as a matter of law or of conscience, but rather as a matter of our relationship to God**. "The carnal mind," says Paul, "is enmity against God. For it is not subject to the law of God, neither indeed can be." Before we become Christian our whole attitude towards conduct is in terms of law, in terms of conscience. The first thing the Holy Spirit does is to make us see that this whole question of conduct and behaviour is not a matter of law and rules and regulations but rather a matter of personal relationship to God. God is holy and God's laws are nothing but an expression of God's character and of God's nature. If I may so put it, God has given His law to man, not because He delights in giving laws, but, I say it with reverence, because He cannot help doing so. The nature of God is holy and therefore the laws of God are an expression of the character, the person and the nature of God. It is therefore futile and idle for anyone to say that he loves God if he hates God's laws. You cannot divorce God from His nature and you cannot divorce His nature from His law. The law is the expression of His being and the Holy Spirit makes me see therefore that when I express my opinion of God's law, what I am really doing is to express my opinion of God. If I feel God's demands are rather stringent, it means I think God is stringent. If I think that these laws are unfair, it means I think God is unfair. He takes me out of the realm of law and makes me view conduct in terms of my relationship to God.

Or look at it like this. He makes us see that what matters in the realm of conduct is **not so much our individual acts and actions and sins, as our state and condition**. You notice that Paul keeps on emphasizing the state of the heart. Ah, says the apostle, what matters primarily is not what kind of actions you are performing, in practice, it is the state of your heart towards these things. You remember how our Lord himself said, "It is not that which goeth into the mouth that defileth a man, but that which cometh out of the mouth, these are the things which defile a man" – not the things that are eaten and taken in at the mouth. That is exactly the doctrine the apostle expounds here. We must be more concerned primarily about the state of our hearts and about our attitude than about our individual actions. Is not that where so many tend to go astray? They put certain questions, "Do you drink alcohol? Do you gamble? Do you go to cinemas?" – particular actions. And so long as a man can say "No" to these things he is regarded as a Christian. That is not the apostle's test. You may be a person who never does any one of these things and yet be entirely devoid of the Spirit of Christ. The Pharisees were very good men; they fasted and they gave tithes of all they possessed. They did not do the things that the tax-collectors did and yet you see it is their spirit that puts them outside Christ. When the Holy Spirit teaches us about conduct, He makes us see that it is the state and condition of the heart and the desires, and the whole attitude towards the things that matter.

Another way of putting it is to say that **the Holy Spirit makes us see that conduct is never meant to be a thing in and of itself**. Conduct is nothing but the expression of our whole position ultimately in the sight of God. It is not saying a daring or a dangerous thing to say that the Bible does not want us to become just good men; the Bible wants us to become God's men, like God, truly Christian, indwelt by the Spirit of God. In other words, there is that essential difference between morality alone and true biblical holiness and sanctification. We should be concerned, therefore, not so much about our conduct as such and about the standard that we have set up, and as to whether we can pass certain prescribed tests, as to our whole state in the sight of God.

Lastly, **we must not think of this question of conduct in terms of happiness or in terms of blessings that we may enjoy**, but rather in terms of God's will and of God's plan for us, and God's plan for the whole church. Often this doctrine of holiness is presented in the following manner. An address is given, the whole purport of which is that if you want to be happy, well then, you must be holy. Certain questions are asked such as, "Are you lacking in joy and in happiness and in resilience? Do you really want life with a capital 'L'?" Then you are told that if you want to live this happy, joyous, carefree Christian life, you must be holy. The motive for being holy is that you may be happy and enjoy your Christian life. I do not say that this is false teaching, but I do say that it is a very false **emphasis**. The reason for being holy is not that we may be happy; there is only one reason for being holy and that is that it is God's will for me. It is God's purpose for me. It is God's desire for me. "This is the will of God, even your sanctification." So that even if the way of holiness should make me utterly wretched and miserable and the most unhappy of men, yet I must be holy because God wants me to be holy. We must take this question out of the realm of subjective feelings and experiences before we can put it into its right New Testament setting. These are some of the ways in which the Holy Spirit gives us a new attitude towards this question of conduct.

2. New arguments

The second proposition is that **the Holy Spirit gives us a new set of arguments with respect to conduct**. This is again of very great importance. It not only gives me a new attitude towards the question, it supplies me with a number of very powerful arguments with respect to it. Let me try to summarize the arguments.

The New Testament doctrine shows us that **it is utterly illogical for us not to be holy**. The argument of the New Testament is this. Here is the doctrine, here is the truth. If you see these things and believe them, well then you must be holy. Holiness is not to be presented as a law, it is to be presented as an inevitable deduction from these propositions. What are they? The Holy Spirit shows me **the true nature of sin**. No man knows what sin really is until the Holy Spirit begins to work in him. Without the Holy Spirit we seem to recognize certain things as right and others as wrong, but that does not give us a true understanding of the nature of sin. It is the work of the Holy Spirit alone that can show a man what sin really is. As you read the words of our Lord Himself you begin to see the enormity of sin. It is only the Holy Spirit that can enable man to say that "we wrestle not against flesh and blood, but against principalities, against powers, against the rulers of the darkness of this world, against spiritual wickedness in high places". It is the Holy Spirit alone that shows us that sin is this foul canker which has entered into life and which vitiates every part of man's being. The moment one begins to realize that, one has a new argument with respect to this question of conduct and behaviour.

The Holy Spirit also shows us that God made this world perfect and meant man to enjoy its good gifts, but this foul thing called evil came in and in the person of Satan persuaded man he was going to improve him, was going to give him liberty and enable him to live a wonderful life. The **Holy Spirit makes man see sin as the greatest enemy** which comes between him and God, and which has robbed him of the image and glory of God. The Holy Spirit makes us see sin as something that is dragging us down and which will condemn us to all eternity. The moment man becomes aware of and sees that he has a new argument against sin. The Holy Spirit then shows us **the amazing love of God towards us in spite of sin.** Is not that the whole record of this Book? It tells us that though man sinned in his folly, God did not turn His back upon him. God planned salvation. Here is the love of God in spite of our sin! No one knows anything about that apart from the work of the Holy Spirit and when a man begins to see God's love to him in spite of his sin, another irresistible argument emerges for conduct and for behaviour.

It is the Holy Spirit alone that reveals unto man **the love of Jesus Christ**. Look how Paul puts it in the third verse: "For what the law could not do in that it was weak through the flesh, God sending his own Son in the likeness of sinful flesh and for sin, condemned sin in the flesh." It is the Holy Spirit alone who can enable us to see what this means. It means that Christ the Son of God, the second person in the blessed Trinity, forsook the courts of heaven and was made in the likeness of sinful flesh. He came on earth and endured the contradiction of sinners against Himself. He staggered up Golgotha, was nailed to the tree and to the cross. Why? In order to bear your punishment and mine, in order to rescue and redeem us. He gave His life, He gave Himself. There is no need to command holiness; there is no need to consider holiness as a law. There is the argument – Calvary! He suffered that for us. Why? In order that we might continue in sin? No! In order that He might separate unto Himself a peculiar people, zealous of good works, in order that He might prepare us for the sight of God.

Then go on to the next argument which is **the prospect of the resurrection which awaits us**. Again, this is only revealed to us by the Spirit. Observe how Paul argues: "If the Spirit of him that raised up Jesus from the dead dwell in you, he that raised up Christ from the dead shall also quicken your mortal bodies by his Spirit that dwelleth in you." In other words, the doctrine of the resurrection. Do I believe it? Well, if I believe it, this is the argument. When I die this is not the end of my life and existence; there is a glorious resurrection coming, and the Spirit of Him that raised up Jesus from the dead is coming to raise me up also from the dead and present me in the presence of God. I believe that. I believe I am going to stand before God and see Him. But I also remember the words of our Lord, in which He said, "Blessed are the pure in heart, for they shall see God." If a man believes that, there is only one logical deduction and here it is: "He that hath this hope in him purifieth himself even as He is pure." This is how Paul puts it in the twelfth verse: "Therefore" – you see the logic – "Therefore, brethren, we are debtors, not to the flesh, to live after the flesh; for if ye live after the flesh, ye shall die, but if ye through the Spirit do mortify the deeds of the body, ye shall live." So one of the most powerful arguments for holiness is the doctrine of the resurrection. I do not desire to condemn interest in particular sins or actions, but I am here to ask you to think of the resurrection and to relate the question of your conduct constantly to that mighty event. That is the New Testament way of preaching holiness.

3. New power

Let me go on to the third principle. **The Holy Spirit not only provides me with an argument about conduct, He provides me with a new**

power with respect to conduct. Let me read verse 3. You see there is a new hope. "What the law could not do, in that it was weak through the flesh, God sending his own Son in the likeness of sinful flesh, and for sin, condemned sin in the flesh." By giving men and women a law, they are not enabled to live a good life. God gave a perfect moral law to the people of Israel but they could not keep it. That is where all moral systems break down; the flesh of man is too weak. "What the law could not do because it was weak . . . " "The carnal mind is enmity against God, it is not subject to the law of God . . . " "They that are in the flesh cannot please God." But, thank God, this doctrine of the Holy Spirit puts me in an entirely new position. "If ye, through the Spirit do mortify the deeds of the body, ye shall live." Thank God I am not confronted with a new set of demands and told in my weakness and helplessness to live them. I am given the gift of the Holy Spirit, the Spirit that was in Christ Himself and which enabled Him to live a perfect life. Thank God I am no longer under the condemnation of sin; I am no longer under the thraldom of sin. The Spirit has raised me up and I have every possibility of succeeding. I am a new man with the love of God in my soul.

So then, what is the result of all this in practice? Surely these are the deductions. The Christian is a man who loves the law and desires to keep it. In view of all these things which we have seen the Christian now has a new mind on these matters. He can see that the law of God is pure and holy; he now loves God and therefore he wants to love and to keep it. The result of this is that the Christian is not a man who just does the moral thing. He does not just live within the law. He does not just want to avoid punishment. He is above the law; he views the law from above; he lives with freedom. Where the Spirit of the Lord is, there is liberty. He is not in bondage. And that of course means that in actual practice and conduct and behaviour he is, through the Spirit, mortifying the deeds of the body. In other words, he works out this great argument. He sees that sin is there trying to stand between him and God and his inheritance in Christ, but he sees the love of God and the sacrifice of Christ and he therefore hates the sin that made it necessary for Christ to go to Calvary. He hates the sin that has marred God's glorious universe and he longs to live a life which is well-pleasing in God's sight. He looks for "new heavens and a new earth, wherein dwelleth righteousness". He seeks "those things which are above, where Christ sitteth on the right hand of God". He "sets his affections on things above, not on things on the earth". He follows "peace with all men, and holiness, without which no man shall see the Lord".

CHAPTER 14

Assurance of Salvation

(Romans 8:16)

"The Spirit itself beareth witness with our spirit, that we are the children of God."

We continue our series of studies of what I have ventured to describe as the "tests of the Christian life", and come now to still another test which, in a sense, is a summing up of what the apostle has all along implied. For as we have considered the new mind and outlook, the new relationship to God, and the new attitude towards ethics and morals and conduct, we have all along been stressing that these things are true of the Christian because he has the Holy Spirit within him. It is not that man decides upon a new outlook and philosophy; it is not that he decides to live a better life and to become a Christian. Rather it is the action of God whereby the Holy Spirit comes to live within him as a result. A Christian man is a man who has a new nature; he is one who is born again. You will remember that the ninth verse puts it perhaps more perfectly than any of the others, "But ye are not in the flesh, but in the Spirit, if so be that the Spirit of God dwell in you. Now if any man have not the Spirit of Christ, he is none of his." There is no need to argue about it; without the indwelling of the Holy Spirit we are not Christian. Without this new nature we do not belong to Christ. That is why these tests become of such great importance. Now that is the argument that runs right through the passage – the Christian is a child of God. The apostle has been saying that implicitly right through. "For as many as are led by the Spirit of God, they are the sons of God", and again, "Ye have not received the spirit of bondage again to fear; but ye have received the Spirit of adoption, whereby we cry, Abba, Father."

But here in this verse it is stated in perhaps a more explicit manner. "The Spirit itself beareth witness, with our spirit, that we are the children of God." The Christian is a child of God.

Is everyone a child of God?

But today we cannot just make that statement, for there are loose ideas current about the whole question as to who is a child of God. There has been a great deal of talk in this century about what is called the universal Fatherhood of God and therefore the universal brotherhood of man. There are those who would have us believe that every person who has lived on the earth is a child of God and that therefore we have no right to draw these distinctions between those who are children of God and those who are not. The argument, I say, has been that all are children of God and therefore brothers and sisters together. That is a statement which flies in the face of biblical teaching. The argument is sometimes brought forward that Paul states the brotherhood of the entire human race when preaching to the people of Athens (see Acts 17:27, 28). He said that "we are also his offspring". From that they try to deduce this doctrine and theory of the universal Fatherhood of God. However, the very context of the apostle's statement shows quite clearly that when he talks about all men being the offspring of God, what he means is that all ultimately derive and have their being from God. God is the Creator; God has given origin and life to all men and women; and apart from that action man would not exist at all. In that sense, of course, we are all the offspring of God. But it is only in that sense, because nothing surely is clearer in the whole of biblical teaching – and this applies to the Old Testament as well as to the New Testament – than that there is a great distinction and division between God's people and those who are the people of the world. Since God originally created man there has come in the fact of sin and the result of that is that our Lord said of certain Jews, "Ye are of your father the devil, and the works of your father ye will do." That is our Lord's own statement. Those people, He says, are the children of the devil and, therefore, clearly not the children of God. He likewise talks about such people as being the children of the world, as belonging to the world. But let me quote some other Scriptures which put this beyond doubt. You remember those words in the prologue of the Gospel according to John, "But as many as received him, to them gave he power to become the sons of God, even to them that believe on his name" (John 1:12). In other words they were not already the sons of God. The picture painted is that as a result of sin we are none of us the children of God, we are children of the earth; we are, if you like, the children of Adam. We have inherited the nature of Adam plus all the consequences of the Fall. We have ceased to be the children of God; we are children of the devil, children of the world, children of Adam. It is only to those who believe in the Lord Jesus Christ that He gives power and authority to become the sons of God. This point is made abundantly plain and clear in the teaching of the New Testament elsewhere, where it is pointed out that "As in Adam all die, even so in Christ shall all be made alive" (1 Corinthians 15:22). Adam is the head of the old humanity; Christ is the first born among many brethren. He is the beginning, the origin of the new humanity, a new race of people, the children of God. That is the contrast to be found running right through the whole of the biblical teaching.

This is seen still more clearly when we come face to face with the New Testament doctrine of the new creation or regeneration. This talks about Christians being "partakers of the divine nature" (2 Peter 1:4). What makes us Christian, according to the New Testament everywhere, is that we are born again. Indeed we have to be born again before we can become Christian people and children of God. Therefore it follows of necessity, if a new birth is essential, those who lack that new birth are not children of God. It is only by receiving the new life and the new birth and the new nature, by being created anew, that we become children of God. That is the doctrine you will find right through the epistles, so that this idea that all men and women are the children of God is a blank contradiction of the teaching of the Bible itself.

The danger of detached reading

Paul emphasizes all this in these verses which we are considering. He points out that we have the Spirit of adoption within us; that we are aware in the depths of our being of a new relationship to God. Though we are sinful and unworthy there is that within us which cries out "Abba, Father," and makes us say like the apostle Peter, "Lord, Thou knowest all things; Thou knowest that I love Thee." But, says the apostle, this is not all, there is something further, "The Spirit itself beareth witness with our spirit that we are the children of God." Now that, surely, is one of the most glorious statements which is to be found even in the New Testament itself. Before I go on to analyse it permit me to make this one remark which I am sure you will all accept and with which you will all agree. Is there not a terrible danger in our reading of the New Testament of our reading it in a detached and impersonal manner? Isn't there this curious danger of reading it without realizing that its statements apply to us? Paul says that if we are Christian "the Spirit itself beareth witness with our spirit, that we are the children of God". Do we have that assurance? Can we all make that statement? Are we ready to take our stand by the apostle and make this mighty claim? Now the danger is, I say, in reading these statements, to think that the apostle is referring to himself and to other people. But let me remind you that he uses this word "we". "The Spirit itself beareth witness with our spirit, that we are the children of God." Nothing is more important as we read our New Testament, therefore, than to remind ourselves constantly that every "we" applies to us and every "our" is ourselves. We must ever remind ourselves of this personal and direct application. I therefore ask, again, the question, do we have this assurance? Can we all say, "I am a child of God?" If not, why not? Why is it that so many Christian people are in difficulty about this matter and would hesitate to say this? Why is it that there are so many who long to say it and yet who feel they have no right to say it?

1. Why important?

Let me say first of all why we should all be concerned about this and why we should desire to be able to say this and have this assurance. We are not discussing something vague and theoretical and academic. There are so many today who think that Christian preaching should be nothing but a constant series of statements about the world situation and they would be tempted to say in their complaining way, "My dear friend, look at the world and its problems! What have you to say about them? Why spend your time in dealing with this personal question?" Let me then try to show you the vital importance of seeing whether you are or are not a child of God and why you should be concerned about it.

Here is the first good reason. **It is something that is offered to us.** It is something that is stated in the New Testament itself. It is something that God Himself is holding there before us and wants us to possess. Therefore not to receive it is an insult to God. There is a sense in which it is to make God a liar to say no man has a right to make this claim, for God says you ought to be able to say that you are a child of God.

Another reason for being concerned about this is that **according to the New Testament we are incomplete without it.** That is just another way of saying that not to be able to say this is dishonouring to God. God has certain plans for the Christian. God, in this great salvation, proposes certain things for us and He wants the Christian to be complete and perfect according to His pattern. According to the New Testament, as I am trying to show you, a part of the Christian position is that we should be able to make this statement. In other words, God wants complete Christians, not apologetic Christians, not uncertain Christians. He desires Christian people like the apostle Paul and those first Christians who stand there before us full of power and certainty. Therefore not to arrive at this standing is to be dishonouring to God, because we represent a partial and incomplete Christian.

But the third reason and perhaps the most urgent one today for the need of this testimony and this certainty is that **it is necessary in order that we may work as we should amongst those who are outside the Christian faith.** Here is something that I need not press. Is it not abundantly plain and clear that it is always the Christian who knows where he stands and who has this assurance who makes the best ambassador for Christ? Look at those first Christians. There was no need to argue as to whether they were or were not Christians. Everybody knew it. There was a radiance and peace and joy; there was a happiness and a certainty about them and wherever they went they carried this message with them. Likewise, if you read the accounts of the Reformation and every revival in the church you will find exactly the same thing. In times when the church is truly alive, Christian people unmistakably assert that they are the children of God. They know whom they have believed and where they stand. I was interested to hear from young men who were in the various armed forces during the Second World War that the people who helped them most, and who encouraged them most in the Christian life, were those Christian men who had the assurance of their salvation. In times of crisis and of trouble and of peril, these men, they said, stood out. It is the man who has a certainty, a testimony, who is always able to help others most.

2. What are the difficulties?

There are some good reasons for desiring to have this testimony of the Spirit. But let me move on to deal with the second principle. What are the difficulties about this matter? Why is it that people lack this certainty? Let me mention some of the difficulties.

There are those who lack this testimony **because they believe that it is meant only for certain exceptional Christians**. They believe, in other words, that Christians are to be divided into great and small, exceptional and ordinary. "Ah," they say, "a man like the apostle Paul is such an exceptional and outstanding man. He is a man whom one would expect to have this assurance, this certainty. But I," they add, "am just an ordinary Christian." Now this is really serious, for what the apostle says here is this, "The Spirit beareth witness with our spirit, that we are the children of God." He includes all those Christian members of the church at Rome with himself. Nowhere does the apostle teach us, or any other of the apostles, that these blessings of the Christian life are reserved only for a certain chosen and special few. Every Christian is a child of God, every Christian is called to be a saint. It is to me not only pathetic but even tragic that in our Protestantism we still persist in recognizing so many unchristian and unscriptural divisions and distinctions. We persist in allowing the Roman Catholics to influence us into thinking that only certain people are saints and that therefore only certain people can have this assurance of salvation. The answer of the apostle is that every Christian should have it and again the history of the church proves abundantly that it is a blessing and a testimony that all sorts and kinds of people have possessed. In the church there is to be none of these artificial distinctions. In this respect we are all, if we are Christian, children of God.

Then there are those who are unable to say this **because they fear that it will be claiming too much**. They feel that it would be a kind of presumption. They say, "As I see and know myself it surely would be wrong for me to claim that I am a partaker of the divine nature; that I am a child of God or that I am a son of God. I shrink from making such a claim. I am not yet fit to be a child of God. I am unworthy to make such an exalted claim." Now the simple answer to such people is this, that we are made the children of God by God's action and that it is not what we may think of ourselves but God's action in us that matters. A man in a natural sense may feel very unworthy of his father, but his unworthiness does not make him cease to be a child or a son of his father. What makes us children of God is our relationship to God; our receiving of the divine nature. So we must regard it in terms of relationship and of nature rather than in terms of a general view of ourselves. Perhaps I can put this best in this form. There are those who feel that the only ones who have a right to make this claim are those who are sinless and those who are perfect. "I dare not," they say, "be guilty of bringing disgrace upon the great name of God by saying I am a child of God and then sinning or living unworthily. If only I were sinless or perfect then I would say I am a child of God, but until I am, I am afraid to use this term because of its implications." Now again the answer is this, that the apostle Paul does not claim for himself that he is sinless or perfect, and he certainly did not claim it for the members of the church of Rome or any other church. Sinlessness and perfection are not taught in the New Testament, but it does tell us that all Christians should be able to say that "the Spirit beareth witness with our spirit, that we are the children of God". It is not my perfection that makes me a child of God, it is my receiving of the divine nature.

The last difficulty to which I will refer is **the identification of this assurance, this testimony, with particular and special manifestations**

that are to be found in certain outstanding cases. People read Christian biographies or hear of certain people to whom this witness and this testimony came suddenly. They read of people who for many a long year had been trying to live the Christian life but who lacked this assurance, and then, suddenly, in a meeting it came to them and they were thrilled with a great joy unspeakable. They may have seen things unseen and they were thrilled by some marvellous experience. Now the danger is to postulate that that must happen before anyone can claim to be a child of God. There is always this danger of our coveting particular manifestations and experiences, and of arguing that because we are not identical in our experience with some other person we are not really children of God at all.

3. A positive statement

The best way perhaps of dealing with all these difficulties is to put the matter positively. How does the Spirit testify with our spirit? Men and women are in trouble because they misunderstand that matter, because they think that it must be some thrilling experience or that they must see a vision or have some marvellous mystical experience. It is because of these errors that they are in trouble and unable to say that they are children of God. So then, how does the Spirit bear this witness and testimony with our spirit? Here, I think, the answer can be best divided into two main sections. There is first of all what I would call a direct witness of the Spirit and then there is an indirect witness of the Spirit.

Now **the direct witness of the Spirit** is something which is rather difficult to describe because it is of necessity something that is mainly subjective and there is a sense in which it is an experience that almost baffles description. But it is something like this. There are times and seasons at any rate when a man who is truly Christian is aware and conscious of the fact that there is a testimony and a witness within him assuring him that he is a child of God. Now we have to differentiate this I think from the Spirit of adoption whereby we cry, Abba, Father. That is something that should be **constantly** in the Christian. He should never lose that Spirit of adoption; he should always think of God as his Father;

there should be no variation in it. But what the apostle has in mind here is a further testimony that is born to our spirit by the Spirit Himself. I can put it in no clearer language than that. It is one of the most priceless experiences that the Christian man can ever know in this world and in this life. He is given that unmistakable certainty and assurance. He does not hear audible voices, but it is equal to an audible voice. There is this testimony born in his spirit that he is a child of God and it is unmistakable. The apostle has that in his mind.

But let me go on to **the indirect witness**. I think that perhaps this indirect testimony is more valuable to us than the direct because it is easier to define. I am anxious to emphasize that the indirect testimony of the Spirit is just as much a testimony as the direct testimony. That is why this passage is so comforting and consoling; it shows us how "the Spirit itself testifieth".

Let me remind you of some of the ways. One way in which the Spirit indirectly testifies with our spirit that we are children of God is that He makes the promises of the Scriptures real to us. You read your New Testament and find the various promises that are given to the children of God, to the Christian, and as you read them the Holy Spirit assures you that these statements apply to you. He assures you that you have got an interest in these matters and that they are talking to you and talking about you. It isn't something of which you persuade yourself. As you read them, the Spirit gives you joy in your heart. He shows how all the promises apply to you, the promises that the very hairs of your head are all numbered. He promises that nothing can happen to you without God. Did you not know something of that during the air raids of World War II? Didn't you find at times that there were certain of those promises that seemed to stand out and you felt they were meant for you? That is one of the ways in which the Spirit testifies with our spirit. He enables us to appropriate the promises and to realize that they are speaking to us and about us.

Another way in which the Spirit does this is to produce the fruit of the Spirit in us. "The fruit of the Spirit is love, joy, peace, longsuffering, gentleness, goodness, faith, meekness, temperance." Are you aware of that fruit of the Spirit in yourself? Are you aware of the new disposition? If you are, it is the work of the Spirit. He assures you thereby that you are a child of God. These things can only come from the Spirit and therefore if we possess them we can be certain that we are the children of God.

Then the other general way in which the Spirit does this is to produce the various things which have been occupying our attention in the previous chapters. Do I "mind" spiritual things? If I do, I can be certain that the Holy Spirit is in me. Do I love God? Do I know this Spirit of adoption? Am I taking a new view of conduct and morality and ethics? Can I say honestly that I delight in the law of the Lord and am I anxious to be pleasing to Him? If I can, all this is certain proof that I am a child of God, for the man who is not born again is at enmity against God. He is not subject to the law of God, neither can be. He does not love God. These things we are discussing do not interest him. In other words, if these things mean nothing to you, the Holy Spirit is not in you. But if these are the things you regard as first and important, I say that is proof positive that you are a child of God and the Spirit is testifying with your spirit that you are a child of God.

Sometimes the Spirit bears this witness indirectly and in a negative manner. This, to me, is the most consoling thing that the New Testament tells us. Sometimes the Spirit bears this witness with our spirit by chastising us. Have you ever thought of that, Christian people? That is the argument of the twelfth chapter of the epistle to the Hebrews. If you are being chastened it is a proof that you are a son of God. "Whom the Lord loveth he chasteneth." Has that ever occurred to you? A period of chastisement is in itself a proof that you are a child of God. Let me put it like this. According to the New Testament, God is fashioning us and preparing us for heaven. Heaven is perfect, God is perfect, and we must be perfect before we can arrive there. The process is to go on, so that if I am conscious of being perfected, of being chastened by the hand of God, it is the proof that He is perfecting me for that. "Whom the Lord loveth he chasteneth." If we only view our chastisement aright we shall see in it a testimony of the Spirit that we are the children of God.

Then another way is that we are conscious of sin and we grieve because of sin. If I can honestly say that I grieve because of sin in my life, it is the witness of the Spirit that I am a child of God. I do not mean that I am just sorry because I am suffering the consequences of sin, but if I grieve that I ever desire to sin against God, that is the testimony. Likewise a desire to know God better and a grief and concern because of my lack of love for God. Are you concerned because your love is so cold, because your love is so weak and faint? If you are it is the assurance of the Spirit that you are a child of God.

The very desire for assurance itself is in a sense the assurance. You remember the great words of Pascal, "Comfort yourself, you would not seek Me if you had not found Me." The man who is grieved because he lacks the assurance, the man who longs for it, is a man who, in a sense, already has it. It is because he is a child of God he desires to know God for certain. So that in this marvellous and wondrous way, even negatively, the Spirit bears witness with our spirit.

Let me sum it all up like this. Complete absence of the testimony of the Spirit in every form means that we are not Christian. If I have never known a direct or indirect testimony of the Spirit, then, according to Paul, I am not a Christian at all. Indirect testimony means that I am a Christian, but that I am failing in my life and in my obedience. I say that that negative testimony does prove I am a child of God, but to have the full experience, not only the indirect witness, but the direct witness is necessary. How may I have it? The apostle tells us. Look to Christ's perfect work. Do not start by looking to yourself. Look at that cross on Calvary's hill and the work of God in Christ. See that. If you look at yourself you will see nothing but blackness and darkness and sin and it will lead to uncertainty and despair. Look at Him in His entire, perfect work. Start there. Then search for the evidence of the Spirit. Search for that indirect witness. Then be obedient to the life of the Spirit. Obey His movements, His encouragements, His leadings. Finally, ask God to give you this certain assurance. Those are the steps: the work of Christ and then the evidence of the working of the Spirit in me in any form; a concern about this and a crying out to God for it,

"Tell me Thou art mine, O Saviour,
Grant me an assurance clear;
Banish all my dark misgivings,
Still my doubting, calm my fear."

That is the way and if we offer that prayer on the basis of obedience and surrender and a searching for any kind of evidence of the Spirit within, all on the basis of Christ's work, we can be certain that we shall have this assurance. Let us make certain that we have it. It is not only the highway to personal happiness but also the guarantee of effective service. The world is arrested by the calm and joy and peace of the true Christian, attracted by him and prepared to listen to him. Those who have always been most used of God have always had assurance of their salvation and have known that they are children of God.

CHAPTER 15

The New View of Life

(Romans 8:18)

"For I reckon that the sufferings of this present time are not worthy to be compared with the glory which shall be revealed in us."

This verse from Romans 8 introduces and virtually summarizes a subsection in Romans 8:18–25. The word "For" connects it of necessity with what has gone before, where the apostle argues that "The Spirit itself beareth witness with our spirit, that we are the children of God, and if children, then heirs; heirs of God, and joint-heirs with Christ; if so be that we suffer with him, that we may be also glorified together. For I reckon . . ." and on he goes with this argument until the end of the twenty-fourth verse. Judged from the standpoint of literature this is one of the noblest passages that was ever written by the great apostle Paul. I constantly find myself trying to decide and determine whether his eloquence reached its greatest height here in this eighth chapter of Romans, or in the fourth chapter of the second epistle to the Corinthians. It is a fact, all must agree, that his eloquence certainly never reached greater heights than it does at this point. We can perhaps say that that this passage beyond all others reveals the imaginative and poetic element in the mind of the great apostle. Here, as you remember, he paints this extraordinary picture of the whole of creation waiting and looking and longing for ultimate deliverance and the manifestation of the sons of God. It is one of the boldest and most striking images that has ever been placed on record, this picture of the whole brute animal creation straining as it were, and waiting, for the final consummation of the work of our Lord Jesus Christ in this world. That is the picture with which we are dealing.

Now the question arises, how did Paul come to write this? The answer is that it follows of necessity and in logical sequence from what he has been already telling us. In this entire section the apostle set out to picture and to delineate the character and the lineaments of the Christian man. His ultimate object was to comfort and console and to encourage these Christians living in Rome. But incidentally he draws a picture which once and forever must become the standard by which we examine ourselves and test ourselves to see whether we are truly Christian or not.

The Christian

Now these are the things that he tells us about the Christian. The first thing that is true of him is that he or she is free from condemnation. The Christian is a person who has been delivered from the condemnation and the curse of the law. "There is therefore now no condemnation to them which are in Christ Jesus." The Christian is someone who realizes and who has come to see and believe that, in the Lord Jesus Christ, and as the result of His atoning death and resurrection, the guilt of sin has been dealt with. The law is no longer condemning him. Christ has satisfied the law; sin has been condemned in the flesh and he is therefore free from the law, and free from guilt in the sight of God. Not only that, he is also a person who is living and desires to live a holy life, and he is one who is being enabled to do so by the power of the Holy Spirit. In other words, the Christian is one who has not only been delivered from the guilt of sin, he is also one who, in a sense, has been delivered already and is being delivered still from the power of sin.

But it does not even stop at that. The Christian is one who has within him the Spirit of adoption whereby he cries "Abba, Father." He knows God in a way that no one else can know Him. God is not someone in the far distance, a law-giver or a judge; He has become to the Christian a Father, one whom he approaches with feelings of filial affection. Indeed beyond that, the Christian is one who knows what it is to have the Holy Spirit testifying with his spirit that he is a child of God. The Christian, in other words, according to Paul, is a new creature. He is a man who has been born again. He is one into whose life the very Spirit of Christ, the Spirit of God, has come to live and to dwell, and the result of this is that he is a man who knows love and peace and happiness. That is the apostle's picture.

Life in this painful world

But this person is also someone who is still living in this world and in this life, and there, at once, arises a problem. Though this person is born again and is a "new man", though he is no longer of this world, he is still in this world. And the world is a place of suffering and of trials, of troubles and uncertainties and contradictions. That was something which constituted a very real problem to many of these early Christians. It still comes as a perplexing problem to many Christians at the present time. The argument is something like this. You tell us in the gospel, says the Christian, that we have had all this wonderful deliverance from the law and from guilt, that we are being delivered from the power of sin and that we are the children of God, that the very hairs of our head are numbered. You talk about these gracious promises and yet look at the world in which we live! We are tried, we are troubled, we suffer, we have to endure things. How do you reconcile these things one with the other? That is the problem. It is a problem, I say, that clearly exercised many people in the first days of the Christian church, because every one of these New Testament epistles, in a sense, deals with that very question. That was obviously the whole point of the epistle to the Hebrews. It certainly was the great theme of the Book of Revelation and you cannot read any one of these epistles by Paul without, in a sense, finding yourself face to face with that selfsame question. How can you reconcile the picture of the Christian man with the man who has to endure and suffer in this present world? That is the problem and the question with which the apostle proceeds to deal in this section. I think we shall find once more that the apostle makes it abundantly plain and clear that the Christian is an utterly unique person who stands out apart from all others, entirely distinct, in a unique position and with a unique outlook. I have already suggested that we have once more a very delicate and subtle test which we can apply to ourselves in order that we may know exactly whether we are truly Christian or not.

Another test

Here is the test. How do we face the problems and the sufferings and the trials and the troubles of this present time? For those who are interested in Christian doctrine (and every Christian should be) it is interesting to note the logical sequence that the apostle follows in his thinking. This is the sequence. Paul never departed from this Christian logic. The Christian is a man who has been **justified**, delivered from the guilt of sin and from the law. He is a man who is **sanctified** in Christ and is being perfected. But, thank God, he says it does not stop there. He is also one who is, in a sense, already **glorified**, but will eventually be actually glorified together with Christ. Justification, sanctification, glorification! That is the doctrine. But here Paul puts his doctrine in a very practical manner. He asks a question. Here, he says, is the Christian faced with this world and its trials and problems and tribulations. But how is he going to face them? His answer, for me to put it in a general phrase, is that the Christian does so in terms of the truth he has already believed; the truth that he has already experienced. That is the only way in which the Christian does face these difficulties.

The apostle does not encourage and comfort these Roman Christians by trying to tell them lightly and superficially that their troubles after all are not quite as great as they imagined they were; that is not his argument. His method is not to minimise their trials and tribulations and their problems; the gospel of Jesus Christ never does that. It is always realistic and never romantic. The gospel does not insult our intelligence by just trying to administer a soothing syrup and by getting us to turn our backs upon the blackness of the picture, to persuade us that all is well. It does not use a psychological method of treatment; neither does it promise us lightly and glibly and optimistically that our problems will soon be less and that we are about to turn some magical corner which will lead us to prosperity and happiness and affluence, and that in a moment all will be well. There is no suggestion of this. There is nothing of your light optimism that is so characteristic of the politicians and the superficial philosophies; that is not his method at all. The apostle's method is this. He takes these Christian doctrines that he has already been laying down and he shows them how to apply them to the situation in which they find themselves. In other words, the gospel of Jesus Christ has no consolation and comfort to offer us unless we believe its truths. The comfort of the New Testament is theological comfort and unless we believe its doctrine, it, in a sense, has nothing to give us. But, thank God, if we do believe its doctrine, then it not only has comfort and consolation and encouragement, but it has the only comfort and the only true and real encouragement that the world can know.

1. A realistic view of the world

Now let me divide up that statement in the manner that the apostle does in this argument. How is the Christian enabled to overcome the sufferings of this present time? The first answer is that **the Christian has an entirely new view of the world and its troubles**. Surely half the difficulties which men and women find in connection with life at this time are due to the fact that they start out with an entirely false view of the world and life in this world, and the history of the world. Men and women are made unhappy in this life and in this world because they have false expectations with respect to it. If our view of life essentially and basically is wrong, we are doomed of necessity to disappointment and unhappiness, and the view of the world outside Christ is a view, I say, that of necessity must disappoint us. The non-Christian view of the world is that this world is a good place. Its view of life is that basically everything is all right and that life is something that one ought to enjoy to the full; that there is nothing inherently and of necessity wrong. It admits that at times on the surface there are certain contradictions and disappointments, but it feels that that does not imply anything essentially wrong. It is just an unfortunate turn that things seem to have taken for the time being. Life in this world and man himself, it claims, are essentially right and essentially good. Such people, starting out with such a view, look to this world for happiness, for joy and peace. They look for conditions which will enable them just to eat, drink and be merry and never to have any trials and tribulations at all. They expect a kind of perfect life in this world without contradictions and the things that sadden the heart of man. It is because of that, that at the present time they are baffled and bewildered and troubled and perplexed. Holding that view of life and the world, they cannot understand why we have had to suffer world wars in the middle of the twentieth century and similar troubles ever since. It seems quite unfair to them and quite contradictory to the philosophy that they have been taught to believe for the last hundred years. With their idealistic picture of man as such a noble creature, and with all the efforts that have been made to improve the lot of mankind and the world during the last hundred years, the world as it is today is contradictory and baffling to the vast majority of men and women. They cannot understand it. That is why they are so depressed by it. That is why they are baffled. They fear what is going to happen and that is why the greatest danger of all is that of sinking into a kind of despair and of saying, "What is the use of anything? Let's just go on and do the best we can and have the maximum amount of enjoyment and not try to think about it." That is the great danger confronting us and it is based entirely upon that false view of man and of his life in this world.

The Christian has an altogether different view. The Christian view of this world, and of humankind, and of life in this world, is based entirely upon the teaching of the Bible. It is a teaching which we can summarize like this. The world was made perfect. So why is it as it is? The answer is that sin has come in. The biblical diagnosis of humanity and of the world therefore is a profound one, a deeper one. It tells us that a false element came into the life of man and the world, something which we call sin. It tells us that that condition at the very vitals of man's being is a principle of contradiction. Man was made in the image of God and he was to conform to God's pattern. But man rebelled against that and therefore he is fighting against God, fighting against the law of his own nature. The result is that he has ruined and spoilt his world. That is the biblical teaching with regard to the world and man's life in it. But it goes further and says that sin and disobedience in men have produced a curse not only on man himself but also upon the whole of creation. This is put in the Book of Genesis in this form. It tells us that as the result of man's sin, God cursed the very earth itself and that the result is briars and thorns and troubles. The apostle puts it here in these words. He says, "The creature was made subject to vanity, not willingly, but by reason of him who hath subjected the same in hope." That is Paul's way of saying that the whole world even of nature and of brute creation has suffered as the result and the consequence of man's sin. Everything on the face of this earth has fallen from God. The world is suffering from the consequences of evil. The world, according to the Bible, is in the grip of sin. It is being controlled by what it calls "the god of this world", or "the prince of the power of the air". The world, therefore, according to the Bible, is full of evil. "Ah," says someone, "what a depressing doctrine!" It all depends upon how you look at it. Is to face facts to be depressing? Is to be realistic to be depressing? Surely there is nothing so depressing as to be told smugly that this world is a wonderful place, on the point of becoming perfect, and then suddenly to be plunged into another war and to hear of nuclear weapons and to see all the contradictions of life. The way of true optimism is to face the facts and according to the Bible these are the facts. This world is against God; it is against man and his highest interests. The moment we begin to realize that we are more than half-way to the solution of the problem of existence in this world. A Christian is a man who starts out realizing that the world is sinful. He realizes that the world is against him; he realizes that there is this principle in the world that leads to a condition in which "there is no peace, saith my God, unto the wicked". He realizes, therefore, that he must not expect a perfect life in this world. He must not expect it to be a round of joy and happiness and affluence. He must not think it is going to be an easy world or a smooth passage. He realizes that it is a fight and a struggle, and that there is this principle of contradiction. Surely to realize that at the very beginning is to go more than half-way to the solution of the problem. If you realize that the world is like that you will not be disappointed when you find that it is like that! If you realize this world is under Satan and under sin, you can expect nothing but the consequences of sin. Thus when war comes the Christian philosophy is in a sense confirmed and the

Christian is not surprised; he is not baffled. The Christian today is not at all surprised at the troubles on the international scene; he anticipates it. He realizes that there is selfishness and sin and evil and lies in the human heart, and that not only in individuals, but in nations and gatherings of people. Since that is his understanding of life he is not surprised at the manifestations of this principle of contradiction in life. The Christian, therefore, starts with that new view of the world and its troubles.

2. A new view of the future

A second principle is **that the Christian has a new view of the future course of the world and its history**. This, again, is equally important. The Christian not only starts with a different view of the world as it is, he has an entirely different view of the future course of the world and its history. We are all familiar with the non-Christian view, so I need not stay with it. The non-Christian view is that the world is inevitably and automatically improving and getting better and better. The non-Christian, therefore, is always waiting for something marvellous and wonderful to happen. He has always got the feeling that whatever may be true at the moment, we are going to enter upon a new era. He always thinks there is a magical corner which we are about to turn. He believes that by Acts of Parliament and better education and improvements socially, that somehow or another we shall be delivered and emancipated from all our troubles. There is that fatal optimism in the non-Christian view of life – that belief that man somehow or another is suddenly going to emerge out of all these trials and tribulations. There is a false optimism.

But the Christian view of the future of the world is a very different one. It is that according to the Bible the world is heading up to a great crisis and that there will never be a radical change in the heart and in the nature of man. Sin is there and it is at the very depths and vitals of our existence. According to the Bible that will persist, so that far from thinking that the world is going to improve gradually and steadily and eventually become perfect, the Christian believes that the world is heading up to a terrible crisis and to a final judgment. The ultimate end of this world, according to the Bible, will be the return of the Lord Jesus Christ to judge the world and all its peoples who have ever lived, and it will be a critical judgment and a final judgment. The earth will be destroyed, the present heaven will be destroyed. There will be this cataclysmic judgment. Sin and evil and everything inimical to God will be finally cast away and destroyed for all eternity. But thank God there will be a new heaven and a new earth wherein dwelleth righteousness. There will be a new heaven and a new earth which will be entirely free from sin and from all the effects of sin. It will be a world that will be entirely and utterly renovated. That is what the apostle means in this passage when he talks about the "glory which shall be revealed in us". It is something which baffles language and defies even the highest flights of spiritual imagination. But you are familiar with this teaching in the Bible. You get it not only here, you get it in the Book of the Revelation; you get it in the Book of the Acts of the Apostles; you get it in the Gospels and you get it in the Prophets. That is what the apostle has in mind: the glory which shall be revealed. It is something that is surpassing and transcendent in its glory and its marvel and its wonder: the new earth and the new heaven, sin utterly destroyed, taken out of life, and everything in a perfect state and condition! That is the biblical view of history. It is not a matter of gradual improvement as a result of conferences and peace treaties and educational and social enactments.

This is not being pessimistic. It is not to denounce these things. Let us have our peace treaties; let us educate men as best we can, but in the name of God let us not pin our faith to such things. The problem of sin is beyond the power of man and the end of the world is judgment and the destruction of evil and sin and of the very earth itself. Then will come the new heaven and the new earth and the new order – the "glory which shall be revealed in us". Here in Romans 8, the apostle, with his spiritual imagination, tells us that the very beasts of the earth and the flowers in the field are in a sense looking forward to it. You remember how the prophets have anticipated it, how they talk about the trees clapping their hands and the whole of nature in this glorified state expressing and telling forth the glory of God. That is the future history of the world.

3. A new view of ourselves

But that brings us to the last principle. How is the Christian man related to all this? **The Christian has a new view of himself face to face with all these things**. That is the apostle's argument. The Christian is a man or woman who has been assured by the Holy Spirit that he is a child of God. He has got within him the Spirit of adoption whereby he cries, "Abba, Father." The Spirit testifies with his spirit that he is a child of God. So, says Paul, this is the argument. If I am a child of God, I am an heir of God; for the child is an heir. And if I am an heir of God I must therefore also be a joint-heir with Christ, for He is the heir. What does that mean? It means that we look at Christ and we see ourselves and our own future through Him.

The first thing I observe when I look at Christ is that **He came into this world and even He had to suffer in it**. He was without sin, He never disobeyed God, He never broke the law, He was never guilty of any neglect. But look at Him in this world. What was He? "A man of sorrows and acquainted with grief." He suffered in this world and it is only He in a sense who knows what it is to suffer. He endured the contradiction of sinners against Himself. This world is such that even the Son of God when He comes into it has to suffer. He is tried, is troubled in it. You see the logic. If, therefore, says Paul, we suffer with Him we shall be also glorified together with Him. I find myself a child of God, an heir of God, suffering in this world and I begin to wonder why. I cannot understand it. But there is the answer. He suffered and I am only experiencing what He experienced. I am suffering together with Him.

But he does not stop at that. **I am one with Him; He is in me**. His Spirit is in me. I suffer with Him. Let us look at Him again. What do I see? He died, yes, but He rose again; He ascended. He is seated at the right hand of God. He is in glory. He will come again into this world which is going to be created anew and He will reign upon it. I therefore argue that if I am one with Christ, though I die and my body be buried in a grave, it is not the end of my story. I have died with Him, but also am risen with Him. The day is coming when the last trumpet shall be sounded and the dead shall rise. I shall rise and my very body shall be glorified. I shall be made like Christ. He is the firstfruits of them that slept. He is the firstborn among many brethren and as He is risen and has become glorified I shall rise. My body shall be glorified and I shall reign with Him. That is the picture. "If so be that we suffer with him, that we may be also glorified together." That new heaven and new earth is not only for Christ, it is also for all His people. That is my consolation in this world of time and my comfort and my encouragement.

That is what the gospel holds out for us. The apostle puts it like this. He tells us that the whole of brute animal creation groans and is looking forward to it. In its groaning and travailing in pain there is this contradiction that has entered into it, but the earth has a feeling that it was meant for something better and that a new day shall come and all will be perfect. It is all straining for it, waiting for it, longing for it. But "not only they," says Paul, "but ourselves also, which have the firstfruits of the Spirit, even we ourselves groan within ourselves, waiting for the adoption, to wit, the redemption of our body." That, being interpreted, can be put like this. The Christian is a man who, because of what he believes and what he knows, knows what it is to groan in this life and in this world. It is only the Christian who does groan in this world. Other people are trying to forget the problems and the troubles, drowning their sorrows and having their fling of pleasure. The Christian, like Christ, sees the cause of it and he groans in it. But he does not merely groan because of the suffering, he is experiencing something that the world does not know. The Holy Spirit within him is giving him a foretaste of that which is to come. He knows what it is at times in a church service, or when he is alone on his knees, to have some experience in the realm of his inmost being. He knows something of the music of heaven; he catches something of the glory of God. Having seen it and felt and tasted it, he longs for more of it, and he groans over things as they are here because he knows something of the glory of God. It is not the groaning of despair, it is the groaning of anticipation. It is a groaning and a longing for the coming of the day when he shall be delivered and emancipated and shall share in this everlasting glory of God, world without end.

That is the Christian philosophy of history! That is the way the Christian faces the sufferings of this present time. It is because of that that we can join the apostle in saying, "I reckon that the sufferings of this present time" – the wars and bombs and pestilences and famine, the tribulations and trials and all that you can ever mention – "are not worthy to be compared with the glory which shall be revealed in us." Have you seen it? Do you know about it? Has the Holy Spirit given you the firstfruits of it? Is this language real to you or is it mere imagination? Does it sound like some flowery poetry, or is it a fact? This, according to the New Testament, is what is offered to every Christian. I go further, this is the demand made of every Christian. The test of the Christian in a sense is this: that he has seen himself and knows himself to be a new man. He is given an entirely new view of the world and of life, and he has at times, by the grace of God and by faith, had a glimpse of the glory that is yet to be; and he has moments and hours and days when he longs for it. The ultimate glory, the final consummation, the eternal perfection of the children of God, are to him the only solid realities. "The sufferings of this present time are not worthy to be compared with the glory which shall be revealed in us!"

PART 4

A Preview of History

CHAPTER 16

The Right Perspective

(Revelation 4:1–2)

"After this I looked, and, behold, a door was opened in heaven: and the first voice which I heard was as it were of a trumpet talking with me; which said, Come up hither, and I will shew thee things which must be hereafter. And immediately I was in the Spirit: and, behold, a throne was set in heaven, and one sat on the throne."

In this verse of Scripture I want to emphasize particularly the words, "Come up hither, and I will show thee things which must be hereafter. And immediately I was in the spirit."

A well-known and deservedly popular American commentator, Mr Raymond Gram Swing, once published a book to which he gave the rather striking title, *A Preview of History*, and in this book he attempted to lay down what seemed to him would be the future course of the history of mankind and of the world, and the future course, especially, of international relationships. Now that title, I think, is rather a significant one at the present time. The whole world would give much to have this preview of history. It is something for which almost everyone longs. The desire for this view of the future, for this preview of history, is not, I believe, a mere matter of curiosity or idle speculation. It is rather something which arises out of the terrible state of the world at the present time and especially because of what has been taking place in the world during the recent decades. In a world which has become as uncertain and as terrifying as this world of ours has become at the present time, men and women naturally are concerned about the future. They are concerned about themselves. They are concerned about their children. Many are asking the question, "Is life on these terms worth living at all?" The problem becomes a very serious and important one from the high standpoint of the state itself, when we realize that there are many who are saying, "Have parents the right at all to bring children into such a world as this? Has one the right to expose children, and those who are going to grow up, to the possibility of constant warfare and trouble and anguish?" This concern, I say, about history, about the future story of mankind, is one which is playing a very serious and very important part at this hour, and is, in many ways, likely to control the thinking of mankind with respect to political, international, social, economic and every other type and kind of question. That is why so many, therefore, are trying at this present time to give us this preview of history. But, of course, neither Mr Raymond Gram Swing, nor anyone else, can really give us this preview of history. All they can do is to tell us what they think; what they imagine is going to happen or is likely to take place. They can never go beyond the realm of their own personal opinion, prejudice, or idea, and what shakes our confidence in them is that we have already had so many experiences of similar forecasts and previews which have been given in the past. Indeed, I suppose, in a sense, there is nothing which is quite so sad as one looks back across the last hundred years and reads again its literature, whether it be its prose or poetry, as to see the way in which the confident, hopeful, sanguine, optimistic predictions have been so utterly and so completely falsified. Our grandfathers were particularly fond of this preview of history and they talked about the days which were coming when we should see federations of men, and when knowledge would grow from age to age, and when, as a result of social enactments, the whole realm of mankind would make this great leap forward. They prophesied confidently the coming of a golden age, but we have lived through times and through events which have utterly falsified all that, and the result is that we have become somewhat sceptical of these previews of history. Surely at long last we have come to the point of realization that what has ultimately accounted for the failure of all these efforts and prophecies has been the fact that they have altogether ignored the principle of which we are reminded in my text from the Book of Revelation. In other words, and to put my main point immediately, **if we would have a preview of history,**

the first step must be that we must obey the exhortation that comes to us as with a trumpet call, and says, "Come up hither." Then, and then only, shall we see "things which must be hereafter".

Now that is the way in which John was given the preview of history which is recorded in this well-known and familiar book. John, you remember, wrote this book as a result of what had been revealed to him. He lived at a time of terrible trouble. Let us again remind one another that there is nothing new about present events. These things have all happened before. John lived in an age of conflict and turmoil and war and persecution and trial. Certain horrible things were beginning to emerge and to manifest themselves. John, an apostle of Jesus Christ, in the midst of a world like that, with the care of the churches and with the problems of individual Christians weighing heavily upon him, was here given this preview of history which he was able to write in order that he might comfort and console that first generation of Christian believers.

Now my object is not so much to work through the Book of the Revelation and attempt to interpret and explain the exact and the precise meaning of all its varied and weird symbols, pictures and signs. I am concerned, rather, with the message of these two chapters, chapters 4 and 5, which to me are all-important, because here we have the introduction to the history. Here we are shown how any correct view of history is alone possible. Here are enunciated those first fundamental principles without which man can never understand at all the story of mankind, and of the world.

1. A total view

Here we have the first of these great principles. It is put in the form of this striking exhortation. John was an apostle, a good man, a saint, but because he was on earth he could not give this preview of history. In order to have it he has to be addressed in these striking words. "Come up hither, and I will shew thee things that must be hereafter. And immediately," says John, "I was in the Spirit, and, behold, a throne was set in heaven, and one sat on the throne." So what does this mean? What are the principles that we can deduce here by way of introduction? The first is that **the story of mankind, and of the world, must always be viewed us a whole if it is to be understood rightly.** What I mean by that is that our constant danger is to regard history piecemeal. We are creatures of the world and of time and of our own age. Very naturally, because of the immediate problems and difficulties and circumstances, we tend to be concerned solely and exclusively with what is happening in our time and in our own immediate generation. It is because we give this exaggerated importance to our own particular section of history that so many of our ideas are false. That has surely been the great trouble during the past hundred years. Men have said, "Of course, various things may have happened in the past, but the world is different now." They think that we are living in a new world and that we have a different outlook and a different mentality. Their whole view of history, and of the immediate future, is solely in terms of the present. But the Bible tells us everywhere that if we would understand any section of history aright, we must put it into the context of the whole. If you read this Book of the Revelation you will find that it always indulges in these grand sweeps. When it begins to talk about things that are going to happen, where does it start? It starts in heaven! The Bible is very fond of doing that. Have you noticed how in the Old Testament when we are given those genealogical tables, they sometimes go right back to Adam. If they are dealing with problems in the life of the people of Israel they always go back to the very beginning and talk about Abraham and about the Red Sea. They cannot deal with the immediate present without putting it into the complete context. Now that is something which is vital and all-important. History must be taken as a whole. There is a sense in which it is the simple truth to say that if we try to understand the history of our own times merely in terms of our own times, we shall of necessity fail. But if we adopt the biblical method we shall find light being flooded upon our immediate problems from all directions. The Bible regards the study of mankind as a unity; it regards it as continuous. It does not believe, as so many modern thinkers believe, that one age can be entirely different from the previous age. It sees a connecting link in the whole story of the human race. Or, to put it in the precise terms of my text, you will never understand history until you view it from the right perspective. Our difficulty is that we are down in this valley called life and because we are immersed in the problems and surrounded by the difficulties and perplexities of life, our perspective is entirely wrong. The Bible tells us, in fact, that if we want to see our bit of history truly then we must "Come up hither." We must get the right perspective. We must climb, in a sense, into the heavens, before we can truly understand the story of earth.

2. The enigma of humankind

The second principle is that **the story of mankind, and of the world, can never be understood solely in terms of man**. Here again, surely, we see the great error of the past century. We have been worshipping man. We have put man in the centre of the picture. We have regarded man as supreme and all-important. We have believed that the powers of man are endless and almost eternal. Never has mankind believed so firmly and so intensely in the power and understanding of man as during these past hundred years. Attempts have been made time and again to explain the entire story of the human race solely in terms of man. We have put man, I say, in the centre. I need not detain you with the various theories concerning man which have been propounded. Men have talked about biological man, about economic, about political, about social man, and so on. But surely, today we are beginning to realize that all these various attempts to explain man have proved to be totally and completely inadequate. Humanity has baffled explanation. Constantly there have been things which, somehow or other, have seemed to smash the philosophies. Man himself is bigger than the attempted explanations. If you try to explain history solely in terms of man then, I say, there are immediately many things which can never be explained. The very uniqueness of man cannot be explained if you start with man alone. Take the various attempts of the past century to explain the origin and the genesis of man. Have you observed how, increasingly, the greatest scientists are having to admit and confess that the unique thing about man is something that cannot be explained? There is that essential gap between the highest animal and the lowest man. The unique character of man is something that cannot be explained solely in terms of man.

Then there is the curious contradiction which is to be found in man. What a strange creature man is! That is why all these explanations break down. There are things in man which make you feel at times that Shakespeare was almost right when he said, "What a piece of work is man! How noble in reason! How infinite in faculty! In apprehension how like an angel" and so on. There have been those during the past hundred years who have idealized man in that way. They have thought of man as intellect and reason only. They imagined that man was nothing but a pure idealist who was out for the uplift of mankind. They saw him as a thinker, an idealist, ever reaching out to the heavens. That man is capable of astounding and noble deeds we know to be true; but that is not the only truth about man. Man at the same time is capable of doing things that an animal would never do. There is a smallness about him, an ugliness, a foulness, a vileness. The same man who is capable of doing heroic deeds at one moment can, at another, act as a cad and be capable of unutterable and cowardly deeds. The contradiction of man! Greatness and smallness. Like an angel, and yet lower than the beasts. This curious link with the divine and the eternal; and yet how earthly, how beastly at times! Mere theories cannot explain this curious contradiction in man.

There is not only the contradiction in man himself, but the consequent strange contradictions that are to be found in the realm of history. In other words, I am suggesting that the history of the past can simply not be understood at all if we view it wholly and solely in terms of man.

Let me take a supreme example. Take the case of the Jewish people. Can the story of the Israelite be explained if you look at him solely in terms of man. Take that nation and look at it especially as its story is given in the Old Testament. The uniqueness of the Jew, the separateness of the Jew, the individuality of the Jew. It is not, as the Bible tells us so often, because he was better than anybody else. In many ways he was worse. Yet think of what that nation did. Look at their literature. Read their psalms and their prophecies. Observe how this one nation stood out to represent the only true God. Look at their story, their code of morality, and their incomparable literature. How can you explain the

Jew except in the terms in which the Bible itself explains him? How often does God say, "You are what you are because you are My people. I did this for you, not because of you, but for My own great name's sake." They rebelled against God constantly, they broke His laws, and yet in spite of all that they remain this unique nation. The story is inexplicable if you regard it merely from the human level. From the standpoint of sheer ability and reason, the Jew does not stand comparison with the Greek. He never produced the great philosophers that the Greeks produced. But in spite of all, here is the greatest nation that the world has ever known – this unique people. It cannot be explained solely in terms of man and yet what an essential part it is of the past history of mankind!

Turn to the New Testament itself and observe how Jesus of Nazareth stands out. The world today that does not believe in Him as the Son of God has to admit that He is the most unique person that the world has ever seen. He has affected the whole of history. Our very dates are in terms of BC and AD. The whole history of the world has been affected by this one Person. Think of His life, His teaching, His death. Think of His church. They have profoundly affected the story of mankind. Can it be explained solely in terms of man? Is a human explanation sufficient? Can Jesus of Nazareth be explained as some kind of biological spurt that was thrown up nearly two thousand years ago, but which has never been repeated? It is inadequate scientifically. These great facts of history defy any attempt to explain the story of mankind purely in terms of man and of the human race. There is this something extra, this something that seems to be coming down from above.

As you follow the subsequent history of the race you find exactly and precisely the same thing. Look at the great movements of the Spirit. Think of the Renaissance and the Protestant Reformation, how these influenced the whole story of the world! You cannot explain the United States except in terms of the Protestant Reformation. You cannot explain Britain, you cannot explain Holland. History would be altogether different were it not for Martin Luther and John Calvin and the Protestant Reformation. But what is the explanation of these great tides and movements of the Spirit? Can you explain these things in terms of man only? Surely, had it been merely the story of man, there would never have been these great upsurgings and uprisings in the history of mankind.

Man always tends to go downwards. Take the great civilizations of China and of Egypt. What wonderful knowledge they had! What astounding influence they exerted! But what happened to them? As I have said, man tends to go down. He tends to obscure the light and to lose the knowledge that he has gained. Man's tendency is ever downwards and yet we know that history is characterized, above everything else, by these mighty movements of the Spirit within these great upreachings of the soul, these great mountain-top epochs. These things, I say, can never be understood or explained if you try to understand history solely in terms of man. No! No! If you would understand history, "Come up hither." Look into the heavens. Start with God. Get up on top of the great peaks and look down upon the earth. "There's a divinity that shapes our ends, rough-hew them as we may." Look at history and what you will find everywhere, and always, is not a story of the gradual ascent on the part of man, but this constant interfering with the story from above, this strange irruption of God into the human scene, this constant visitation from on high when everything had become hopeless, and when man was immersed in darkness. It is God coming in, God interfering, God disturbing. Would you understand it? Then, "Come up hither." Start in heaven. View the story from the beginning, from eternity, from the ultimate. Is not that obvious as a principle?

3. Only revelation helps

I would lay down as my third principle that **man can never understand the story of mankind, and of the world, by his own unaided efforts**. Here we get it in these graphic terms: "The voice which I heard was as it were of a trumpet talking with me; which said, Come up hither, and I will shew thee things which must be hereafter. And immediately I was in the spirit; and, behold, a throne was set in heaven, and one sat on the throne." Even the apostle John could never have seen it and could never have recorded it were it not that "immediately" he was "in the spirit". The preview of history that is given in this book is a view which is beyond the reach of human understanding and the human intellect. History is to be understood, finally, not by making an analysis of past history, but by accepting the category of revelation. The story of man is not to be understood by studying man. The story of man is to be understood by accepting God's revelation of Himself and His revelation concerning man. In other words, if we would understand the times in which we live and if we would understand the future that is coming, we have to make this great act of surrender. We have to accept this Book as the revelation of God. We shall have to admit that we have come to the end of our human understanding and ability. We shall have to accept the category of the eternal and supernatural, the miraculous and the absolute. We have to believe those things that to the natural mind are folly. Now that is our trouble. You remember how the great apostle works that theme out at length in the first epistle to the Corinthians. The whole thing to the Greek, says the apostle, is foolishness. He cannot understand it; he cannot believe it. He wants to be able to explain it with his mind and his understanding, but the things of the Spirit of God cannot be understood by the natural man. The things of the Spirit of God can only be understood by the Spirit which God gives. There is the key to the understanding of the human story and of mankind at large. If we stop at our own understanding, with our own ability, and our own attempt to reason, why then, as the wise man tells us in the Book of Ecclesiastes, the whole thing is foolish. "Vanity of vanities; all is vanity." What is the point of having your Acts of Parliament? What is the point of popular education? We have had it for nearly a hundred years, yet look at your modern world! Like the pessimist and the cynic, you will say, "There is nothing in it." The river flows to the sea, it goes back to its beginning. The sun rises, it sets, and it rises again. Everything is as it has been. It is a mad thing to go in for wisdom. "Let us eat and drink, for tomorrow we die." It is futile if we attempt to understand life it solely by our own unaided efforts. We are doomed to disappointment and to final failure. But, thank God, there is another way. History can be understood. The meaning, the sense and the purpose of life, and of everything that is, has been revealed. God has revealed it. It is the great story of this Book. It is this story we are considering in these sermons. It is this unfolding from above. But the first step is the acknowledgment of our own inability; it is the admission of the inadequacy of human reason and understanding, and the childlike acceptance of the revelation of God in Jesus Christ. That, I say, is the introduction to the understanding of human history. It must be taken as a whole. We must have the right perspective. We must never view it only in terms of man. We must never place our final confidence in our own ability to understand it.

Would you see the future? Would you understand the meaning of life and of the world? "Come up hither." Surrender to the Spirit of God. Ascend into the heavens. And if we are but ready to respond to that invitation we shall find, as the apostle found of old, that we shall receive the Spirit and we shall begin to see things as they truly are.

CHAPTER 17

The Throne in the Heaven

(Revelation 4:1–11)

We are attempting, in the light of chapters 4 and 5 of this Book of the Revelation, to understand something of the meaning of the days through which we are passing and still more to try to understand something of the meaning and purpose of history.

There is nothing which the average person so desires and so covets as a preview of history. We realize that we are creatures of time, that we are subject to the various changes and clashes of history. Life has become uncertain and there are many who have ceased to think, feeling that everything is vain and hopeless. One of the great dangers of the hour is that a spirit of despair will descend upon the nations on account of the wars and tragedies that face us – and as a result of the present situation and of everything which can be described as modern history. Nothing is so important, therefore, as that we should try to understand clearly and grasp what the Bible itself has to say concerning this all-important, urgent and vital matter. Here in these two chapters we are given what is, perhaps, in many ways, the clearest view of history which can be found anywhere. The apostle John, you remember, on the Island of Patmos, is given this vision. Here he is addressed by a voice from heaven which says to him, "Come up hither, and I will shew thee things which must be hereafter. And immediately", he says, "I was in the Spirit, and, behold, a throne was set in heaven, and One sat upon the throne."

Now we must look at this matter in a more positive way. In other words we are going to heed this exhortation to "Come up hither" more directly and more immediately. John hearkened unto the exhortation and immediately he was in the Spirit, and he began to receive the vision.

He went up to heaven and at once he was confronted by a throne and by one who was seated upon the throne.

Now why does this preview of history which was given to John start in that way? Why is it necessary in order to see things which must be hereafter, that the apostle first of all has a vision of heaven and of God? I would answer that question by putting it in the form of a principle.

The first essential

The first essential step to a true knowledge of history is to know God. That is a principle which is fundamental and vital. History is meaningless apart from God. The way to learn history and to understand it is not to start with your secular history books, it is to do something which seems paradoxical and almost, in a sense, ridiculous. If you would learn history, start by turning your back on history and looking at God. The key to history is a knowledge of God. That is how the preview of history that was given to the apostle began. Now may we ask, with reverence, why it begins in this way? Why was it, before John began to see the opening of the Book, and the opening of the seals, and the blowing of the trumpets, and the pouring forth of the vials, and all the amazing things which are outlined in this Book – why was it that before all that was given to him in a vision, before he was told about it, and told something of its meaning, that it had to start with this great vision of God upon the throne?

I want to suggest the following answers – and they are as applicable to us today as they were to the apostle. I must put these answers in terms of John's teaching.

John was given this vision, first of all, **in order that he might be reminded that man's relationship to God is more important than his relationship to history**. Or, to put it the other way round, more important than my relationship to history is my relationship to God. Here again is one of those first principles. Our whole trouble is that we take ourselves so seriously and we take history so seriously. There is a sense in which it is very right to take history seriously. But if we put ourselves and history before our relationship to God, then we are doing something which is unutterable folly. But this has been the temptation, especially during the last hundred years. We have placed man in the centre and God has been relegated to the background. He is very valuable and useful on our Days of National Prayer when we need His blessing on our efforts, but God has not been central. God is one whom we call in and whose help we invoke when we are in desperate need and in a case of dire necessity. History has been the all-important thing to us and we all want to know what is going to happen; what is going to be the future of our nation and of the "Commonwealth of Nations" and other groupings of nations? What is going to be the future course of mankind and of history? Can we look forward to a period of affluence and prosperity, or can we not? These are the things which mankind is concerned about and all our energies are devoted to the elucidation of them – of these things that have become central.

But here, at the very commencement, we are reminded that of infinitely greater importance than my relationship to history is my relationship to God. That does not derogate from the value of my nationality or citizenship in "the Commonwealth" or whatever. But infinitely more important than my nationality, or my membership of any group of nations, is my relationship to God. This is not to depreciate the importance of history, but it is to say this: that kingdoms may come and go, empires may rise and wax and wane, civilizations may appear and vanish, but God remains; and my relationship to Him is something eternal. In other words, this is the first blow that is delivered to our pride, and this pride is something of which we are all guilty. We are all guilty of it as individuals. We are all guilty of it as members of nations. Every nation loves itself and takes pride in itself; and it is this national pride that ultimately accounts for war. Here is God's answer. It is not our history that matters primarily, it is our relationship to God. It is as if God said to John, "John, you are concerned about the church and about the world and about human history. That is all right. But lest it should absorb you, let us start in the right place. More important than any of these things is your relationship to Me." I do not hesitate to say, therefore, even at this critical hour in the history of this country, and of the world, that more important than the date of the turning-points of any wars or conflicts, and even of their outcome, is our relationship to God. For though we win the war against any monstrosity in our world, if our relationship to God is wrong, there can be no lasting peace and prosperity, and ultimately and beyond it all, we still meet and face God, the judge eternal. Therefore we must start at this point. More important even than my relationship to history is my relationship to God.

The second reason why, I believe, John was granted this preliminary vision was that he might be reminded that **everything, history included, starts with God, is under God, and will end with God**. God is at the back of everything. God is the Author of everything. God is the originator of history. There would be no history but for God. It is God who made the world. He set this process going. He has created time. He has set the machine going and He is sustaining it. Even history itself is subordinate to God. Now we are in the warp and woof of history, and we are subject to the changes and to the clashes of history. The result is that there is a school of philosophy – and it is a very popular one at the present time – which would almost make us just cogs in this great wheel. There are many who are given to that form of pessimism and who say that man is nothing but the plaything of history. They even go on to ask the question, "Is it worth enduring? Is it worthwhile? Should a man continue in it? If this is all that it means, why not get out of it?" That is a pessimism which results from regarding history as the master-force and failing to realize that history itself starts with God, is ever under God, and will certainly end with God. It is God who started the process and it is God who will wind up the process. That is, of course, the teaching of the Bible from beginning to end. The whole of the historical process is under God and John was reminded of all that by this great vision of the eternal temple with the throne in the centre and the one who was on the throne. History is put into its right place and into its right perspective.

But I imagine there was another reason, a very beautiful and tender one, why John was given this initial vision before he was given to know the exact details of the future. It surely was, in the third place, **to enable him to bear the preview of history that was about to be given to him**. I see here a very wonderful display of the love and the compassion and the understanding of God. John was going to be shown some terrible things.

Read for yourselves again the account of the seals and the trumpets and the vials. John was to be given a terrible picture of conflict, of war, of the dragon, of the beast out of the sea, and the beast out of the earth; those forces inimical to the church, those terrible powers that were going to make havoc of her. He sees blood being shed and the whole world in a state of turmoil. How can he stand such a vision? How can he bear such a spectacle? There is only one way. He is shown the throne and its Occupant, first. He starts with the vision of the eternal and of God. He is given a sight of God, so that when he comes to the vials and the trumpets and the seals, and all the havoc and bloodshed of war, and when he feels at his wits' end and is about to collapse, he will remember the original vision and be comforted, strengthened and fortified.

Now all this, I say, is equally applicable to us today. In our ignorance and in our folly we long to have a view of the future. Yet do we not begin to feel at times that it is by the mercy of God that we are only given to see one step at a time? Would you have liked a few decades ago to have been given a preview of the past twenty years leading right up to this hour? Do you really want to know about the future? Have you any conception of what it is going to be like? The Bible gives us a preview. It is not a very cheering or comforting one. It is not the kind of thing that is said by the politicians. They would have us believe that these conflicts are "a war to end war", and in the future we are going to enjoy peace and plenty. No, the preview that is given here is not an optimistic one. It does not take that rosy view of human nature and of subsequent history. But, thank God, it does give us this vision of heaven and of the throne of God. I do not hesitate to aver that were it not for what I have seen of this vision, I would prefer not to know the future. I would prefer to remain ignorant of history. I would, indeed, despair of the human race and of the whole story of mankind. But, given this view, history is supportable, history is bearable. It is something that one can venture to look at, because one already has the key.

What is the vision?

What then is the vision that was granted to John? It is likewise granted to us as a result of John's record. I merely desire to summarize it. John was given this astonishing and amazing vision of God. What does he see? It is put here in the form of very strange and beautiful imagery. These are symbols, these are pictures, yet they represent eternal truths. First of all, John is shown certain things concerning God Himself, God in His essence, God as He is. What does he see? Well, first and foremost, he sees that **God is eternal**. "The four and twenty elders fall down before him that sat on the throne, and worship him that liveth for ever and ever." "And the four beasts had each of them six wings about him; and they were full of eyes within; and they rest not day and night, saying, Holy, holy, holy, Lord God Almighty, which was, and is, and is to come." God the eternal one. Surely, I need not show the application of that. We are interested in history, we are concerned about history, we live in time and we feel that we are so much the creatures of time. When we are given to such thought, and tend to become the victims of such thoughts, the antidote, remember, is to realize that God is eternal, God is timeless, God is ageless, God is absolute, God is everlasting. God is above time, God is above history. We are in the vortex, we are in a state of war, things are about to happen here, we are involved in it all. How can we bear it? How can we face it? Remember your relationship to one who is above it all, beyond it all, and superior to it all. God is not involved in time. God is not in the flux of this world and its history. God rideth upon the heavens; He is seated on the throne that is above the cosmos. God is eternal and the time process does not affect Him. He is above it and beyond it. He has brought it into being and though independent of it, He is behind it and at the back of it. God the eternal one. Do let us remember, therefore, as we feel immersed and engrossed in these things of time, that we are related to one who is above it and beyond it all and who, whatever may take place in the realm of time and of the world, can never be affected by it and can never be changed by it. He is "the Father of lights, with whom is no variableness, neither shadow of turning".

But John is also given a vision of **God as the Holy One**. We have already been shown that the one that sat upon the throne was like a jasper, like an emerald, like a diamond, perfect in its purity and in its holiness. What relevance has this to history? Its relevance is simply this: that in view of the fact that history is the creation of God, it is of vital importance to remember that God is holy, that God can do no wrong. God cannot be tempted with evil, whatever may be happening in time. Remember that God is holy and you can say that "all things work together for good to them that love God". Whatever your experience may be, there is no unrighteousness in God; there is no unfairness in the treatment meted out to you; God is holy. He is absolute in His perfection. Let us, therefore, never even dare to raise certain questions. Let us never criticize Him. Let us never say, "Why does God permit this or that? Is God being fair to me? Is God answering my prayer? Is God honouring His own word?" "The four beasts ... rest not day and night, saying, Holy, holy, holy, Lord God Almighty." There can be no wrong, there will be no wrong; never dare to suggest it. Do not allow your view of history to cast the slightest suspicion of a cloud upon the holiness and righteousness of God.

Remember **He is the Lord God Almighty**. Are you tempted to think that history has got out of hand? Are you tempted to say, "Surely God cannot be controlling. Look at these wars and conflicts. Look at these dictators. Look at the godlessness and the irreligion. Look at what is happening in the world"? If ever you are tempted to ask the question, remember the answer: "Holy, holy, holy, Lord God Almighty." Nothing can escape Him. His power is illimitable, absolute and eternal. Everything is under His dominion. Remember the throne and its almighty occupant. That is the vision given to John, in its essence, of God Himself.

Then he is given a vision of **God in His relationship to the world**. Here he is shown two things. First of all he is shown that God is the Creator. "The four and twenty elders fall down before him that sat on the throne ... saying, Thou art worthy, O Lord, to receive glory and honour and power; for thou hast created all things, and for thy pleasure they are and were created." You cannot understand the world apart from God. Creation is meaningless apart from Him. Even the scientists are beginning to see that and to admit it. With their own pride and arrogance, and confidence in man's reason, they say you must postulate a Mind. He is the Creator and there would be no history apart from Him and His creation.

But let me emphasize another aspect of this question. Even this modern world is God's world still. God in His infinite wisdom – we can never understand it – has permitted certain things. He has permitted evil. Why? We do not know. We may understand better when we reach the glory. He has permitted sin. He has allowed the devil to do so much. He seems to permit what is happening today. Yet, my dear friend, never lose your grasp on this thought: it is still God's world. He owns it, He fashioned it and sustains it. He is its artificer and the world today is God's world; He is not going to let it go. He is pledged to keep His hand upon it until the end when it shall be perfected, and when it shall be handed back to Him by the Son. God the Creator is the owner of the world, and, therefore, we are assured, whatever may happen, finally all will be well.

In other words, I have anticipated the next part of the vision, which is that God is not only the Creator, but **He is also the King of the earth** and the Ruler of the world. He is upon the throne and the throne suggests rule, a dominion, a government and an authority. I say again that whatever we may be seeing and witnessing, we must never forget that God is the King eternal. He is the Ruler of the world and of the whole universe so that "not a sparrow falls without your Father knowing", and all things are in His hands. God in His relationship to the world is the Creator, the King and the Ruler.

Lastly, John is given a vision of **God in relation to a world of sin**. Now this, of course, is essential, because history is so much the product of sin, and the vision does not merely start with some idealistic future apart from God's relationship to the world. He is shown in His relationship to this actual world in which we live. God in His relationship to this sinful world is revealed in two aspects. First, we see Him as the righteous judge. We are told that He is seated upon the throne and that He is like a sardine stone, as the Authorized Version puts it, and that "out of the throne proceed lightnings, and thunderings, and voices". This is a vision of God's judgment, God in His holiness and in His absolute perfection, hating sin, judging sin, denouncing sin, punishing sin, dealing with sin – the sardius stone of God.

So we can be confident of that, whatever is happening in our world. History is very largely nothing but a demonstration of the righteous God dealing with sin. History is the judgment of God upon sin. That is, for me, the only adequate explanation of this war. It is God allowing mankind to reap the consequences of its own action. It is God punishing, God judging sin, God the righteous Judge of sin. Here we are given the assurance that finally all that is opposed to God and inimical to Him shall be judged and shall be punished. But, thank God, the story does not end there. For God, in His relationship to sin, is revealed in another character. "And He that sat upon the throne was to look upon like a jasper and a sardine stone: and there was a rainbow round about the throne, in sight like unto an emerald." Thank God for the rainbow! I look at the throne and I see clouds, I hear thunder, I behold flashing and I hear voices. God the Judge. But, thank God, there is a rainbow like an emerald. God the Saviour. God in His infinite love and compassion. God the Father of our Lord Jesus Christ. God who "so loved the world that he gave his only begotten Son". The rainbow in the cloud – the mercy and compassion and love and the great salvation of God.

There is the essential preliminary to an understanding of history. God the eternal. God the holy One. God the Almighty. God the Creator. God the King and the Ruler. God the Judge eternal. God the Saviour of my soul. It is in that way alone that a true view of history is understandable. All things are in His hands. What matters supremely, therefore, is my relationship to Him. As we think of today, as we think of the future, as we wonder what is going to happen, as we tremble on the brink of terrible things, let us with John turn aside and turn away from it all for a moment and turn to God. Let us look to the throne and, with the elders and the beasts, prostrate ourselves before Him and cry out and say, "Holy, holy, holy, Lord God Almighty."

CHAPTER 18

Two Types of History

(Revelation 5:1–4)

In the early twentieth century there developed a new tendency in the approach to history on the part of the authorities. History, in the past, used to be regarded mainly and chiefly as a record of events. The popular conception of history was that it was an account, a record, of kings and of countries, of births, marriages and deaths, of wars and conquests, and things of that type and kind. But, during the twentieth century especially, there has been a new outlook upon history – a new approach towards history which has described itself as an attempt to understand the philosophy of history, or some would even say, perhaps, the psychology of history. This new outlook was put very well by a certain professor of history in London, Professor Pollard, when he said, "The important thing is not when did Columbus discover America, but why Columbus discovered America." That reminds us very perfectly of this new view of history, this new outlook. It is not the mere fact that Columbus discovered America, or the date on which he made the discovery, that really matters. What really matters, they tell us, is what were the forces and factors that conspired together to make him do that. So they begin at once to analyse the condition of the Old World. They point out that with the Renaissance a new curiosity arose in the minds of men and a sense of dissatisfaction. A spirit of adventure came into being which sent men, not only to study literature, but to investigate science and even sent them out upon those hazardous journeys across the ocean. Why did Columbus discover America? This whole approach is interested not so much in the events themselves as in their meaning, in their explanation, and in a true understanding of them. Its concern is to discover the principles that explain history and that produce history. It is no part of my business to consider with you the various schools of thought in which this modern approach to history expresses itself. Many explanations have been put forward. Some would explain history in terms of economics; others would explain it solely in terms of population and biology.

The biblical approach

What I am concerned to do is to show the biblical approach to history, which is in a sense very similar to this modern approach. I mean that one of the first things we have to grasp as we look at biblical history is that the Bible is not merely interested in events as such. The Bible is interested in explanations. It is interested in what we may call the philosophy of history. Events, as such, do not matter. It is the significance of events that matters so tremendously. In other words, biblical history is very definitely prejudiced. It does not pretend to be a detached, scientific view. It is history written from the standpoint of God and of man's relationship to God. The whole of the history of this Book is coloured by that thought. It is determined by it and entirely controlled by it. The Bible is not merely concerned to record history in and of itself. What it is anxious for us to do is to understand the meaning of history and to see in these records, and these events, the working out of the mighty purposes of God amongst men. So that here, at any rate, we can say that there is a very close parallel and similarity between the modern approach to history and biography, and the biblical view and presentation of the history of mankind, and of the world.

Here in Revelation 4–5 we are reminded of this principle in a very forcible manner and nowhere, perhaps, in a more striking way than in Revelation 5:1–4. We are told by John that he "saw in the right hand of him that sat on the throne a book written within and on the backside, sealed with seven seals". John, therefore, has this vision of God seated upon the throne, with a book in His right hand, sealed with seven seals. In that book is the account of the future history of mankind and of the world. Now another important point to remember is that the history which is revealed and divulged in this Book of the Revelation is, as regards its type and order, exactly and precisely the same as the history which is revealed in the Old Testament. The latter leads up to Christ and His coming; the former leads on from the first coming of Christ to His second coming. But the type and nature of the history is exactly and precisely the same. In other words, we must approach the history which is recorded in the Revelation in exactly the same way as we approach the prophecies recorded in the Old Testament canon. They both belong to the same type of history. In the Old Testament prophecies you have a preview of history; you have this forward glance, this foretelling of what was going to happen. In this Book of Revelation you have a similar preview of history, a similar predicting of that which is going to take place.

Two general principles

Certain principles are taught us here very clearly. Standing therefore as we do, at a crisis in history, and on what many people regard as the threshold of a new world, surely nothing is more important than that we should test these great principles of the biblical view of history. As suggested by this text, it seems to me that we can best look at them in this way.

First of all, there are two general points indicated here; they are perfectly obvious and simple. The first thing is that **everything is known to God**. John sees God seated upon the throne with the book in His right hand. God has the history in His hand. He knows the contents of that book. The angels do not know them; no one knows them save God. But God knows them. Now this is the principle which is to be found running right through the Bible. How often do we read of things happening according to the "foreknowledge of God the Father". "Known unto God are all his works from the beginning of the world", says James in the Book of the Acts. Nothing that can happen is unknown to God. The very omniscience of God guarantees this. God sees the end from the beginning. God is aware of everything that has taken place and ever can take place. God, being outside time and above time, does not see things in sequence as we see them. God sees them as a whole, and this picture of God seated on the throne, with a book in His hand, should remind us of the foreknowledge of God. So that as we look to the future, with a sense of insecurity and with a certain amount of trepidation and alarm, is it not a comforting thought to realize and to know that everything that is going to happen is known perfectly to God already? There are no surprises for God; there are no contingencies in the life and mind of the Eternal. The whole of the future is known and open and plain to God. The book was in the right hand of Him who sat upon the throne.

The second general point is that all **history is ultimately controlled by God**. I want to emphasize that word "ultimately", for a reason which I will explain when I come to the detailed analysis. God sits upon the throne with this roll, this book in His right hand, with the seals upon it. The history is sealed; it is settled and fixed and final. It is all in the power of God; it is all in the hand of God. History, in its entirety, is ultimately controlled by God. Now we need not stay with that point this morning, as we were referring to it before when we emphasized that it is of the very essence of the biblical view of history. God started history and keeps it going, and it is God who is going to bring it to a final conclusion. Yet it is good that we should hold these two general principles in our minds before we go to the details. This picture of God, seated on the throne with the book in His right hand, of necessity compels our attention. He knows it all finally; it is all in His hand and can never get outside His control. What a wonderfully comforting and consoling thought that is at a time like this.

1. Two types of history

Let us go on to consider the particular principles which seem to me to be suggested in a very striking manner by this vision which was granted unto the apostle. The first is that there are two main types of history. First, there is the history that God permits; then there is the history that God produces. Now this is a very important distinction. **The history that God permits is the only concern of secular history**. Take all your history books with all their accounts of countries and nations and empires and kings and battles, and all those things that go to make up history books on the secular plane. All those things, according to the Bible, are simply the history that God permits. Civilizations come and go, empires rise and wax and wane. Take the great story of the world, as far as it is known, with all the rivalries and jealousies, quarrels and warfare, and activities of mankind. Now all that, according to the Bible, is mainly the history that God permits; it is the history that God allows. When you come to look at that type of history in the Bible, you are immediately impressed by certain striking things. Have you observed how the Bible treats in a brief and cursory manner this history which occupies so much space and attention in our history books? Have you noticed how the Bible dismisses the history of Babylon in just a few sentences? Yet what a mighty civilization it was! Can we picture to ourselves all the wealth and the military prowess, the art, the culture, the learning and the wisdom of a great empire like Babylon? Yet it is dismissed in a few sentences in the Bible. Think of Assyria, of Egypt. Think of the Medes and the Persians, and all those other great dynasties and empires. Secular history makes a great deal of these empires; they are tremendously important. It talks about the great battles of history and about the great leaders, and the great generals, as if they were great and important factors in life. Yet they are dismissed in the Bible in the briefest compass, the reason and the explanation being that all that kind of history, according to the Bible, is merely the history that God allows and permits. But to be strictly accurate I must point out that the Bible not only tends to dismiss such history in a very brief space, but sometimes it almost deals with it in tones of contempt. There was a very striking book published just before the outbreak of this war by a Swiss preacher and theologian of the name of Walther Luthi on the Book of Daniel. In it he puts this point very perfectly. Concerning the prophecies of Daniel he makes this very penetrating and interesting remark. He says that the man whom the world recognizes and refers to as Alexander the Great is dismissed in the Bible as a he-goat! What a profound and penetrating observation![8] Read again for yourselves the Book of Daniel and just bear in mind the

8. Pastor Walther Luthi's sermons on Daniel were published in Basel in 1937 shortly before the Second World War (see *Die Kommende Kirche: Die Botschaft des Propheten Daniel*). Dr Lloyd-Jones had read the English translation.

fact that when you read that account of the he-goat you are reading about Alexander the Great! He was great in secular history, but from the standpoint of God, a he-goat! Those great captains and kings who cut such a great figure in the text books of secular history come in and are given their place because, ultimately, they belong to the realm of the history that God permits.

The second type of history is **the history that God determines**, the history that God brings to pass. That is the great theme of the Bible and that, of course, is something of which we are reminded in a very special way in this Book of the Revelation, and very particularly in Revelation 5:1–4. For let us never forget this, that the breaking of the seven seals that bound that Book that was in the right hand of God does not merely mean that God is giving to His servant a preview of what was coming to pass. The breaking of the seals brings that God was bringing history to pass. It says that as every seal was broken something happened. It does not merely mean that the Book is opened in the sense that these things were originated at that point; no, it brings into being things that are already determined. That is a reminder that the second great type of history is the history that God brings to pass. This history is a record of God's intervention or, if I may use a better word, God's irruptions into the realm of human history and into the story of mankind. It is the history which records God bringing to pass His own great and gracious purposes. Or, to put it in a single phrase, the second type of history is the grand history of God's redeeming purpose on this human plane.

That is our first principle. There are these two types of history: the history that God permits and the history that God determines. But to make it complete I must point out this. **These two types of history are constantly intersecting and they intersect according to God's ultimate purpose.** That is why the Old Testament, for instance, has to mention Assyria and Babylon, the he-goats, and all the rest of them, because they impinge upon God's history and God's history impinges upon them. In the forty-fifth chapter of Isaiah we read that God girded Cyrus. It was God that was doing it and Cyrus is of consequence, not because he was a captain and a great king, but because God used him to bring His people back to Jerusalem from the captivity of Babylon. The two histories intersect frequently and the two histories thus come together at certain points. Ultimately and finally the two histories will be blended into one and God will reign and rule over all, and evil will be destroyed, and there will be only one history, the history of redemption, the history of the redeemed, the history of the perfect world. That is our first principle – that there are two types of history.

2. The significance of history

But let us hasten on to the second principle, which is that **the true significance of history is only discovered when it is seen as a record of the conflict between God and evil**. That is the history that matters and counts, and this is, surely, the thing we are to grasp at a time like this. The Bible does not tell us exactly how evil originated; that is a great mystery that still remains. We are not given the final explanation of the origin of evil. There are many ideas and theories about the great cosmic fall when Lucifer, the son of the morning, fell. Why did he fall? We are not told. All we are told is that God, in His infinite wisdom, permitted evil to come into existence and the fact is that it is there. We are told that it is terribly powerful, that it has entered into the life and story of mankind. It has brought havoc, it has brought discord, it has brought misery into the world. God made a perfect world. God made man perfect. Men and women were made to enjoy the fruits of the earth and to have communion with God. How do you then explain the modern world? It is this terrible thing, this awful cancer, that has entered humanity, devastating everything. It has come in and God has allowed it. The Bible tells us also that this power is much stronger than man; it conquers man; it defeats man. And it would have finally destroyed man and the world, were it not for the fact that God came in. God gave the original promise concerning the seed of the woman and that is the beginning of the sequence of history. You notice how the Bible starts with that. It tells you the story of the creation and it tells you of that which came in and spoiled it, and then it tells you of God coming in. This conflict between God and evil, heaven and hell, this mighty conflict, has been going on ever since. The grand process of redemption that originated and was initiated by God, and that has been set upon its way, has continued ever since.

Now what the history of the Bible is really concerned about is the conflict between these two things. You see it, as I have already reminded you, in the Old Testament. It is also the whole meaning of the Book of the Revelation. Read it for yourselves again starting with these two chapters and going on to the end – the dragon, the beast out of the sea, and the beast from the earth, the city of Babylon – all these powers trying to destroy the saints and to destroy God's work. This conflict between God and evil – on and on it goes.

But we must make some special points because they are elaborated at very great length in this Book of Revelation. **Evil, we are told, may take many different forms** and we can never truly understand the conflict between God and evil unless we are very clear about that point. Evil does not always appear the same; evil takes many different shapes. Sometimes it appears in a very ugly form, in all its vileness and degradation. Evil as it is incarnated in certain men who seem to be the very embodiment of the spirit of antagonism to God; evil which is anti-God and anti-Christ in its various localised human forms; and evil in nations and in dynasties that are godless. But evil does not always take that form. It can sometimes be highly respectable. Evil, according to the Bible, may emerge sometimes as a false religion. It may sometimes manifest itself as a highly spiritual form of religion. Evil may show itself as idealism, as humanism, as materialism, even as love of country, as love of learning, as love of culture. It has an almost infinite and endless variety of forms in which it may appear.

The second point is that **these various forms often contradict and fight against one another**. The world regards these subsidiary fights as being important. Take your history books and observe the time, the space and the attention they give to the fight of knowledge against ignorance. Take the great pride of mankind during the past hundred years in education, in culture, and the talk there has been about enlightenment, about fighting the ignorance and the darkness of mankind, about the reform of society, the doing away of the slums, and the improving of housing conditions. Now the world regards these things as being of supreme significance. Of course, in a certain sense, they are significant, but from the biblical standpoint they may have no significance at all. For, according to the Bible, these things may be nothing but internecine or civil wars. What the Bible is finally interested in is this, the relationship of every human being to God. The Bible has no interest in learning and understanding which is godless. The Bible does not differentiate between the nation that has an anti-God movement and the nation that forgets God and ignores Him. The significance of that at this hour is that according to the Bible we shall have achieved nothing in the defeat of Hitlerism and Fascism if, having done so, as a nation we simply settle down to a life of ease and enjoyment and forget everything about God. Yes, evil takes many forms, according to this Book. There are several beasts. There is the dragon, there is the city of Babylon, the great whore, as she is described. All the kings and the captains came and paid their court and attention to her. Is not all culture superior to the filthiness of certain of the beasts? Not at all! If it is opposed to God it belongs to the realm and kingdom of evil and of sin. Let us, therefore, not be misled by these false divisions and distinctions. One thing matters. The fight between God and evil. And what matters is not which regiment of evil we may belong to, but are we on the side of God? God and evil. Anything which is not of God belongs, of necessity, to the kingdom of darkness and of iniquity.

3. Pessimism and optimism

Lastly, I must say a word about what I would describe as the pessimism and optimism of biblical history. You observe that when John had this vision of God on the throne, with the roll in His right hand, he then heard an angel proclaiming in a loud voice, "Who is worthy to open the book, and to loose the seals thereof? And no man was able to open the book, neither to look thereon. And I wept much, because no man was found worthy to open and to read the book, neither to look thereon." Why did John weep? He wept because he saw, first, the pessimism of biblical history. He saw man as the slave of sin, man as the helpless victim of Satan and of hell, man ruined and destroyed by the forces of iniquity if left to himself. The other element in this pessimism is that the Bible tells us everywhere that in the interim we have nothing to expect but apparent defeat and temporary suffering. If you take the biblical view of history you can put it like this. In the immediate it is pessimistic. But, thank God, that is only in the immediate. In the ultimate it is optimistic. The Bible always pours scorn and ridicule upon the various movements of idealism in human history, for they never come to anything. Civilizations rise and wane. The world seems to be reaching what seems to be perfection and then it crashes down. In 1914 all seemed to be going well; then came the crash. It has always been like that. In the immediate the Bible is always pessimistic. You read about the opening of the seals and the pouring out of the vials and everything seems to be against the elect; there is immediate suffering, apparent defeat. But it is only immediate. The ultimate is always optimistic, for always at the end we are reminded of the power of Christ. At the end we see everything that has raised its arrogant head against the Lord of glory defeated and cast into the lake of fire, utterly destroyed. God and His saints triumph over all and there is a new heaven and a new earth, and the glory of God is revealed.

There briefly and inadequately are the great basic principles of biblical history. Let us try to remind ourselves of them. This is not a theoretical disquisition. We are in history; we are in the world. We have to face these things. God knows what is going to happen. But whatever may happen, put it all in the context and see it in the light of that great and glorious background. Keep clearly in your mind the two types of history. See the significance of the fight between God and evil. Above all remember that the ultimate outlook is glorious because of the power, the invincible power, of Almighty God.

CHAPTER 19

The Lord of History

(Revelation 5:1–5)

"And I saw in the right hand of him that sat on the throne a book written within and on the backside, sealed with seven seals. And I saw a strong angel proclaiming with a loud voice, Who is worthy to open the book, and to loose the seals thereof? And no man in heaven, nor in earth, neither under the earth, was able to open the book, neither to look thereon. And I wept much, because no man was found worthy to open and to read the book, neither to look thereon. And one of the elders saith unto me, Weep not: behold, the Lion of the tribe of Judah, the Root of David, hath prevailed to open the book, and to loose the seven seals thereof."

An impressive chapter of the Bible

Any man approaching this particular chapter must be more than usually conscious of his unworthiness and his insufficiency. For it is, I think all will agree, one of the most majestic and one of the most glorious chapters which is to be found anywhere, even in the Bible.

It is a matter of great interest to observe how this chapter has been the means of inspiration to large numbers of poets and to large numbers of musical composers and musicians. There is something about it which calls out that which is best in any man who has any understanding whatsoever of the Christian truth and of its glorious nature. Probably all of us, as we read the chapter at the beginning, and as we have been singing our hymns, have thought of Handel's *Messiah*, and some of those great choruses that found their direct inspiration in this very chapter. It is something which is transcendent in its glory and in its majesty and in its note of triumph. That particular note of triumph comes out when we take this chapter, as it should be taken always, in connection with the previous chapter. There, you remember, in the fourth chapter, John was given that great vision of God upon the throne and the chapter ends with the four beasts and the four and twenty elders joining together in that great song of creation, ascribing the glory and majesty unto God who is the creator and sustainer and ruler of all things.

But you will see that at the commencement of chapter five we are given a somewhat different picture. There we see that sin has entered in and we find John weeping. He wept for this reason: that there was no one in heaven or on earth, or anywhere else, who was fit to take this book out of the hand of God and to unloose the seals. In other words, sin had entered in and had created a problem; a problem that was baffling to all. "I wept much," says John, "because no man was found worthy to open and to read the book, neither to look thereon." There is a note of sadness and of pathos and of unhappiness; all seems to be lost. Then you come to verse 5 of the fifth chapter. "And one of the elders saith unto me, 'Weep not; behold, the Lion of the tribe of Judah, the Root of David, hath prevailed to open the book, and to loose the seven seals thereof.' " Immediately, the whole scene changes and we are given the privilege of listening to these mighty angelic choirs singing forth the praises of the Lamb and of Him that sat upon the throne.

Now the danger that confronts us when we read a great chapter like this is, curiously enough, the danger of being overawed by its very majesty and greatness. The danger is to regard it only and solely as literature, and there are those who would even go so far as to say that it is almost sacrilege to attempt to analyse it, or to consider, or to discuss it. It is a matter of poetry, they say, and you must not come with your analytical minds and try to analyse it. It is something so transcendently glorious that while you may look at it, to attempt to analyse it is like removing the petals of a rose. Yet, surely, that approach is quite wrong, for these chapters were written with a very practical object and intention. This book was not written as literature merely for the sake of literature. It was written to the infant church that was facing terrible days and still worse days were to come. If ever a book was written with a practical pastoral intention, it was this book, written to comfort and to help them, and if it is to be of any comfort and help and benefit to us, then we must take the trouble to analyse its contents and to discover what exactly is its practical teaching. We shall never be able to join with those angelic hosts unless we realize the reasons which moved them thus to pour forth their praises.

Two principles

In other words, we must remind ourselves once more of two vitally important principles. The first is that **John is here being given this preview of history**. That is the object of the book. The scene starts in heaven because it must start in heaven, yet we are not meant to stay there regarding the heavenly host. The word that comes to us is the word that the angels spoke to the disciples after their Lord had been taken up from them. "Ye men of Galilee, why stand ye gazing up into heaven?" We must come down to earth and work out these things on the practical level. Here is a preview of history; it is an account of things that are certainly going to happen.

The second general principle is that **real history is the history of redemption**. That is a principle which we must never lose sight of. We must maintain our hold on these two types of history and we must realize that the whole message of the Bible from beginning to end is that real history, the history that is going to matter in the end, is the history of redemption. God made the world perfect and He intended it to remain perfect. Man was placed in a state of bliss in paradise, but unfortunately sin entered in and everything was marred. The creation was, in a sense, ruined, and havoc entered in. But God, in His infinite mercy, did not turn His back upon the world. He did not say, "Well, man has ruined it and despoiled it by yielding to sin. I will allow it to fester in its iniquity until it has come to nothing." No, God, in His infinite mercy and love, planned that the world which had gone wrong should be put right again. God initiated this great movement of redemption. There is a purpose in history, a continuing and growing purpose, and there is an end to history.

This purpose is something which is slowly, yet surely, being worked out by God. The plan is to rid the world of evil and of sin; to restore it, not merely to its original pristine condition, but, indeed, to make it even more wonderful and glorious – a perfect world inhabited by perfect men, all giving thanks and worshipping God and glorifying His holy name. That is the purpose.

Now this purpose of God has had to meet much opposition. The story of the Old Testament is the story of that opposition. The story of the New Testament is the story of that opposition. And here it was given to John to see that there would be still more opposition. It is the picture of the attempt of evil to frustrate that purpose of God, but this is the great point. The purpose of God is going to succeed. Victory is certain and assured. What we have in this glorious fifth chapter of this Book of Revelation is just a kind of proleptic vision of the rejoicing in heaven because of that ultimate and final victory. "Proleptically," I say, we are given a vision of the ultimate triumph of God. When we go back to the ordinary turmoil and battle and discords of life, we carry in our minds and hearts the vision which we have seen. In the strength of that, and of its inspiration, we are enabled to continue and to go on to the end, come what may to meet us.

Now that is the background of this great chapter. But we must analyse it in a little further detail. There are certain great principles which stand out here on which we must concentrate, and especially at a time like this.

Further details

The first thing is that **the Lord Jesus Christ is the lord of history**. We can put that negatively by putting it like this. The world without Christ is hopeless. Here is a theme which one could very easily elaborate. But let us confine ourselves solely to the way in which it is put in this book itself. God is seated upon the throne and there in His hand is this scroll, written on the inside and on the outside, rolled up and sealed with seals. There is God's purpose, the purpose which we have already defined as the purpose of redeeming the world and delivering it out of the shackles and tyranny of evil and of sin.

But how is it to be done? What can be done for the world? A strong angel sounds forth the challenge. He proclaims with a loud voice, "Who is worthy to open the book and to loose the seals thereof?" What can be done for mankind? How can this purpose be brought to pass? "And no man in heaven, nor in earth, neither under the earth, was able to open the book, neither to look thereon." That is the first point with which we must start. Man is incapable of saving himself. Man has failed. That, again, is the great theme of the Old Testament. Look at those men who are called by God one after another; wonderful men, godly men, and yet every one of them fails and falls into sin. Every one of them has an imperfection. Good as they are, they are not good enough. Here we are told of something still deeper. Neither in heaven nor in earth is there any being that is capable of solving this problem. Man will never rid this world of sin and evil in and of himself. There is a sense in which it is astonishing that it is necessary still to make that statement. It was, was it not, Hegel who said, "We learn from history that we learn nothing from history." Still man harbours this pathetic illusion that by his own efforts and organizations and endeavours, he can rid the world of evil, and of all its consequent problems. But he cannot. He has tried to do it all through the centuries. Look at your great philosophers and teachers. Look at all your reformers on the secular plane. From the very commencement men have been trying to do it, but they have always failed, and here it is proclaimed that man always will fail. Man can never conquer sin and evil. He is too weak. He cannot conquer it in himself, leave alone in society and in the world round about. "There was no man able to open the book." Try in your imagination to take Christ out of history and what have you left? Take the message of this book out of the future and what have you to look forward to? Try to banish the Son of God out of your thoughts and what remains? He, and He alone, is the Lord of history. There was no man in heaven, or earth, or under the earth who was worthy, which means not only "worthy" in the usual sense of that word, but also strong and capable enough to take the book and to unloose and open the seals. But He steps forward and the result is that He is the Lord of history and the final arbiter of history. The future of the world is in the hands of the risen and glorified Christ. That is the first principle.

The second principle is that **the coming of Christ to earth, and all that He did while He was here, is the central point of all history**. That is the centre of history. Here is a point which we need not elaborate. It has already been recognized. Time is divided, and very rightly, into BC and AD. Before Christ and after Christ. He is the centre; He is the pivot. We are reminded of that in this verse. You observe that He is described, first of all, as "the Lion of the tribe of Judah". He is also described as "the Root of David". Why are those particular appellations attached to Him? Why is He described in these terms? The meaning, surely, is this. What one of the elders said unto John was, "Here is the one of whom God spoke so long ago to Jacob." Back in those early days of history the promise had been given, the original promise about the seed of the woman that was to bruise the serpent's head. Then nothing seemed to happen, but God was going quietly forward. He called Abraham and Isaac and Jacob, and spoke to them of "the Lion of the tribe of Judah"; of one to come, the Messiah, the Deliverer, who would deliver the world from sin and evil and iniquity. The elder here says to John: "Here is the Lion of the tribe of Judah, the fulfilment of that ancient prophecy."

But he is also "the Root of David". The promise was likewise given to David. We are told exactly where He is to come, and when, and the whole of the Old Testament looks forward to Him. Everything in the old dispensation is looking forward to this coming of "the Lion of the tribe of Judah", this offshoot of David, this sproutling that comes out of David, of the very line of David. He appears; He comes. That is why in the Gospels, in the account which we have of His birth and genealogy, these points are constantly emphasized. All the ancient history leads up to Him.

But you observe another very significant thing that is told us here in this description of Him. "I beheld," says John, "and, lo, in the midst of the throne, and of the four beasts, and in the midst of the elders, stood a lamb, as if it had been slain." If the whole of the Old Testament history looks forward to Him, the whole of the subsequent history looks back to Him. Even when He is seen in heaven He is seen in terms of the Lamb that was slain. There on the right hand of the throne, the throne of authority and power, is something that reminds us of His birth, yet still more of His death. Ancient literature looks forward to Him; all subsequent history looks back to Him, back to the Jesus of history, back to the Jesus who died on the cross, back to the Christ who was made a sin-offering for mankind. I say, therefore, that the coming of Christ to earth and all that He did while He was here on earth, is the central point of history. I sometimes feel that if only we could grasp that as we ought to, it would revolutionize everything. Is it not our constant danger to be spiritualising these matters? Are we not in danger, the danger of which the apostle Paul warns us, of turning the cross of Christ into a matter of philosophy and of forgetting that these things are facts? The fact is that the very Son of God has walked this earth; that God has intervened in history; and that there is a central turning-point of all history – the biggest thing that has ever happened. We are so absorbed by our own age and our own time. We talk about the greatest war of history – the Second World War – and it is perfectly true. But greater than all these things was that event that happened in such apparent obscurity away back in Bethlehem and on Calvary's hill. They are the central points of the whole of history.

Then that, in turn, leads me to the next general principle, which is to consider for a moment **Christ's programme for history**. What is our Lord's programme for history? He is the Lord of history. Well then, what does He propose to do? We are reminded in this chapter that His programme is not simply to exert a general influence upon history. He is not proposing merely gradually to improve the world and its denizens. His idea is not that His teaching shall come as a kind of refining influence upon mankind, and that gradually His ethics shall percolate through the various teachings of man and gradually permeate them, and so produce a higher type of humanity. No, that is a false idealism; that is humanism. It is not the teaching of this Book. Christ is not going to deal with the world merely in a vague, general sense. It is not going to be some diffuse influence.

The programme as we see here very clearly is the formation of a new kingdom. "Thou art worthy to take the book, and to open the seals thereof; for thou wast slain, and hast redeemed us to God by thy blood out of every kindred, and tongue, and people, and nation; and hast made us unto our God kings and priests; and we shall reign on the earth." Here is the point at which the biblical view of life and history clashes most vividly and obviously with secular history, and with the ideas and thoughts of the secular man. Biblical history is essentially apocalyptic; it is essentially eschatological. You may not like these terms, but I defy you to give me better terms. History is crisis. It is something critical. It is not a gradual development or evolution. It is not a gradual climbing up towards perfection. No! No! It is God coming in; it is God coming down. It is Christ intervening. It is God in Christ returning finally. It is Christ forming a new Kingdom. The kingdom is being formed within while we are living. He started it away back in the dawn of history. God took hold of men. He chose them from tribes and nations. He marked men out for special purposes. He began to use particular people. He was drawing them out in the old dispensation and He is still drawing them out. A new kingdom is being formed. It consists of men and women who have come out of every kindred and tongue and people. This does not mean that there is no ultimate meaning in the nations of the world. There is. It is not a false internationalism, it is a higher kingdom; it is something altogether above this. It does not denounce earthly kingdoms, but it says that the ultimate kingdom of the world is the kingdom of men who have been bought by the blood of Christ out of every tongue and nation and kindred and tribe. They will be gathered out and are being gathered out. Christ is forming a kingdom and the day will come when He will have gathered out what the Bible calls the total, the full number of the elect. The day will come when He will have called out of the nations, and out of the Jews, the complete number that was in the Eternal Mind. And then will come the end, the crisis, the cataclysmic event, the apocalypse, the unveiling, the return of that once-crucified Lord, the judgment, the renovation of the cosmos, and He will reign amongst His perfect people on a perfect earth. That is the programme.

Go back to the beginning. God made a perfect world. God intended this world to be perfect. Is it conceivable that God is going to allow sin and evil to defeat His purpose? No! The world must end perfectly as it began perfectly and Christ's programme is to produce that perfect world, that perfect people, and His method of doing it is the method that is here described. He is taking men and women to Himself; He is gathering them out; He is calling them out and finally the kingdom will be complete. That is biblical history. Men laugh at it and scoff at it. But let me remind you that they laughed and scoffed at the Old Testament prophecies. They laughed and scoffed at Noah. They ridiculed Lot. Men laughed at the prophets. They have always done that. They even laughed at our blessed Lord Himself. And yet the world that dismissed His talk about the resurrection was shocked by the resurrection. As certainly as these ancient prophecies have been fulfilled already, so these New Testament prophecies shall be fulfilled. The only hope for the world is that Christ is forming this perfect kingdom of a new and perfect humanity.

Why Jesus alone?

How does He do this? He is the Lord of history. We have seen His programme for history. What entitles Him to do this? **Why is it that He, and He alone, is worthy to produce this history?** What is the real meaning of the breaking of the seals and the opening of the roll? The answer is given to us. He alone can do it because He is the Lamb that has been, as it were, slaughtered. For the first problem is this: the problem of the sin of mankind. That perfect world which is to be will be a world of people who will desire to glorify God and to spend their time in communion with Him. Yet how can a sinful creature do that? God cannot dwell with sinners. He cannot have communion with those who have sinned against Him and who have sought to wound His eternal heart. The problem of sin and guilt and iniquity – how can it be dealt with? The answer in the Bible is this. No man can deal with it. No man can cleanse his soul and get rid of the stain of sin. No man can erase the past. No angel in glory can do it. There is only one who is able to do this, the very Son of God Himself, who took on Him our human nature and became man, who was born in the likeness of sinful flesh and who, in this great mystery, took upon Himself as a cloak the sin of mankind and was dealt with on the cross by His holy Father. "He hath made him to be sin for us, who knew no sin; that we might be made the righteousness of

God in him." He saved us, first, because He is "the Lamb of God who taketh away the sin of the world". Apart from that He can do nothing, for my sin stands between me and God. "I beheld," says John, "a Lamb, as it had been slain." If only we realize this fully we shall understand increasingly why these men burst out crying, "Worthy is the Lamb that was slain to receive power and riches and wisdom and strength and honour and glory and blessing." So He has there dealt with the first problem. He has rescued us from the law and from the guilt of sin.

But who are we to face sin? Who are we to face Satan? Who are we to face this organized might of iniquity? We cannot. We fail inevitably. But, thank God, He is also "the Lion of the tribe of Judah". Satan met Him in the days of His flesh and He dismissed him with a word. He conquered him. He has defeated the strong man armed. He has conquered sin and death and the grave. He has satisfied them all. There is no power in heaven, or earth, or hell that can, in any way, stand up to and meet Him. He has triumphed over all. He calls us out. He keeps us. He holds us. He strengthens us. "Temptations lose their power when Thou art nigh." So sang one, putting in terms of his own experience the very message of this fifth chapter of the Book of the Revelation.

"I need Thee every hour
Stay Thou near by.
Temptations lose their power
When Thou art nigh."

"The Lion of the tribe of Judah", the one who has already conquered sin and iniquity, He holds and keeps those whom He has already called.

But the process is going on and, finally, before it will be completed these inimical powers must not only be controlled and held in check, they must be routed and destroyed altogether. That is the whole message of the Book of the Revelation. Observe that one after another they are destroyed: the beast, the false prophet, and finally Satan himself, the ultimate source of it all. They are taken and thrown into the lake of destruction. Every evil power will finally be destroyed by the Lion of the tribe of Judah. He must be the Lion before the programme can be carried out. He must also, prior to that, be the Lamb that was slaughtered before it was carried out. But He satisfies all the demands; He meets all the needs. He is the perfect Saviour and in His mighty hands the programme is safe, its ultimate consummation and fruition are certain and assured.

My dear friends, the one question for you and me is this: Are we in the new kingdom? Are we sure that we have been called out? Do we know that this is the thing that matters above everything else among the things that are engaging our attention and concerning us at the present time? Are we members of the new humanity? Do we belong to the new race? Are we brethren of Christ? Do we feel the desire to join in the angelic anthem and to mingle our voices with the eternal choir? Do we know him as the Lamb slain for our sins? Are we confiding in Him as "the Lion of the tribe of Judah" who alone can perfect us and enable us finally to reign with Him in a perfect world? As we think of Him and look at Him do we desire to join with those who sing, "Worthy is the Lamb that was slain to receive power and riches and wisdom and strength and honour and glory and blessing"? Yea, "Blessing and honour and glory and power be unto him that sitteth upon the throne, and unto the Lamb for ever and ever."

PART 5

Paul's Order of the Day

CHAPTER 20

General Introduction and Strategy

(1 Corinthians 16:13–14)

"Watch ye, stand fast in the faith, quit you like men, be strong. Let all your things be done with charity."

One thing which must strike us at once as we look at 1 Corinthians 16:13–14 is the extraordinary way in which this exhortation suddenly makes its appearance in this chapter. In other words, we cannot but be attracted, and somewhat fascinated, by the context of these verses. You will notice in reading the chapter that it is a kind of postscript to this great letter, in which the apostle has been dealing with the many and varied problems that had arisen in the church at Corinth. Having dealt with those great questions he comes here, in what can be regarded rightly as a kind of postscript, to a number of odd statements concerning matters which are more or less practical in nature. He deals, for instance, with the question of the collection of money for needy churches. He gives them advice and detailed instruction and information as to how, as Christian people, they are to make provision in that respect. He tells them to lay aside on the first day of the week that which they feel they can give. He goes on to give them certain detailed information concerning himself and his future plans and proposals. He proceeds to tell them of what is happening to certain of his fellow workers, such as Timotheus and Apollos. He has a number of things on the purely practical plane to tell these people. Afterwards he goes on to tell them how they are to behave, and to conduct themselves, with regard to certain people, such a Stephanas, and others who labour together with them. Then comes the final salutation. That is the nature of the chapter in general: a number of odd matters on the practical level which come crowding into the apostle's mind as he finishes this great and long letter. But suddenly, into the midst of these mundane, practical things, comes this mighty exhortation. *"Watch ye, stand fast in the faith, quit you like men, be strong. Let all your things be done with charity."*

Some deductions

Now before we come to our analysis of the actual statement, I cannot refrain from deducing certain things, looking at the message in general, about the great apostle himself. For I want to suggest to you that these two verses cast considerable light upon Paul himself and tell us a great deal about him. As we look at him we, surely, must be made aware of certain things concerning ourselves. For nothing is so helpful and important as that we should look at such a man and carefully scrutinize his conduct and behaviour in order that we may discover certain principles of conduct for ourselves, and especially at such a time as this. Paul, I do not hesitate to say, sometimes reveals himself much more in these postscripts than he does in the main body of his epistles. It is always important to watch his introductions and his conclusions. The man suddenly appears and reveals himself and it is as we examine those introductions and conclusions carefully that we come to know him as he was and we begin to acquaint ourselves with the man in addition to the great apostle.

One thing which must strike us at once about the man as we look at these verses is **his fervent, passionate, energetic nature**. That is one of the outstanding things about him. In several places in his letters he tells us something about his labours, about his journeys in different continents, about his crossing oceans, preaching the gospel to all and sundry in different lands and in different places. But, somehow or other, it is in a statement like this in these two verses that we really get a true impression of his fervent, passionate nature, his energy, the strenuous character of the man's temperament and of his whole outlook and activity with respect to life. We see it here in the way I have already indicated. Though he has come to the level of business matters, though, in a sense, he has finished with the doctrine, so intense is the man, and so concerned is he about the church, that he allows the form of his letter to be left aside and suddenly he breaks in upon it with a great doctrinal statement. That is one of his characteristics. As a stylist he is often guilty of what are called anacolutha. He suddenly breaks the sequence. Something comes to him, a great vision, a great inspiration, some vital message, and out it comes, in spite of the form and the arrangement of the letter. That is a characteristic of Paul's various epistles. So here we are reminded of the fervent, passionate, energetic nature of this man.

I emphasize and stress this point, because, surely, there is nothing of which we need to be reminded quite so forcibly at this present hour as this particular quality in the great apostle. There is nothing which is more salutary and more valuable than this emphasis upon the energy which was ever displayed by this mighty servant of God. The tragedy of the time through which we are, and have been, passing in church and in state has been very largely the tragedy of a lost enthusiasm. The world in which we live seems to have become tired. It is not for me at present to seek to state the precise and exact causes of this curious characteristic of our age. Is it not the case that we have adopted a blasé attitude towards life? We have regarded fervency of spirit and intellect, enthusiasm and a passionate nature as something which is incompatible with true greatness; as something which is the antithesis of knowledge and culture. Surely for the last hundred years in church and in state we have been guilty of deliberately curbing what was the outstanding characteristic of this mighty apostle Paul. We have regarded any manifestation of feeling as something which is unworthy of the man of culture and education. It has been a part, indeed, of the very educational system that has had main sway in this country to discount such things and to discourage them. We have become negative creatures. We have been repressing ourselves. Not even by the flicker of an eyelid are we prepared to manifest any feeling or concern. We have returned to the condition which prevailed at the beginning of the eighteenth century. The taunt which was then frequently hurled against the Methodists at the beginning was that they were guilty of "enthusiasm", and were therefore inferior. Enthusiasm in connection with religion has been at a very serious discount. Our idea of the general standard to adopt is to display no emotion, or fervency of spirit in relation to any matter. We have rather cultivated a philosophical calm and detachment, and the result is, of course, that in our actions and activities we have become more or less paralysed and slow moving. We take time to awaken to any situation. That was true of Britain with respect to the origin of the Second World War and it is still more true with respect to the obvious moral declension which has characterized the last twenty years. If we deliberately cultivate the suppression of fervency of spirit and the display of emotion, the logical effect must inevitably be that we shall not only become slow in awareness of what is happening around us, but we shall become paralysed in the realm of our activities. As we look at the life of the church in general today we must acknowledge and confess that of all the criticisms which can be brought against her, this is the first thing to be said. How little enthusiasm is to be found in the church! How apathetic we are! How slow to realize the significance of the cataclysmic events that are taking place round and about us. When we contrast ourselves with men at a football match, or at the various places of amusement, or even when we contrast ourselves with the enthusiasm and the zeal and the fervency that was displayed on the continent of Europe by the men and women who have been beguiled by the various false philosophies such as Nazism, Fascism and Bolshevism, surely we have need to reprimand ourselves and to feel a sense of shame. Nothing was so characteristic of this man of God as his zeal, his enthusiasm, his fervency of spirit. He says to these Corinthians, "They call us fools. Well, we are fools for Christ's sake!" It was true of the other apostles also, for they said, "We cannot but speak the things which we have seen and heard." Thus we see why it is that, in the midst of the business of this postscript, the apostle suddenly introduces this great exhortation in verses 13 and 14.

In the same way we find here a striking sidelight upon **the character of this man as the incomparable pastor**. Paul was a great evangelist. He was also a great teacher and in addition he was a great pastor. Let us remember that he was always the three. Our tendency has been to say that a man is either an evangelist, or a teacher, or a pastor. Here we see the great pastor in Paul shining out. Don't you see here his concern, his solicitude, for these people? Why is it that having finished his letter, having given the postscript as to the business details, he suddenly speaks out like this? There is only one adequate explanation. This man was concerned about the church at Corinth. He could not rest. He tells us elsewhere he was not at ease. He loved them. He was anxious that they should be built up in their most holy faith, that they should derive the full benefit of Christian teaching and salvation. He was concerned about the city in which they lived and he was anxious for the salvation of the souls of the people in that city. It is because of his great concern for all these things that he cannot rest. He has finished with doctrine, in a sense, but he still goes back to it. Here again is something, surely, of which we need to be reminded at the present time. At the final bar of judgment when those of us who are Christians stand face to face with our Maker, the gravest charge which will be made against us will be the charge that we were so unconcerned. We lived at a time and in an age when the very foundations of civilization were being shaken, when the very world in which we lived was rocking, when we witnessed things such as men have never seen before. We saw the spiritual and moral, as well as the political, declension all around us, and yet we did nothing about it. We were apathetic and unconcerned. We did not feel a great solicitude that would not allow us to rest by day or by night. But this man could not contain himself because he was so concerned about what was taking place in Corinth.

Another thing we notice about him as a pastor is **his remarkably detailed knowledge of the particular needs of his particular churches.** You cannot read the epistles of Paul that are included in this New Testament canon without at once being struck by that fact. He knows his churches and his people. Here again is something which is of great significance. We hear a great deal in these days about psychology. The greatest psychologist that the world has ever known was none other than this great apostle to the gentiles. He tells us in this epistle that he makes himself all things to all men that he might thereby gain some. He speaks as a Jew and as a Gentile. He accommodates himself, he takes the trouble to know the people, and to vary his method, and to suit his message to the particular circumstances. I emphasize this point because I feel, and feel increasingly, that here again is a matter on which we need instruction today. So much of our church services and organizations have become purely traditional. This is something which is true, as far as I am aware of it, of every branch and section of the Christian church. But I speak more particularly of the Evangelicals, for to me nothing is quite so sad as the way in which we still persist in adopting the methods that were highly successful at the time of Moody and Sankey. They have become a tradition, hardened and fixed and set, and we seem to think that the evangelistic methods that were of extreme value then are of equal value today, little realizing that a profound change has taken place in the mentality and outlook of the people. Vast changes have taken place in education and culture and in various other ways. We need, therefore, to learn this second lesson from the great apostle at such a time as this, namely, that we must accommodate our method to the time. We have no right to persist with methods which may have been very suitable at the time when they were first used, but which fail to make contact with the age in which we now live. The truth itself is one and eternal, but I am referring now to the presentation of the truth and to the application of the truth. We are living at a time when there is a fundamental ignorance of the Bible and when we can take nothing for granted. We must apply the message of the gospel of Christ to the age in which we live and in a language which it can understand. Paul was always very careful to do so.

Another thing which I notice about Paul as the great pastor is **his constant emphasis upon the spiritual**. The spiritual was always preeminent in everything which Paul did. He is always re-emphasizing and repeating it. Even in the midst of these business matters with which he is dealing, he can no longer hold himself and he cries out, "Watch ye, stand fast in the faith, quit you like men, be strong. Let all your things be done with charity." As if to say, "I am telling you about my future plans and arrangements. I am telling you that I am hoping to come and visit you. I am telling you about Apollos and Stephanas. But in the name of God, never forget the supremacy of the spiritual." Not that the business is unimportant, but the business really becomes quite ridiculous unless it is soundly based upon sure and certain spiritual foundations.

Those then are some of the obvious things with respect to the apostle himself which strike us as we look at our text in general. Another matter which might well engage our attention is **the marvellous way in which, in the space of these two short verses, the apostle seems to summarize completely everything that he has been saying to the church at Corinth** during the course of this long letter. But I shall be able to work that out more in detail as we come to the division of the general exhortation.

The application of these words today

I call your attention to all this because I want to suggest to you that there is a very close parallel between the church as she is today and the church as she was in Corinth at the time when the apostle sent this letter to her. The fundamental question I have at the back of my mind is this: What is the matter with the church? Why is the church so impotent? Why is it that the church of God counts for so little in this modern world? What is it that has gone wrong with the church? The church once occupied a position of influence and power and supremacy. The church once led the way in this country. What is it that has gone wrong? My reply is that we can discover the answer as we look together at the terms of this great exhortation of the apostle Paul. This seems to be his answer, not only to the problems which faced the church at Corinth, but also to the troubles and problems which face the church at this hour.

We notice **the military character of the exhortation**. I do not hesitate to describe this text as Paul's order of the day for the church at this present hour. Here is this mighty general, this great Christian leader viewing the situation, and he issues his order of the day. To carry the military analogy still further, I would put it to you in this way: that the message as a whole can be regarded as his strategy. The detailed parts of the message can be regarded as his tactics. We shall look at the tactics, but as to the general strategy, what is it that Paul says to us? What is his message to the church at this hour in terms of this order of the day? I would put it in language like this: **We are to realize, above all else, that we are members of the church of God**. We need to recapture the great New Testament doctrine of the Christian church. Paul makes it abundantly clear in this letter to the church at Corinth that the real fundamental trouble with them was that they had lost hold of the doctrine of the church. He says, "You divide up into this faction and that, one saying I am of Paul, and another saying I am of Apollos, and another saying I am of Christ. But the church is the body of Christ, and Christ cannot be divided. You have been baptized into Christ." The trouble with the church at Corinth was that it had ceased to believe truly in the doctrine of the nature of the Christian church. If I understand the times in which we live aright, I would suggest that that is our fundamental trouble today. We have lost the sense of a corporate church life. We are interested in religion. We are concerned about listening to sermons and addresses. But I wonder to what extent we really believe that we are members of the body of Christ, not a loose association of people who are interested in religious things, but really members of that mystical body of Christ through which He acts upon earth? Do we realize that we have been bought with a price, that we are not our own? Do we remember that we are co-workers with God? Have we an active and lively sense of the fact that we have been redeemed by the precious blood of Christ, not merely that we might be saved from the punishment of hell, but that God, through us, might bring to pass His own great purposes and plans in this world? Have we seen ourselves in the eternal plan and scheme? Have we seen ourselves as the hands and the feet of this mystical body of the eternal Christ? Surely that is something which we have been tending to lose sight of. Have we, further, realized that opposed to us is a mighty adversary; that all the powers of Satan and evil and hell are arrayed against us? Are we not seeing even in these present times a manifestation of certain evil spirits and malign powers and forces? And if we see in the life of the church the manifestation of these evil powers, how much more so those evil forces that are leading to moral degeneracy in our own land and in other lands. Have we realized that the ultimate object of the enemy is not simply to destroy us, but is, above all, to frustrate the schemes and plans of God? Oh, the tragedy is surely that we are like the church at Corinth, that we are unaware of this spiritual conflict! While the devil and his forces were fighting to destroy the church, they were dividing up into these various factions and were arguing about their respective ideas and respective philosophies. They were dividing themselves up into little groups and little sects, then were comparing their spiritual gifts. And while they were quarrelling amongst themselves the influence of the church was being weakened and her impact upon the evil city of Corinth was becoming smaller and smaller. Is not that the position in which we find the church of God at this hour? We are quarrelling about our shibboleths and arguing about our ceremonies and ritual, differing from each other in the way we dot our i's and cross our t's, and arguing about secondary and third-rate things. While the church is thus divided, and is quarrelling and arguing, the world is in the welter of a great war and the people in this and other lands are departing further and further from a knowledge of God. What are we to do about it? Here is the order of the day. "Wake up," says the apostle. "Rouse yourselves." And having done so, "stand fast in the faith, quit you like men, be strong. Let all your things be done with love."

That is the strategy. We shall go on to look at the tactics and to analyse the general statement into its component parts.

CHAPTER 21

"Watch Ye"

(1 Corinthians 16:13–14)

"Watch ye, stand fast in the faith, quit you like men, be strong. Let all your things be done with charity."

We come now to a consideration of the two words, "Watch ye." It is important that we should again remind ourselves that there is in this great exhortation a very definite logical sequence. We were reminding ourselves that there is nothing so characteristic of the apostle from the mere standpoint of style as the way in which he constantly breaks in upon the matter in hand. Suddenly some mighty inspiration seems to come to him and he interpolates or interposes something which seems to be quite extraneous, and he does that in this particular instance. Yet we were careful to point out that when you come to examine these interpolations you find that invariably they are perfectly logical. They are never haphazard, never casual. What he has to say always follows a definite sequence. He is fundamentally logical. But it is not merely logic in terms of thought and of reason. It is not merely an exhibition of rationalism, but of a higher spiritual logic also. He lays a basis, then he builds on it, then he adds to it. Therefore it is vital that we should take the particular statements in the general exhortation in the order in which they appear. These tactics, using that analogy, are very definitely worked out on a given plan.

This is the first step: "Watch ye." If you prefer other translations we can suggest quite a number. Instead of "Watch ye," you can read it like this: "Wake up," "Keep awake," "Be wakeful." Or, perhaps, adopting our military analogy, it would not be inappropriate if we translated these two words "Watch ye" by the one word "Attention!" For this is exactly what the apostle does. He wants to rouse these people, to awaken them, to keep them in a condition of wakefulness and watchfulness and awareness. Or, if we may borrow the language and the imagery of a well-known Old Testament passage, we might very well translate the words "Watch ye" by the phrase "Sound an alarm!" Or there is still another which might be equally suitable. We might say that in using these two words "Watch ye" the apostle is ordering someone to sound the reveille, announcing to the troops that the time for sleep has come to an end, that they must wake up and put on their uniform and their armour; that each man must go to his post and stand there and watch. It is the sounding of the reveille – the morning wake-up call – a call to attention; a great general ordering his men to their respective positions.

Now those of us who are at all familiar with the Scriptures will remember at once that this is a very characteristic word, a word which is thoroughly typical, not only of the New Testament, but also of the Old Testament. If you read the various recorded discourses of our Lord and Saviour Jesus Christ, you will find that constantly He uses this word "Watch". Sometimes it is used alone and sometimes it is accompanied by other exhortations, such as "Watch and pray." We all remember those words of His towards the end of His life and ministry: "What I say unto you I say unto all. Watch." Nothing is more characteristic of the last chapters of the various Gospels as this exhortation to watch. And when you come to read the epistles you will find, in exactly the same way, that it is a word that is found very frequently. You get it in all the epistles and it seems to be the theme above every other theme in the Book of the Revelation, this exhortation to watch, to observe, to be wakeful, to stand at attention, to mount guard. From which fact, I think, we are entitled to deduce that it is a word that Christian people stand constantly in need of. You never find an exhortation like this repeated frequently in the New Testament without it being perfectly obvious that it was a word that was needed. Our Lord would never have uttered a word like this if He had not realized the dangers that were going to confront His people. So He seeks to prepare them and that selfsame gift of foreseeing the future was transmitted to the apostles. It is a word that is clearly needed by Christian people. Never in the history of the Christian church has this word been more needed than at this present hour. There have been times of lethargy in the past. There have been dark periods in the history of the church. There have been times when the church was decadent. But surely, there has never been a time when we all stood in need of this word more than we do today. "Watch ye." We can, perhaps, best consider the exhortation by putting three simple questions. They are self-evident and yet I think they will lead us directly to the very heart of this matter.

Why?

The first question we must put is this, "**Why are we to watch?**" What is the reason for watching? Why does this mighty Christian general order us to watch, to be on guard? What is the reason for it? The immediate New Testament answer to that question here in 1 Corinthians 16:13–14, and everywhere else where the words appear, is that there is need of watchfulness for the one simple reason that **the Christian life is a life of conflict, is a warfare, is a battle.** Somehow or another this is an idea which we dislike and with which, to a very large extent, we have become unfamiliar. How often do we naturally and instinctively think of the Christian life as a warfare, a battle, a conflict? How often in our reading do we find this aspect emphasized and stressed? I suggest that the church of God, for some reason or another, has lost sight of this vital New Testament truth that the Christian life is a conflict, a warfare, and that the church is an army, a fighting force, left here on earth by God Himself. If we are to correct that impression, we must discover the reasons why that truth concerning the Christian life has been lost. We cannot put ourselves right without discovering why we have gone wrong. What are the reasons? I suggest some such answers as the following.

Surely one of the explanations is that **we have tended to lose sight of the whole idea of the supernatural in connection with religion.** That has been a process which has been going on for well-nigh a hundred years. There has been this tendency to exclude the supernatural. It happens both positively and negatively. The main purpose of the destructive criticism of the Bible has been to exclude the supernatural. Men have tried to exclude the miraculous from the New Testament. In exactly the same way there has been an increasing tendency to cease to believe in the power of Satan and in the power of evil; to cease to believe in a personal devil and in evil forces and evil powers which are unseen, but which are, nevertheless, really there fighting and working. The whole idea of the supernatural, both of the holy and the unholy, the true and the blasphemous, has gradually been excluded from religion, and once we lose that conception of the spiritual nature of life and of being, we must of necessity lose this idea of a spiritual conflict. Or, to put all this in another way, **there has been a tendency to regard Christianity as being nothing but a philosophy**, as being just an outlook on life, or a point of view. The whole idea of the dynamic of religion has gone. So as you do not expect to find any spiritual or dynamic force in a philosophy, so men have argued that there is no such thing in Christianity as a force or a dynamic – that it is merely a philosophy of life which you can either accept or reject.

Or perhaps it is due to the fact that **large numbers of people have thought of Christianity solely in terms of a life to be lived**, as something which is purely practical, as something which is to be applied to life. I think of the so-called social application of the gospel, that emphasis which has been so familiar for a number of years. My point is the same here, that if we think of the Christian gospel and message merely in these terms of practical application, we of necessity will lose the idea of this mighty spiritual conflict between good and evil, between God and Satan, between heaven and hell, which is the characteristic teaching of the New Testament. There are others, I fear, who have lost this sense of the Christian life as a conflict, a warfare, for the reason that **they have accepted false views and teaching with respect to holiness and sanctification**. They have accepted a somewhat vague mysticism or ideas that lead to a state of passivity. They have actually condemned this idea of conflict and instead they represent the Christian life as being supremely something in which a person ceases to be engaged in a conflict; in which, rather, someone relaxes and enters into a passive state and condition.

For some such reasons as I have stated – and there are many others – this idea of the Christian life as a warfare and as a conflict seems to have dropped out not only of our mind, but also out of our vocabulary. All that is, surely, an utter travesty of the teaching of the New Testament. For if the New Testament does one thing more than another, it surely emphasizes everywhere that the Christian life is a conflict, a fight and a battle. We are constantly being urged and exhorted to watch. The apostle talks towards the end of his life about the good fight of faith. He tells us that the Christian life is a life of wrestling, and that "we wrestle not against flesh and blood, but against principalities, against powers, against the rulers of the darkness of this world, against spiritual wickedness in high places". The apostle Peter tells us that our adversary is like a roaring lion seeking whom he may devour. Also, as I have already reminded you, if there is one message which stands out pre-eminently in the Book of the Revelation, it is the message of this mighty conflict, the spiritual entities and powers battling for this world and for mankind.

This impression of the Christian life is confirmed abundantly by all the great Christian literature of the ages. If you examine the greatest Christian literature, and especially during times of revival and awakening, you will find that it always emphasizes this idea of a spiritual conflict. Let me give one example: *The Pilgrim's Progress*, or *The Holy War*. That is a typical New Testament idea of the Christian life, the pilgrim journeying on, beset by enemies, being attacked on all hands, or a fight for the city of Mansoul. You find it also in our greatest hymns and in all the greatest Christian literature. That is the primary reason, therefore, for watching. We are to watch because the Christian life is essentially a conflict. In addition to that, we are to fight for this further reason, that, according to the New Testament, **if we do not fight, we shall be defeated**, we shall be vanquished, we shall fall victims to the enemy.

What?

Having examined the question as to why we should watch, let me ask a still more practical question: "What are we to watch?" Here, again, the answer is perfectly simple and direct. First and foremost, **I am to watch myself**. Anyone who has not yet discovered that he himself is his greatest problem, especially in the Christian life, is just a tyro – a novice – in these matters, a veritable babe in Christ. Before you watch anyone else, watch yourself. What am I to watch in myself? Let me be intensely practical. First of all, I am to watch **against a lowered general morale**. I am deliberately using terms which became familiar during the Second World War, in order that the analogy may impress itself upon us. There is the danger of a lowered general morale. What do I mean by that? I mean this. Am I beginning to feel a little bit hopeless about the church and about the Christian message? I see the masses going everywhere but to God's House. I see a lowering of the moral tone. Am I beginning to think that, after all, there is very little in it? Do I ask myself whether it is worth while going on with it? Hitherto, because of certain loyalties I have still continued to go to God's House, but perhaps I am beginning to wonder whether really there is any point in going on. Is my general morale gradually going down? Am I as keen as I once was; am I as alert? That is one thing.

Again, I have to watch myself **against the constant danger and tendency of a lowered standard**. I think now particularly of a lowered standard in connection with my own life. Have I got the same standard of Christian living now as I used to have? There was a time when I believed in making a clean break from the life of sin. There were certain things which I said were not legitimate to me because I was a Christian, because of my faith in Christ. I had a certain standard of morality. I recognized certain standards in regard to my personal life in the matter of honesty and chastity and cleanliness. Is that still as absolute in my life as it once was? Am I as sensitive to sin as I used to be? Or is there a tendency on my part to compromise in regard to my sins? Have I become an expert in explaining away what I do? Am I an expert in the work of self-justification? Am I spending much of my time in reconciling myself to myself? We must watch constantly against a lowering of the standard.

In exactly the same way we must be ever **watching ourselves for a lowering of our strength and of our power and of our efficiency**. I must be perfectly certain that I am taking my spiritual exercise regularly. Do I find when I meet temptation that I can resist it with the same ease as I used to do? Have I the same reserves of power to call upon in the hour of temptation, of subtle temptation? Are my spiritual muscles in as good a condition as they once were? Do I read the Word of God as I used to? Am I spending time in prayer and in meditation? I have to watch myself in that respect. I know that there is nothing easier than to let the days pass, forgetting these things. Life is so full and active. We are so ready to make excuses for our neglect. We talk about our frayed nerves and our tired bodies. We say that we have no time to read God's word and to meditate. There comes this lowering of strength because of the lessened exercise of my spiritual faculties. I must watch myself.

Again, having watched myself, **I must also watch the enemy**, for obviously it is useless for a man to watch himself unless he also keeps an eye upon the enemy. There are two things in particular that I want to mention in this connection. The first thing I must watch is **the strength and the power of the enemy**. I have already reminded you that Peter describes him as a roaring lion. You remember that word of Paul to the Ephesians where he said that we are not fighting merely against flesh and blood. Some people seem to think that the whole of the spiritual conflict centres around things residing in the flesh. "We wrestle not against flesh and blood" he says, "but against principalities, against powers, against thee rulers of the darkness of this world, against spiritual wickedness in high places." Our conflict is against mighty spiritual forces.

But over and above the power of the enemy is **the subtlety of the enemy**. You remember that Paul, in his second letter to this church at Corinth, describes the enemy as being sometimes "an angel of light". He can transform himself into a veritable angel of light in his subtlety and in his efforts and endeavours to get us away from that simplicity which is in Christ Jesus our Lord. If I understand the signs of the times aright, this is a vitally important and urgent matter today. Regarding the church in general, her greatest danger at this hour is the danger of allowing herself to be sidetracked, the danger of a false emphasis. It was, of course, pre-eminently the danger in the case of the church at Corinth. They were divided up into groups and divisions. They were arguing as to whether they belonged to Paul or Apollos or Christ, while all the time the enemy was getting them down. They were arguing about meat offered to idols; they were wrangling about secondary matters; they were contrasting their various spiritual gifts. While they were thus arguing the enemy was seeking to destroy the church. There is this danger of being sidetracked. There is the danger of putting our emphasis upon secondary matters. Is not this one of the greatest dangers of the hour, the danger of being entirely absorbed by the idea of a visible Christian unity and saying that nothing else matters but that the denominations should come together? And while we are organizing our machinery, the enemy is at work. There is the danger of putting all our emphasis on the importance of Christian education, good as it is in itself. There is the danger of the people of God losing themselves in prophecy, of putting all their emphasis upon the prophetic interpretation of the Scriptures, and, thereby, to use a phrase of the apostle's, being weaned away and attracted from that simplicity which is in Christ Jesus. Read your Bible, try to interpret prophecy, endeavour to understand its special teaching about holiness and sanctification, be concerned about Christian education. Let us do all these things, but let us never forget that the primary business and function of the church is to call men to repentance. It is to denounce the sin and the evil which is at the root of all our problems. It is to preach Christ and Him crucified; it is to make contact with a fallen humanity. There is this danger of being sidetracked.

When?

All this brings me to my third and last question: **"When am I to watch?"** The answer is perfectly simple and plain. I am to watch always. There is nothing so fatal as to leave the watching until something has happened. That was the cause of the tragedy of the Second World War. We did not begin to watch as a nation until the enemy had done something. I must watch now. I must watch always. There is no such thing as a spiritual holiday. There is no such thing as a "national holiday" in the spiritual realm. I must be always on duty. I must ever be on the alert. To use again the words of this great man, this mighty apostle, I must be "instant in season and out of season". Watch! Be wakeful! Ever keep on the alert!

CHAPTER 22

Stand Fast in the Faith

(1 Corinthians 16:13–14)

"Watch ye, stand fast in the faith; quit you like men, be strong. Let all your things be done with charity."

So far we have, in a way, been entirely negative in looking at these exhortations. But now we come to what we can call the first positive exhortation in the text: "Stand fast in the faith." The exhortation "Watch ye" was, in a sense, purely negative. When I describe it as being negative, I do not mean to imply or to convey the impression that it is, for that reason, unimportant. The Bible constantly emphasizes the importance of the negative. But I say that though it is important and vital, it is, nevertheless, a negative command. It was an exhortation which told us to beware of certain things which might happen to us, the danger of flagging in our strength, or of allowing our spirits to droop, or to become discouraged; the danger of lowering our standard of truth, of personal integrity, of personal righteousness; the danger of allowing the enemy to encroach upon our position. It is vitally important, but yet nothing beyond an introduction. An introduction is essential, but if we stop at the introduction, we obviously are failing altogether and entirely. Merely to stop at the exhortation to watch and to be wakeful is similar to an order being given to the army to keep its eye very carefully upon the foe, but to leave the army without any implements of war. It is to exhort a man to beware of any slackness on his own part and to observe the subtlety of the enemy, but, at the same time, to fail to give him the necessary munitions and armaments which are essential before the enemy can truly be dealt with. We must keep awake and alert, for the best armour in the world is of no value at all if we are asleep. But that alone is not enough. We need something with which we can fight the enemy, and here we come to the great source of supply, the Christian armament.

The centrality of the faith

We come here to a description of that without which we can never wage this warfare triumphantly and successfully. I do not hesitate to describe these words as the very centre and nerve of this great exhortation. Here is the pivot, the foundation, the thing above everything else which is essential and vital. Or, if you would prefer it in another way, we can describe our subject as the absolute centrality of the faith, the all-importance of true doctrine.

Now it would be a very simple thing for me to show you how my contention can be fully substantiated and justified in the case of the church of Corinth herself. It would be a simple thing to make an analysis of this letter, to take it chapter by chapter and step by step and to show you that all the things that have gone wrong in that church have really gone wrong because of the failure to grasp and to understand doctrine. The division into groups and sects was nothing but a manifestation of the failure on their part to grasp the nature of the doctrine of the Christian church. The toleration of evil men amongst them is another illustration of the same thing. The vexed question of eating foods offered to idols shows that they have never placed in their relative positions the various centralities of the faith. The dispute about spiritual gifts again, as Paul shows them, is a failure to put first things first – the failure to follow that more excellent way. Similarly, the dispute about speaking with tongues Paul dismisses in those strong words where he says that he would rather speak five words with his understanding than emit ten thousand words in an unknown tongue. This all comes to a climax in the great fifteenth chapter where he deals with the doctrine of the resurrection and where he is at pains to show that if they have gone wrong on a matter of that kind they have gone wrong altogether and they can expect nothing but entire and complete shipwreck.

This matter is of considerable importance in connection with the church at Corinth, but I am concerned about it because of its importance to us at this present hour. I do not hesitate to affirm that here, surely, we have the explanation of the present state of Christendom and of the Christian church. What is the matter with the Christian church? Why is it that the influence of the church has been so visibly waning and declining as the years have passed? Many explanations have been suggested. Some would explain it solely and entirely in terms of the Second World War. They say that we have never recovered from that. People then got into the habit – especially the men in the army – of keeping away from places of worship and they have never got back to the habit again. Others find the explanation in the cinema, others in the radio, others in automobiles which take people away from places of worship on Sundays. But I would suggest to you that there is only one really satisfactory explanation. It is the one suggested by my text this morning. We have failed to "stand fast in the faith".

Authority has gone. The authority of the Bible, the authority of the pulpit, the authority of the church. It is because men have questioned the whole foundation of Christianity. They have ceased to realize its importance. When the foundation goes, the superstructure, of necessity, collapses. Therefore it follows that if we long for a revival in the life of the church, and for a revival of the place of the church not only in the life of the nation, but in the life of the world, the first and obvious thing we have to do is to come back to the position that is urged and stressed by my text, to "stand fast in the faith".

How?

Let us examine this a little more closely by putting two simple questions. How are we to "stand fast in the faith"? Let us start with that practical question. I would suggest the following answers. First of all, we must realize that **there is such a thing as "the faith"**. We have to realize that it is something concrete, a body of doctrine. That is a suggestion which is made by the apostle in many places in this particular letter. You may remember when he introduces the communion service in the eleventh chapter that he uses this particular formula: "For I have received of the Lord that which also I delivered unto you." We find in the introduction to chapter 15 that he says, "I declare unto you the gospel which I preached unto you, which also ye have received, and wherein ye stand." That is his way of reminding us that there is such a thing as "the faith", a given body of truth and of doctrine. Now I need scarcely remind you that this is an idea which we have lost sight of, indeed is an idea which has become definitely unpopular during the last fifty years. We have become accustomed to a slogan which is the very antithesis of what I am trying to say, namely that Christianity is something which is "caught, not taught", that it is a vague kind of spirit, an influence, something infectious as it were. The idea is that it does not consist of a body of objective truth which can be considered and analysed and discussed and studied, but that it is an atmosphere into which one enters and which enters into one's being.

There are others who have disputed our contention because they would have us believe that the very genius and essence of Christianity consists in a search for truth; that a man approaching Christianity is not in the position of one coming to a definite, given doctrine, but rather of one setting out on a great quest, going into an unknown territory. How much have we heard about the great adventure, about the search for truth! You remember the words of an American author in which he said quite specifically and explicitly that if he were offered, on the one hand, the search for truth, and, on the other hand, the truth itself – if he were told that he could take his choice – he would without any hesitation choose the thrill and the excitement of the search for truth. Christianity has been described as a seeking, as a search, rather than the acceptance of a body of truth.

Then there has been a tendency on the part of some to dispute this statement that Christianity really is a given body of doctrine, because they have believed in what is called the spirit of eclecticism and syncretism. There has been much talk about that in recent years. They say that what is really needed is not an exposition or propagation of that which we call the Christian faith, so much as a gathering together of that which is good in all the faiths and philosophies and points of view of the different nations of the world. There have been congresses, so-called, of world faiths. There have been round-table conferences. The idea of "the round-table" has been very popular in the last twenty years. This idea of there being a little bit of good in everything and in a spirit of friendliness of extracting that which is good in Christianity and Hinduism and Buddism and Confucianism and Mohammedanism, and in all the various other religions of the world, was characteristic of the effeminacy, the lack of backbone and virility that characterized the inter-war period in 1918–1939. Recently a service was held in a church building in which, we are told, extracts were read from all the great Scriptures of the world. That is an utter denial of the position which I am trying to define.

Then **there are people who never trouble to think at all**. They just go on happily assuming that so long as one is a church member and attends a place of worship; so long as one attempts and endeavours to live a fairly decent life, that is Christianity. The idea of being a good man, playing the game, doing one's best to put into practice these vague general ideas, seems to them to be all that is necessary. All this is an utter travesty of the New Testament position. The New Testament talks about the faith, about the truth, the deposit, and we are exhorted in the epistle of Jude to "contend for the faith once delivered to the saints". The Book of the Revelation warns us not to take from, or to add to this book. In the Bible we have to start by realizing that there is such a thing as "the faith", that Christianity is not something vague or indefinite. It is not seeking the truth somehow. It is not a coming together and choosing that which is best from other faiths. It is not just the living of a good life. It is something concrete and discrete; it is a body of doctrine. You cannot "stand fast in the faith" unless you realize that there is such a thing as "the faith".

Secondly, you must know exactly what "the faith" is. What is it? The answer is to be found everywhere in the New Testament. Let no one misunderstand me. There are certain things in connection with the Christian faith which are a legitimate subject for dispute and difference of opinion and disagreement. It is no part of my case to say that unless we all repeat exactly the same things that, therefore, we are not Christians; that unless we all repeat the same formulae down to the veriest detail and minutiae of the faith, that we are, therefore, outside Christ. It is nevertheless my purpose to stress and to emphasize the fact that there is a certain irreducible minimum which is absolutely essential, without which we are not even entitled to use the term Christianity at all. What is that? In its essence we were reminded by the great apostle at the commencement of the fifteenth chapter of this epistle that it is this central truth about Jesus of Nazareth. These things are beyond the realm of dispute. According to the New Testament this is the faith. Jesus of Nazareth is uniquely the Son of God. He is not merely the greatest religious genius of all time; He is not only the one who has reached highest in the search for truth. He is God incarnate. He is the eternal substance of God. He came from heaven miraculously. He was born as a baby in Bethlehem. He manifested and demonstrated His unique deity in His work and life and teaching. When He went to the cross on Calvary's hill, He went there deliberately. His death on the cross was not the mere result of political activity. It was the Son of God taking upon Himself the sins of the whole world. "God was in Christ reconciling the world unto Himself." "He has made him to be sin for us who knew no sin that we might be made the righteousness of God in him." Take these New Testament records and you will find that these men preached and said that Jesus of Nazareth came because He alone was pure enough to bear the sins of mankind. On the cross at Calvary He bore the sin of the world and in Him we have forgiveness. The message goes on to say that He was buried in the tomb, but that on the morning of the third day He tore asunder the bands of death and arose literally and physically from the grave. He manifested Himself to certain people and He afterwards ascended into heaven, and there He is seated at the right hand of God. Subsequently, on the day of Pentecost, He sent upon the early church the gift of the Holy Spirit. That is the essential message, surely, of the New Testament. That was what was preached by the apostles and the first preachers. That is the thing which is repeated and emphasized constantly in these various epistles. That, surely, has been the historic faith of the Christian church. That alone is the true "catholic" [that is, "universal"] faith which has been believed always and everywhere and by all Christian people. That, says the apostle, is the faith wherein we have to stand, about which there can be no argument or disputation. We either believe or reject it and our belief or rejection determines exclusively whether we are Christians or not.

Furthermore **we stand fast in this faith by reminding ourselves of it constantly, by reading and thinking about it, by meditating concerning it.** This is something for which I would plead at this present time. We must return to a constant consideration of the terms of the faith. That is specially necessary, perhaps, for those of us who are Evangelicals. I plead, in other words, for a revival of the study of theology. To me the most hopeful sign in the last fifteen years has been that great movement on the continent of Europe associated with the names of Karl Barth and Emil Brunner.[9] Nothing to me is of such significance as the increasing realization that without a given body of doctrine, without a fresh study of Christian theology, there can be no true revival in the church. It is not enough to cultivate the devotional life. It is not sufficient to read certain selected portions of Scripture daily, accompanied by the reading of a devotional commentary, though that is good and excellent and we can never do too much of it. But in addition let us return to a systematic study of theology. Let us view the whole landscape. Let to go back to the great profound biblical expositions of the cardinal tenets of the faith. That is the way to "stand fast in the faith" – to remind ourselves of it, to read it, to study it and to digest it; to soak ourselves in the great expositions of the faith that have come down to us from the past.

Why?

Let me ask the second question, "Why are we to stand fast in the faith?" The first answer, of course, is **because our salvation depends upon it.** You remember what Paul says in writing to these Corinthians in the fifteenth chapter. "Moreover, brethren, I declare unto you the gospel, which I preached unto you, which also ye have received, and wherein ye stand. By which also ye are saved if ye keep in memory what I preached

9. In later years Dr Lloyd-Jones was less enthusiastic about Barth and Brunner. The "neo-orthodox" movement was in the end a disappointment to Bible-believing Christians. But for a while it drew people's attention away from simplistic "liberalism" and back to Christian doctrine.

unto you, unless ye have believed in vain." Our salvation depends upon it. Unless we hold on to this faith and live by it, our whole position is gone.

Another reason why we should "stand fast in the faith" is that the New Testament, and all subsequent history of the church, make it abundantly clear and plain that **the Holy Spirit will finally honour nothing but the faith**. We may pray for a spiritual revival and awakening, but it will fail if we do not preach the faith. We can be eloquent, we can have after-meetings, we can produce certain mechanical results, but there will be no true conversion unless the faith is preached. The Holy Spirit will honour nothing but the truth as it is in Christ Jesus.

Then coming to a much more practical level, it is important that we should stand fast in the faith **because it is always the greatest incentive to the living of the Christian life**. There is nothing that so drives and urges a man to live a truly ethical, moral, Christian life as an understanding of the doctrines of the faith. However good a man may be the time comes when he asks himself the question, "Why should I live a good life? Other people are not doing so. Is it that I am lashing myself unnecessarily? Am I cleansing my steps in vain?" Those questions come and there is only one answer which keeps any man or woman on the narrow path. He sees himself to be a pilgrim of eternity. He knows that only Christ can save him and that he can only plead Christ's merits when he faces God as judge. He realizes that he must live the life. "Whosoever hath this hope in him purifieth himself even as he is pure." Paul puts it perfectly in the fifteenth chapter when he says, "Evil communications corrupt good manners." The man who goes wrong about the resurrection is the man who goes wrong in his daily life. The man whose doctrine is shaky will be shaky in his whole life.

In the same way, also, standing fast in the faith is essential because **it is always the greatest spur to the missionary enterprise**. What makes me interested in the souls of other men and women is that I see them as they are in the sight of God. Nothing has so acted as a spur to the great missionary enterprise of the Christian church as the acceptance of the Christian faith. You always find after a great revival missionary interest and enterprise are awakened. Men are made conscious of the condition of the lost and there is awakened within them a desire for their salvation.

But to be still more practical, **we are to stand fast in the faith for the sake of our own happiness**. There is no other way to be happy in a world like this except by standing fast in the faith. Doubts will come for certain; the enemy will attack you and try to shake you. Paul puts it perfectly when, in writing to the church at Ephesus, he tells them to put on the Christian armour, but, above all things, he says, "Take the shield of faith wherewith ye shall be able to quench all the fiery darts of the adversary." It is essential to "stand fast in the faith" when we are assailed by doubt. And it is essential as against feelings. If we trust to our feelings and to our moods, the time will come when we shall be feeling miserable. We shall wake up in the morning feeling tired and lethargic and the question will come to us, "Why go on with it? I do not feel like going on with it." There is only one answer when you feel like that. It is the faith, the truth! It is our only means of happiness. It is essential also as against the facts of life. There come "the slings and arrows of outrageous fortune". Illness comes, disappointment comes, difficult circumstances arise, a world war takes place, our profession is lost, our business is gone, sorrow knocks at the door of your home and someone dearer than life is taken away. Death comes, either in battle, or on the sea, or in the air, or quietly in a room. How can I face the facts of life? There is but one way: "Stand fast in the faith." It has envisaged all these things. It has provided for them all; it covers them all. It is the faith for life. It is the faith for death. It is the faith for all eternity. "Stand fast in the faith."

CHAPTER 23

Quit You Like Men, Be Strong

(1 Corinthians 16:13–14)

"Watch ye, stand fast in the faith, quit you like men, be strong. Let all your things be done with charity."

Never was it quite so important that we should bear in mind the principle of which I have been reminding you, namely, that in these exhortations there is a very definite, logical and spiritual sequence. The apostle does not utter these words anyhow, or haphazardly. He has a very definite arrangement in his mind and is anxious that we should see the sequence. We need to be awakened, first of all. Then we need to be pointed to the faith and to be told to stand in it. Then comes this word to quit ourselves like men and to be strong. It is vitally important that we should take these words in the position in which they are to be found in the context. Unless we do that we shall entirely fail to understand what the apostle means by them and we shall probably end by entirely misapplying them at the present time.

The context

These words are in a sense extremely dangerous. For nothing would be so easy for me as to use these words simply as a means to a call to courage, to steadfastness in connection with the national effort. Were I to do so I should be violating the Scripture, for whatever else Paul meant here, he certainly did not mean that. The apostle did not start with these words, though there was much in the church at Corinth that called for them. He puts them after he had called the church to watch and to stand fast in the faith. It is not the first thing he says, neither is it an isolated word. In other words, this exhortation is not just a vague general appeal for manliness and courage, or, to use the expression at one time so current, these words are not an inculcation of muscular Christianity. The danger is to interpret them in that sense. They are such stirring, strong and manly words, and there is a very real danger that we should think of them as such and out of their connection and thereby miss their real significance and true import.

Two principles

Perhaps we can best make this point clear by putting it into the form of two general principles. **The danger that confronts us in these words is the danger of regarding Christianity as just a general appeal for courage, face to face with the problems and difficulties of the battle of life**. As you know full well, there have been many who have been very fond of presenting Christianity in some such terms as that. The father of the movement was William James, the American psychologist, who flourished at the end of the last century, and certain British poets were prominent in expressing the same view, as though Christianity was just an appeal for courage, for setting ourselves firmly against the difficulties of life. The late Sir Hugh Walpole put the whole outlook very perfectly in a phrase in one of his books. He said, "It is not life that matters, but the courage that you bring to it." Now that is the philosophy, that the supreme thing in life is courage and strength and boldness and the spirit of endurance. If you have that, it is said, it makes no difference at all what may attack you, so long as you have courage, all will be well. The danger has been to equate that philosophy with the teaching of the Christian gospel and to regard the preaching of the gospel as being a general appeal for that particular quality of courage, and of strength, face to face with the battle of life. The reply to all that is that not only is it not Christianity, but it is in its essence paganism. Nothing is so important as that we should sharply distinguish between what is essentially pagan teaching and Christian teaching, at a time like the present when we are faced with a great need of these particular qualities in connection with the national and international situation.

In paganism the supreme virtue is courage. The Greeks put courage in the highest position; there was nothing that was superior to it. The Greek liked strength and manliness; that was ultimately the reason why he went in for the culture of the human body and the human form. Anything which suggested ability in that natural sense; anything that suggested courage and the spirit of endurance was highly extolled by the pagans. But in Christianity the supreme virtue is not courage, but humility. There, of course, is the differentia of Christianity, and there above all we see the sharp dividing line between pagan teaching and the Christian teaching. The apostle tells us in this very epistle that to the Greeks the preaching of the cross was folly. Why was it folly? It was folly to them because of its sheer weakness. The failure of this man who was called the Messiah, His failure to stand up and defend Himself, the unutterable weakness of the cross was, of necessity, to the Greeks, folly, because they had always been taught to think that of all the virtues, courage and strength were supreme. So it is vitally important that we should keep this distinction clearly in our mind.

This difference is frequently emphasized in the New Testament. You remember what the same apostle says in writing to the church at Philippi. "Let this mind be in you which was also in Christ Jesus." You remember the characteristics of that mind. It was a mind that divested itself of certain signs of glory, humbled itself, and took on the form of a servant which went submissively to the death and shame of the cross. That is the mind which is to be in the Christian. Not courage, primarily, but self-abasement and humility. You remember those words of our Lord which put the whole thing still more clearly, when He turned to His disciple as He was going up to Jerusalem for the final scene of the death on the cross, and said, "Ye know that they which are accounted to rule over the gentiles exercise lordship over them, and their great ones exercise authority upon them. But so shall it not be among you, but whosoever will be great among you, shall be your minister." There, I think, once and for ever, we see the division between the pagan inculcation of courage as the supreme virtue and the Christian exhortation to humility.

But I hasten to add that that does not mean for a moment, or imply, that to be a Christian is just to be flabbily weak and sentimental. The trouble with this distinction, as with many another, is that we so often tend to fly from one extreme to the other. We start by thinking that courage is the all-important thing and then we tend to go to the other extreme and to think that the Christian is a weak, flabby and sentimental person, who never takes a stand about anything, but is one who just smiles weakly and indiscriminately upon all and sundry; one who lacks vitality and virility and backbone; one who has no real strength. That view is as great a travesty of the Christian teaching as the other. We see very clearly from my text that that cannot be the truth.

But how do we reconcile these things? That draws our attention to a second point. **Christianity does call us to be strong and virile**. It demands of men and women courage and strength, but it does so in a way of its own, and in a manner which is entirely different from the pagan teaching. Christianity never puts courage and manliness first. Or, to put it in a better way, courage and manliness and strength in the Christian are always to be the outcome of his faith, of his belief. Christianity is not interested in courage as such. It is not interested in manliness in and of itself. The state, of course, as distinct from the church and her teaching, is interested in courage *per se*, but Christianity never is. It never isolates the thing. It never holds it up as being of value in and of itself. The Christian gospel does not think more highly of the strong man than it does of the weak man. It is only interested in courage in terms of truth. We are not called to "quit you like men, be strong" until we have been told to "stand fast in the faith". However much strength and courage and manliness I may possess, if it is not in terms of faith, it is useless and valueless from the Christian standpoint. In other words, the Christian gospel is not interested in pagan virtues; it is not interested in our natural divisions and distinctions. "In Christ there is neither Jew nor Gentile, male nor female, bond nor free." It is not interested in great intellectual attainments or in our social distinctions. To be "in Christ" is the important thing. It is only if we are "in Christ" that we are called upon to "be strong", to "quit you like men". Christianity is only interested in courage in the context and setting of the faith. In other words, we must always bear in mind the logical and spiritual sequence in these great exhortations of the apostle Paul.

How?

So with that as a background, let us work out exactly what the exhortation does mean in a little more detail. We can best do so by asking two simple questions. First, how are we to "quit ourselves like men and to be strong"?

First of all, we answer in a negative manner. We are to quit ourselves like men and to be strong **by not being children**. Those of you who are familiar with this great epistle will recall that the apostle frequently plays on that particular theme. Some of the intelligent people in Corinth had been complaining that the apostle had not given them much philosophy in his preaching and teaching. They said, "He has only spoken to us about the cross; he has not taken us on to the higher doctrine." The reply which the apostle gives is this: "I could not do it, for you were still babes, still carnal, still dividing up into these sects and groups and comparing me with Apollos and Cephas. You were not fit for such doctrine; you could not stand anything but milk. Indeed you are yet children." And he works out that principle in other ways throughout the epistle. Not only were they acting as children in dividing themselves up into groups and sects, but they were being childish also with respect to the question of eating meats offered to idols. Some of them had come to see that there was no sin in that. The weaker brethren could not quite understand that and they were being offended and they were complaining. The intellectuals on the other hand were boasting of their understanding and despising the others. "That is childish," says the apostle. Then there was that whole question of spiritual gifts. Some had the gift of tongues, others had gifts of healing and miraculous power, others possessed gifts of interpretation and understanding. As you remember, the entire church was divided up in that manner, some saying that this particular gift was the only thing and that if you did not possess it you were not a Christian at all. Others claimed the same for some other gifts. "Quit you like men, be strong," says the apostle. "You are arguing like little

children, desiring each other's toys and gifts. Put these matters into
the background of that great faith of which I have reminded you. Play the
man!"

Now, surely, this is a word which we need to lay to heart at this
present time. I have been trying to point out to you that this exhortation
seems to be such a direct word to the church today. With the need of the
world as it is today and the apparent apathy and sleepiness of the church,
is not this one of the things which needs to be stressed? Look at the
pathetic way in which so many churches bicker away their opportunities.
Those of us who travel about the country are far too frequently brought
into contact with those who call themselves Christians who quarrel over
little offices and places of importance in the church, and who argue as to
who is the senior and who is the junior worker. These petty things often
destroy the life of a church and utterly nullify its influence and its
usefulness in a particular district. Then there are petty squabblings about
vestments and ceremonies, and this addition to a service or that
subtraction from a ritual. Is it not a tragic thing when the world is on
fire and men have lost their sense of values in connection with life, that
the church of the living God which has the message that the world needs,
should be playing as children with these trivialities? "Quit you like men,
be strong," says the apostle. Have done with these manifestations of
mere childishness.

But to be a little more positive in our interpretation, we are to be like
men and strong, very especially, **in the matter of understanding**. You
will remember that the apostle puts that very perfectly in chapter 14,
verse 20, where he deals with this matter. You remember that he tells
them that they are to "be not children in understanding: howbeit in
malice be ye children, but in understanding be men". In this final
exhortation he has that very thing in his mind. We are to be men and to
be strong in understanding. What does he mean? Surely it means this: we
must not be afraid of exercising our intellects in connection with our
religion. Now that may sound perfectly obvious, and yet, if I am at all
aware of what has been happening in the church during the last forty
or fifty years, there has been, especially in Evangelical circles, a fear, a
distrust of the study of theology in connection with religion. This fear

can be easily understood. As the result of the exaltation of philosophy which characterized the end of the last century, and the devastating higher critical movement in connection with the Bible, men quite naturally began to take up the position of saying that the best thing to do was to read no theology. They said, "Let us live our devotional life, but do not let us use our minds. Above all, do not look at textbooks on theology." A friend of mine, now an ordained clergyman, told me how that twenty years ago when he felt called to enter the ministry, he went to consult a man who was prominent in religious circles to ask his advice as to what he should do. The advice he was given was this. He was told, "There is one thing I can tell you for certain. If you go to Cambridge don't study theology if you want to keep your faith. Take history, or economics, but, above all, avoid theology." That has been the attitude which has been far too prevalent. Now you cannot "stand fast in the faith" unless you know it, unless you are aware of its arguments, unless you can give a reason for the hope that is in you. Let us not develop exclusively the mystical and pietistic side of our religious life. Let us "be men in understanding". Or, to put it in another way, we must not be content merely with an experience which we had at the beginning of our Christian life. There is ever a danger for men to live on their first experience. Many never grow; many do not desire to grow. They realize that they have had a great deliverance and they rest content with it. I remember some men describing the Welsh Revival of 1904–1905. They waxed eloquent about it at great length, but after they had finished, I said, "But that is not the end of the story." "Yes, it is," one man said, "I was gloriously saved. It happened to me there," and he began to describe in most graphic terms how he had there and then been delivered from certain sins. "But you have not finished your story," I said. "You did not die in 1905. What has been happening in the intervening years? How have you grown in grace and in knowledge of the Lord? Have you grown in your understanding of the faith?" This man was living on his first experience; he was looking back and remaining a child in Christ. He had not become a man in understanding. But, perhaps, in some senses the most important way of all in which we are to be men, and to be strong in understanding, is the way in which the apostle puts it in Ephesians 4:14.

"That we henceforth be no more children tossed to and fro, and carried about with every wind of doctrine, by the sleight of men, and cunning craftiness, whereby they lie in wait to deceive." In other words, we are to quit ourselves like men in such a way that we so firmly grasp the doctrines of the faith and the vitals of these eternal verities that we shall not be overtaken by the latest cults which may spring up. To me there is nothing more tragic than to observe the way in which people suddenly follow the various movements that arise. First there is one movement and suddenly that vanishes, then there is something else. Christian people far too often rush after new cults and lop-sided gospels and fail to stand four-square in the faith itself. There is only one way to avoid being carried to and fro like a bubble on the surface of the waves and that is by being strong as the result of studying and understanding the truth; by developing a knowledge of biblical theology, by reading, by developing a knowledge of what has been written by the great saints of the past in the interpretation of the word of God. "Be strong" in the realm of understanding.

Another way in which we are to be strong is **to be consistent, to be dependable, to be reliable**. It is so characteristic of the child that he gets these spurts of enthusiasm, but he never persists. A child takes up a toy and it is everything for the time being. But soon he drops it and takes up something else. He hears a sound and he rushes after it. We do not expect a child to be dependable. But a man must be dependable and reliable and strong. He must not have these fitful enthusiasms. He must always be at his post; he must always be one upon whom one can depend.

But above and beyond all this, we are to "quit ourselves like men, and to be strong" in the sense that **we must be ready for persecution**. You remember what Paul said to Timothy, who had been having a hard time, and who was suffering persecution. Paul wrote to him, and said, "All that will live godly in Christ Jesus shall suffer persecution." If you "stand fast in the faith" you will soon be persecuted. You will be told that you are behind the times, that you are a back number, that your theology is the theology of Adam. You will have men hurling their criticisms at you. You will become a joke in the office; people will laugh at you. You cannot be a

Christian in an army barrack-room, or camp, or shop, or office, but that men will cause you to suffer. They will attack you with the arrow of ridicule and sarcasm and scorn. It is not always an easy thing to stand firm. It is a much easier thing to give in and to compromise, to do what others do. "Be strong," says Paul.

Why?

Let me come to my second question. Why are we to "quit ourselves like men"? Because of **the greatness and worthiness of our cause**. Appeals are made to men to fight for their country, but here is a cause infinitely bigger, the truth of the gospel. "England expects that every man this day will do his duty." God expects that every Christian shall quit himself as a man and be strong.

Another reason why we are to be strong is **the present precarious position**. The enemy is powerful and strong and mighty. He commands his big battalions. The church is small and weak; it is not a popular thing to be a Christian. The crowds do not come in our direction and for that very reason every man amongst us counts, and counts tremendously. Therefore, let us be strong. Let us quit ourselves like men.

If you are very conscious of your weakness, let me tell you something else. **Consider our Lord Jesus Christ**. "Quit yourselves like men, be strong", looking unto Jesus, the one who trod the winepress alone when all His disciples fled and left Him. He never flinched; He set his face steadfastly to go to Jerusalem for your salvation and mine. If He did that for us, He, surely, has the right to demand of us that, for His sake, we should "quit ourselves like men", and that we should "be strong".

CHAPTER 24

Let All Things Be Done with Charity

(1 Corinthians 16:14)

"Let all your things be done with charity."

The last statement in the fourteenth verse is the last of the steps in this great injunction which we have ventured to describe as Paul's order of the day for the Christian church. There is a sense in which it may be regarded as the last of the distinctive steps, or instructions, in the general exhortation. But it also can be regarded, as I hope to show you, not so much as an additional exhortation, but as a statement which tells us how to interpret accurately and correctly all the separate exhortations which the apostle has previously given us. It can be interpreted in both those ways in quite a legitimate manner. As we have looked at this text this has been a principle which I have tried to enforce, that it is vitally important that we should observe the sequence in these exhortations. They are not chosen haphazardly. Paul started with the exhortation to "watch" simply because it was the right thing to start with. Then he bade them to "stand fast in the faith" because that was the next step in the sequence. Then he called upon them to "quit you like men, and be strong". It would be dangerous to call upon men to "quit themselves like men and to be strong" without, first of all, having told them to "stand fast in the faith". All these things have a particular reference to one another and they must be taken in the order in which we find them in the text.

If that has been true about the exhortations with which we have dealt hitherto, it is especially true of this final exhortation. Here again we cannot but turn aside for a moment and express our admiration of this amazing man of God, the apostle Paul. In our first discourse we spent some time in describing him as the incomparable pastor. We pointed out how thoroughly he knew the churches, that he never wrote to any two of them in exactly the same way. He writes to one church in one way and to another church in another way. He knew his people so perfectly; he knew their weaknesses and their special dangers. He knew the human heart, he knew the strength of sin, he knew all about the adversary. He tells these people that he is not ignorant of Satan's devices. Now here he displays all that again in a very striking and remarkable manner. It was after he had told them to "watch", to "stand fast", and to "quit them like men", that he adds these words: "Let all that you do be done in love." How thoroughly he knew this church at Corinth! And how remarkably well does he know us! The point is that the apostle knows perfectly well how we are constituted, and, particularly as a result of the perverting effect of sin upon our lives, how we invariably tend to go from one extreme to the other. Perhaps by nature we are most liable to be slothful and lethargic and to go to sleep and not to care. So the apostle calls upon us to watch. But he knows the danger is that we should then switch over to the other extreme and so become guilty of those things which I hope to mention later. Likewise with regard to the exhortation to "stand fast". He knows the danger of our resting upon experience. He knows also that having told us to "stand fast", we may go so far to the other side that we shall finally do more harm than good. Likewise in regard to the exhortation to "quit us like men, and to be strong" we may go from one extreme to the other. We either do nothing or we are carried away by excessive and false zeal. So he guards against that particular danger by winding up this great order of the day with this general statement, "Let everything be done with love."

Two general statements

As we approach these words, there are two general statements which I feel constrained to make with respect to them, and especially with regard to this word "love" or "charity". First, note that **the apostle says "with love" not "with sentimentality"**. That is a warning, surely, which is necessary. The apostle, as you know, found it essential to write a whole chapter on this question of love. The ancient world knew very little about it. They regarded it as mere sentimentalism. The apostle wrote that thirteenth chapter of the first epistle to the Corinthians in order to define love. You notice in that chapter a number of negatives. He starts by saying what it is not. People will persist in equating love with something that is weak and flabby, and so at great length the apostle has to tell them what love is and what love is not. They need to know **exactly** what it is. Christianity has brought this word into the vocabulary of mankind. People did not know what love was until Christ carne. It is still a difficulty which constantly confronts missionaries when they go out to pagan lands to ensure that this word be not misunderstood. Surely it is equally necessary and important that we should call attention to the true nature of this word at the present time. Love, as is shown so clearly in that thirteenth chapter, is something which is positive and strong. We are so much influenced by the daily press and the cheap novels and the films and the hoardings, that we allow our ideas quite unconsciously to become influenced by such forces. Surely one of the most serious problems that will confront this country is the problem of safeguarding the education of the people. People are deriving much of their education from these things that I have mentioned and there is no more striking evidence of the debasing effect of those popular ideas and agencies than in the notion of what is meant by the word "love". It is to them a weak, flabby, sentimental thing. How different from the conception which Paul gives us of it in this thirteenth chapter of the first epistle to the church at Corinth!

Secondly, we cannot but observe here **the amazing and remarkable way in which the Christian gospel blends and harmonizes things that seem to be antitheses and opposites**. It is rather a striking thing that this exhortation should come immediately after the previous exhortation, "quit you like men". Love and strength! There is something which is quite unique. Nothing but the Christian gospel brings words like that together. There are endless examples of the same thing. If you want another illustration of it you find it in 2 Timothy 1:1, "For God hath not given us the spirit of fear, but of power, and of love, and of a sound mind." There is nothing incongruous, as far as the gospel is concerned, in mentioning "power" at one and the same time as "love". The world cannot do it. To the world power is utterly opposed to love. Think of it in terms of Nazism and the many modern conflicts. When you are thinking of power in such terms as that you cannot think of love. That is how the ancient world thought of power! It was something hard, brutal and fierce. And you can never harmonize a thing like that with the idea of love. But the New Testament does so, because, as I have been trying to point out, the whole New Testament idea of love is of something positive and strong and manly. Here, I say, we find this remarkable blending of opposites, this synthesis, which includes all the virtues and covers them all by this canopy of love.

A general approach – why?

Now having made those two general remarks about the nature of love let us approach the text directly along two main lines. These words can, first of all, be applied in a general way and then we shall look at them in a special way. First of all they can be applied generally. We are told that "all", that "everything", is to be done in love. Let us ask the question, "Why are we to do all things in love? What is the meaning of this exhortation?" The answer is perfectly obvious. The first answer that Paul gives is this: **If you do not, everything you do will be useless, and worse than useless**. That is a very good reason in and of itself. "Though I speak with the tongues of men and of angels, and have not charity, I am become as sounding brass, or a tinkling cymbal." The most eloquent preaching the world has ever known, apart from that love, would be useless and valueless. I may have the gift of prophecy and the understanding of mysteries and all knowledge; I may have faith so that I could remove mountains, but apart from love, says the apostle, I am nothing. So that is a very good reason for doing everything that we do with love. Apart from love all that I do will be a waste of energy, which will lead to nothing, and, perchance, it may even be worse than useless.

Another general reason why all things should be done in love is that **it is the supreme essential to the life of the church** and the basis of the usefulness of the church. I have been at pains to point out that I am interested in this text because it seems to me to have a message for the church today. There is an analogy and a parallel between the church at Corinth and the church today. The church at Corinth was becoming ineffective because they were divided up into groups and sects, and the result was that the morale and spiritual tone of the church was going down, and the impact upon the immoral and dissolute town of Corinth was becoming more and more feeble. The apostle writes this letter to them in order to put them right. He knows that there is no hope for Corinth until the church has been put right. It is a waste of energy to start evangelizing the world before the church herself is right. And that is equally true today. The great principle which is absolutely essential to the life of the church is this principle of love. It is only when we who are Christians, and who claim to be members of the mystical body of Christ, are in a right relationship with one another that we can truly function in relation to the world. It is a vitally essential principle to the harmonious life of the church and, therefore, to the usefulness of the church.

Another general reason given in the thirteenth chapter of 1 Corinthians is that **love is the supreme grace of the Christian life**. We were mentioning before the virtue of humility. There can be no argument or dispute that the highest grace of all is the grace of love, for "God is love" and Christ was the incarnation of love. It is only in Him that the world has seen a perfect manifestation of love. So that when we are exhorted to do all things in love, we are simply called upon to be like Him, to be what He was, to live as He lived and to do everything as He did it. It is the topmost pinnacle. The apostle speaks of knowledge and understanding and tongues and prophecy. He does not disparage these things, they are all-important; they are vital and essential. Faith and hope are included. But the time comes, says the apostle, when nothing will be left, because nothing will be necessary but love, and love will be inevitable, because we shall see Him face to face and realize the love that God has for us. That, surely, is the reason why very close and special attention should be given to this exhortation, because you have been made anew in order that you may be like Him.

A particular approach

Let us now apply the text in a special sense. I have no doubt at all, myself, that it was this special reference which was supreme in the apostle's mind when he penned these particular words. He had been talking about watchfulness, about standing fast in the faith, about quitting themselves like men and being strong. I do not hesitate to assert that without my text this morning the other injunctions would be extremely dangerous. That is why I have already emphasized the wisdom displayed by this man as a pastor. Simply to tell a man to watch, to stand fast in the faith and to be strong, would be the most dangerous thing that could be said to a man. That is the danger of those who are most orthodox. It is the danger of those who are most aware of the fact that the Christian life is a conflict. It is the danger of those who are most concerned about the truth and who are most anxious about the work of the church. It is the danger of those men and women who are burdened by the sin and the iniquity which they see in the world around them. To all who fall into this category are these words necessary, "Let everything be done in love." When we considered that exhortation to watchfulness, I pointed out it meant this: that any person who was in the Christian fight had to be careful to watch himself and to watch the enemy. It is a dangerous exhortation if the watching be not done in a spirit of love. If a man is not watching in the spirit of love he will very soon be in that state in which he is not so much watching himself and the enemy as watching every other Christian. That leads to a spirit, and to an atmosphere, of suspicion and distrust. It produces self-appointed spiritual detectives. We realize that we have to watch and we forget that it must be done in a spirit of love, with the result that it leads to a critical spirit, to a state of mind in which men are constantly criticizing each other. The apostle tells us in the thirteenth chapter that "love thinketh no evil, that it hopeth all things". Yet how often are good orthodox Christian people, in their desire to be watchful, guilty of becoming critical of their fellow Christians. Perhaps a simple incident will illustrate my point here. I remember once preaching on the third chapter of the Acts of the Apostles where we are told that "Peter and John went up to the temple to pray, at the hour of prayer being the ninth hour." I said that just before they went into the prayer-meeting they saw an impotent man sitting at the gate of the temple who had never walked in his life. And seeing the man, Peter said, "In the name of Jesus Christ of Nazareth rise up and walk." As a mere aside, I said, "Peter and John were actually at that moment hurrying to a prayer-meeting in the temple, but they saw this problem as they were passing by, and for a moment they forgot all about the prayer-meeting and dealt with the problem. Perhaps," I said, "it would be a good thing if some of us occasionally forgot our meetings and prayer-meetings in order to deal with problems of need and of sin that exist in the world outside." Later on I was approached by two young ladies wearing the uniform of a certain Bible school and they came up to me, notebooks in hand, and they said, "Do we understand that you do not believe in prayer meetings?" That is what I would call a hypercritical spirit. These good girls had been taught to be watchful, so they came to listen to a preacher, ready to discover some error, some apostasy, some heresy which they might detect. They were self-appointed spiritual detectives. Such an attitude, I say, leads to a hypercritical spirit. But, alas, it can sometimes lead to something even worse. It may come to this, that we even delight in finding error in others. Not only do we become suspicious and hypercritical, but it sometimes reaches the stage where people really rejoice in the discovery. They enjoy exposing what they consider to be heresy. Yet here is something which the apostle tells us is utterly opposed to love. "Rejoiceth not in iniquity, but rejoiceth in the truth." Dr Moffat translates it, "Love is never glad when others go wrong." There are some who watch so carefully, who become so hypercritical, that they are almost glad when someone does go wrong. In exposing the error the spirit of watchfulness is not controlled by the spirit of love. Thomas Charles Edwards, in his great commentary on this epistle, says very much the same thing. "There is no malice in love." How difficult it is to be watchful without becoming malicious!

Let me say a word about the second injunction. "Stand fast in the faith." We were at great pains to point out that nothing is so disastrous to the life of the church as a false spirit of eclecticism. Nothing is so pathetic as the way in which men run after this cult and that and believe in some body of doctrine which is not firmly grounded upon fundamental principles. We must stand fast in the faith, but if we fail to do so with love we may do more harm than good. "Love," says Paul, "vaunteth not itself, is not puffed up." Yet you know there are some people, who, in announcing that they are orthodox are guilty of that very thing. Orthodoxy can sometimes be thoroughly objectionable. I remember once, in my medical days, I was asked to examine a certain man and as I proceeded to do so, he said, "Probably it is not often you get the privilege of examining a truly Christian chest!" "Love vaunteth not itself, is not puffed up."

Another way in which danger may arise at this point is this. In standing fast in the faith, if we are not animated by the spirit of love, we may not always differentiate as we should between faith in its essence and certain peculiar interpretations and expositions of our own. Here is a theme which might very easily occupy our minds on many occasions. There is nothing so tragic, I sometimes think, in certain circles as the way in which men fail to differentiate between that which is of the essence of the faith and certain other matters about which there can be no certainty. You cannot, I am told, be a member of the World Fundamentalist Association unless you believe in the "pre-millennial" return of our Lord and if you happen to be a "post-millenarian" you cannot be a Christian! If you are an "a-millenarian" you are just unspeakable. There you have an illustration of the importance of differentiating between the essence of the faith and the interpretation of a particular matter about which there has always been a difference of opinion. There is the same difference of opinion as to when the rapture of the saints is to take place. Men separate from each other about matters of that nature, where there is no certainty, and where there can be no certainty, though the return of the Lord is certain. Who can decide who is right, whether those who hold the pre-millennial, or those who hold the post-millennial view? I could mention great names on both sides, equally expert theologians. Surely these are matters where there can be a legitimate difference of opinion. Let us bear in mind the adage: "In essentials, unity; in non-essentials, liberty; in all things, charity." "Stand fast in the faith." Yes, but in a spirit of love.

Then the exhortation prior to this one: "Quit you like men, be strong." The apostle points out in many places in this epistle that you are not to ride rough-shod over the feelings of other people. To be strong did not mean that the more enlightened Corinthians were at liberty to eat meats offered to idols. Paul says, "I will eat no flesh while the world standeth, lest I make my brother to offend." That is love and strength combined, love and strength in one. "Love beareth all things, believeth all things, hopeth all things, endureth all things." You remember also how in the sixth chapter there is the question of the disputes which they were taking to the public courts. There also Paul says the same thing. "Why do ye not rather take wrong? Why do ye not rather suffer yourselves to be defrauded?" Why not be big enough to suffer wrong in the spirit of love for the sake of the church?

That is Paul's order of the day. We are told to watch, to stand fast in the faith, to quit ourselves like men and to be strong. But, above all, let us remember the motive for doing all these things. The motive is to help others and to win others and above all it is to bring honour and glory to the name of our Lord God and His wondrous Christ who came to redeem us.

Let me give you a word of encouragement. If you feel that it is a high calling and a hard task, think of Him and of what He has done for you. He had the right to stay in heaven, but He laid that right aside and came to this earth, to suffer and die at the hands of ignorant and sinful men. He endured it all. Think of Him when you are confronted with these problems and difficulties. Think of what He has done. Remember always that He never calls you to a task without equipping you with power for that task. He offers us His own Spirit. He watched in love. He stood fast. He made a good confession in love. He quitted Himself as a man. He was strong, even to the point of going to Golgotha and to the cross, and all in love.

PART 6

"Except the LORD Build the House..."

CHAPTER 25

Illusion and Reality

(Psalm 127:1–2)

*"Except the LORD build the house, they labour in vain that build it:
except the LORD keep the city, the watchman waketh but in vain. It is
vain for you to rise up early, to sit up late, to eat the bread of sorrows:
for so he giveth his beloved sleep."*

A turning-point in history

We must all agree that we stand, at the present time, at what is one of the
significant turning points in history. We have completed the first half of
the twentieth century and we start upon the second half of this century
about which so much has been spoken, and about which so much has
been written. It is a time, therefore, surely, for review, a time to pause
and look around and draw conclusions and deductions; a time for
assessment. It is our custom as human beings to do this more or less at
the beginning of every New Year. It is not for me at the moment to enter
into the spirituality of such a procedure. On the whole I agree with it. I
think that life is so difficult that it is a good thing at any time, or for any
reason, to pause, and to consider and to examine ourselves, and to review
our lives. We are so disinclined to do this that anything that makes us do
it, whether it be an almanac or anything else, is something which is of
value and benefit to us. But I do feel that this particular first of January
[1950] is of unusual significance and importance. It is a time, I say, which
demands that we should review this century to which we belong.

Now I think that all will agree further with me when I say that no
century in the long history of mankind has so falsified predictions and

prophecies as the twentieth century. There never was a century of which and from which so much was expected. If you read the poets of the Victorian era, and the politicians and the popular writers, the essayists and others, you will find that they were all looking forward to the twentieth century. It was to be the crowning century of all the centuries in the story of the human race.

Standing as we do half way through this century, are we not compelled to say that no century has ever so disappointed the prophets and has so falsified the confident optimistic predictions? Obviously the great questions that must arise are: What is the matter? What is the explanation? What has gone wrong with this twentieth century? Why do we find ourselves in our present condition and in our present position?

Our contention as Christian people is that there is only one adequate answer to that question and it is the answer which is to be found in this Book which we call the Bible. We do not conceive it to be part of the work of the Christian preacher to consider in detail all the various other theories. We are familiar with, and aware of them, and could do so, but that is not the real function of a Christian preacher. The biblical message starts on the assumption and supposition that everything else has failed. Then it pronounces its message. There is no other explanation. You can consider the economic, the political, the social and various other theories, but not one of them will provide us with an adequate explanation. There is always a gap, always something incomplete, and the Bible, I say, asserts without any apology whatsoever that all these of necessity are inadequate because they leave out the most vital facts. Its claim is that it and it alone has the adequate explanation.

The biblical case

In these two verses of Psalm 127 we have a very perfect exposition of the biblical case and the biblical answer to man's dilemma and the problem of the human race. Here it is put in a very brief form and yet in a perfect manner. It is a kind of synopsis of the whole biblical teaching with regard to history and man's destiny in this world. It is probably a psalm written by Solomon, whom the Bible describes as the wisest of men; a man to whom exceptional wisdom was given. Here we find this wise man reviewing history, looking at the whole course of human history. In his wisdom he stops for a moment and out of his vast store of knowledge and experience, having envisaged and looked out upon the entire situation, and especially in the light of all he knew of the past, he comes to this solemn conclusion: "Except the LORD build the house, they labour in vain that build it."

Solomon, of course, primarily was thinking of the people of Israel, but it is a very simple thing to show that what was true of the people of Israel has been equally true of every other nation under the sun and is equally true also of every single individual that comes into this world. This is the biblical pronouncement with regard to man individually and collectively. Man is always seeking for happiness; there is no one who is not seeking for happiness. Whatever his view, whatever his theory of life, every man is out for peace, security, happiness, prosperity and a sense of satisfaction. Man in a sense is always building a house. It may be an actual house and home, it may be a city, it may be a state, it may be an empire. It may be a view of the whole world and the whole state of mankind in general. You go back and read the history of man, not only the biblical history, but even the secular text books of history, and I think you will find that that is what man has been doing from the very beginning. He has always had ideas in his mind with respect to certain things he desires. He wants to enjoy himself, he wants to have something durable, he wants to get rid of the sense of insecurity, and he wants to have happiness, peace, joy, prosperity and to find satisfaction for himself in this life and world. He also wants to extend it as long as he can, so he fights disease, he fights death. He tries to make of this world a kind of house and home in which he can enjoy himself to his heart's content. Now man has always been like that and man is still like that, but the great question is, has he succeeded? What has happened to this great human effort and endeavour throughout the running centuries? Here is the conclusion at which this wise man had arrived. He was very well versed in past history in his day and time and he looked round and about him, and having looked at it all this wise man draws this conclusion. "Except the LORD build the house, they labour in vain that build it." In other words this man teaches here what the whole of the Bible teaches, namely, that in the last analysis there are only two ways of viewing life. If the Christian church were doing nothing else at the present time, she could justify her existence by simply saying this, that there are ultimately just these two views with respect to life. You either face it with God, or else you do not. You either base your ultimate philosophy on the fact of God, or else you are guilty of forgetting Him and of trying to deal with your life and to plan your life without Him and apart from Him.

That is the proposition that is laid down by this man and I want to consider it with you. In the light of the fifty years of this century that have already gone, and as we look at a future that seems full of foreboding, is it not about time that we stopped and reviewed the whole position? Are we content just to go on drifting? What has gone wrong with this century? What is the matter? Why is this, I say again, which was meant to be the golden era and the crowning century of all centuries, why has this of all others gone so disastrously wrong? "Except the LORD build the house they labour in vain that build it."

No encouragement of laziness

But let us be quite certain that we understand what this man is saying. The man is not just encouraging laziness and telling us we have nothing to do but to sit down and to trust that God will do everything for us. That is not his teaching at all; that is a travesty of his teaching. What this man is concerned to say is this, that the ultimate two positions are either one of complete self-reliance or else reliance upon God. He believes in work, he exhorts people to work, he shows the importance of having a number of mighty men in the land and so on. But what he is concerned about is to know in what we place our faith and on what we ultimately rely. So the final contrast is a contrast between self-reliance and reliance upon God. He brings this out very clearly by drawing a contrast between man's methods and ways of building a house and God's way of building a house. How can we find this durable satisfaction for which we are seeking in life? I say there are only two ways – man's way and God's way.

Now let us look at these two ways as we find them compared and contrasted by Solomon here.

The human method

Let us look first at man's method and way of building the house. What are the characteristics of the human method? Here are some of them.

Toil and labour. "Except the LORD build the house, they labour in vain that build it." Here we find toil and labour, not only with sweat but also with sorrow. "It is vain for you to rise up early and sit up late, to eat the bread of sorrows." Now that is undoubtedly a reference to what you find in the third chapter of the book of Genesis, where we are told that man as a result of sin and the fall was doomed by God to a life of toil and of sorrow and told that he would eat his bread by the sweat of his brow. Here in this world we have "to eat the bread of sorrows". As we look round and about us upon life I think that that is perfectly evident. Look at all the toil and labour. Look at all the organizations and all the effort. Look at all the machinery that is involved, the machinery of government without going any further, and as it is obviously increasing from year to year.

Everything has become so complicated. "It is vain for you to rise up early, to sit up late, to eat the bread of sorrows." That is man and it is so typical of him. His method is one of endless complication. It is one of endless strain and fatigue. He is ever rising up early, sitting up late, planning, having his conferences and scheming, sweating, toiling, labouring. We need not stay with this as we are all perfectly familiar with it. The Bible puts all this very hurriedly in a picture right at the beginning. Man started by living in a place called Paradise. His life was a simple life, but the moment sin entered in, life began to become involved and complicated. Because man sinned he had to lie to cover up his sin and then he had to lie again to cover up that sin. Then you have the story of Cain and Abel and of how Cain went and built a city. Immediately you have an involved, complex idea of life. That is always characteristic of man and the busyness and bustling which ever characterize man's work and effort. That is always man's way of seeking for happiness. Read your history text books and you will see it all. Man has ever been seeking for happiness, but look at his involved machinery and the complications he has introduced. Look at the whole system of government in this and every other country today. Look at all the complication and complexity of it all. What are they trying to do? They are just trying to introduce a system that will enable us to be happy. That is all. And here is the result. Look at your typical modern man – harassed and perplexed. Look at him even in his pleasures. How involved they are! Look at all the effort he has to put into his pleasure. Look at the money involved. Look at the time expended. Look at all the organizations that are in existence in order to give him pleasure and entertain him. That is the great characteristic of man's endeavour to find durable satisfaction; it is always characterized by endless involved complications, toil and labour, sweat and sorrow, strain and fatigue and care, rising up early, sitting up late, scheming, planning and yet never seeming to arrive.

But it is still worse than that, according to the psalmist. **There is a constant sense of insecurity**. "Except the LORD build the house, they labour in vain that build it; except the LORD keep the city, the watchman waketh but in vain." Consider the watchman! However successful man may appear to be from time to time, he always has to have this watchman. For everything he plans seems to be insecure. There is always an enemy, there is always the threat of an attack coming from some direction or another. This is true not only of nations, it is true of individuals. "Uneasy lies the head that wears a crown." Most men who are filled with a spirit of ambition and want to get to the top are always afraid someone will out-distance them. You read the biographies of politicians and professional men and you will find there is always this jealousy and envy and fear. There is always need of the watchman. Everything is insecure; someone is always ready to rob you of that which you possess. It is true in every realm and department of existence. It is true of the individual, it is true of a collection of people, it is true of the state and of the whole world. Though man plans and tries to build in a durable manner there is always something threatening and the watchman is always needed. Here is a man who lived long ago, so many hundreds of years ago, and that is the conclusion to which he came. He

—

looks at man without God, trying to make a perfect world for himself, trying to build a house, and that is what he sees, toiling and sweating and after all, insecurity. The whole thing is liable to blow up at any moment; it is all in vain; it all comes to nothing. Yes, that is the result, absolute failure. Everything that man has been trying to build seems suddenly to collapse.

Once more that is not merely something that one deduces only from the Bible. Your secular history books are very eloquent on this theme. Read again of the great civilizations that have arisen in the past and have vanished. Read for instance the view of history of a man like Professor Toynbee and you will find that that is his teaching. Think again of the great civilizations that were once in China and Egypt and Rome and various other parts of the world. Man has been building, but even when he has been most confident that he has built a durable and lasting empire, the watchman was necessary. But even the watchman was never enough – the enemy has always come and the civilization has vanished. We boast of our great knowledge in this twentieth century, but nothing is so amazing as the way in which knowledge and culture have vanished and disappeared. The story of the world seems to be one of alternating periods of enlightenment and of darkness.

There, very briefly, is this man's view of man's effort and man's method when he forgets God.

God's method

But let us contrast that with God's method and God's way. What do we find? The essence of this, says the psalmist, is its **simplicity**. "Except the LORD build the house, they labour in vain that build it; except the LORD keep the city, the watchman waketh but in vain. It is vain for you to rise up early, to sit up late, to eat the bread of sorrows; for so he giveth to his beloved in sleep." What tragic folly it is to be relying upon man, says the psalmist, when God is offering to do so much for us and God's method is such an essentially simple one. This is the great message of the Bible and how often is it illustrated in the Old as well as in the New Testament. How often did God deliver the people of Israel! In a sense they had nothing to do. Sometimes they were hard-pressed and the enemy was at the gate and threatened to overwhelm them. But while they were asleep God sent pestilences, or He would raise up someone to take their enemies away. "God giveth to his beloved in sleep." How often did He bless His faithful followers in that way. While they were doing nothing God did everything for them. Now this is the great principle taught in the Bible everywhere.

It is **the principle of the free grace of God**. It is the whole basis of Christian salvation. It is just this, in a nutshell, that everything that you and I need is being offered us freely by God in the Lord Jesus Christ. It was "while we were yet enemies that Christ died for the ungodly"; it was while "we were yet without strength" God did this thing. Before you and I were born God planned the way of salvation. "He giveth to his beloved in sleep." That is the very essence of the gospel message and that is where this tragic folly of man comes in. Here is man bustling and busy trying to find peace and happiness and joy, trying by means of education and culture and pleasure and worldly organizations and various other things, and always ending in failure and disillusionment. Yet here, in utter simplicity, on the other hand, is the very thing offered us, for which we are looking. In the grace of God, and in the gospel of Jesus Christ, everything that man can need is offered him for nothing. "Love, joy, peace, long-suffering, goodness, gentleness, meekness, temperance, faith" – such are the fruits of the Spirit, the Spirit that God gives to all who truly turn to Him. How amazingly simple is God's method by contrast with the complexity of the world's method that comes to naught. And the result of God's way is that success and happiness and joy and security and peace and everything that man can desire are achieved and guaranteed.

There, briefly, we have watched the psalmist as he compares and contrasts the method of human self-reliance and the method of reliance upon God.

Is it true?

But now I want to ask a question. Is the psalmist's message literally true? My reply is that the history of the people of Israel proves it abundantly.

Whenever they tried to live their lives without God they invariably got into trouble and were always defeated, but the moment they relied upon God and Him alone, they were blessed with prosperity and success. Read your Old Testament and you will find that that is its story. Read the lives of individuals in the Old Testament and you will find exactly the same thing. And it is not only true of the people of Israel and the saints of the Old Testament, it is true of the history of the whole world. My particular purpose is to apply it to ourselves at this present hour.

Is not what I have just been saying the simple truth about the state of the whole world? If you look at the world in general, or if you look at this country at this moment, must you not agree that never have the words and the teaching of the psalmist been so verified as they are at the present time. Has man in all his long history ever been quite so busy in trying to put himself and his world in order as he has been in this twentieth century; as he has been in the last hundred years? I am never tired of repeating it, for it seems to me to be the one thing modern man needs to be told. For a hundred years, by Acts of Parliament and by the multiplying of institutions and organizations, we have been trying to solve the problems of man; we have been trying to build this house. Never has man expended so much energy in trying to put his world in order. But what is the result? What has it come to? Is it not simple and literal truth to say, "Except the LORD build the house, they labour in vain that build it"? Man, during the last hundred years, has been confident he could banish war. He has said, "We only need to be educated, we only need to meet one another, we only need to mix more with one another. That is the way to get rid of war." So now then, humankind has his aeroplanes to land him in any country. We have never mixed so much with one another and yet we have had two major world wars within a quarter of a century. With all our education and our culture, with all our organizations and our efforts, look at the state of society in this country and in the world this morning. No, no, the conclusion of the psalmist is inexorable, it cannot be gainsaid. "Except the LORD build the house, they labour in vain that build it." This twentieth century has proved the truth of the Bible in a way no previous century has ever done. I cannot understand the man who does not believe the Bible today. In a sense I can understand the man who was in difficulty sixty years ago when the world seemed to be going on perfectly. They said the Bible was too pessimistic. But I cannot understand any intelligent man who has not been driven in this twentieth century to believe the Bible. Here is the message. Without God whatever man does, with all his cleverness, comes to nothing. We have had our two world wars and there is the atomic bomb hovering over our head and the possibility of another war. Who would like to prophesy what the next fifty years are going to produce? No, no, man has proved to himself and before the whole world that he is incapable of building this house which he so much longs for and for which he seeks.

But it is not only true of the world and the state. I am anxious to emphasize that **it is equally true of the church.** Let us be perfectly plain and blunt about this. Things are not well with the Christian church. What is the matter? I do not apologise for saying without any qualification that the answer and the explanation are still the same. For the last hundred years, and especially in this present century, in our folly we have been trying to build and to run the Christian church without God. We have forgotten the prayer meeting, we have forgotten the experience and the fellowship meeting, we have given up discussing the problems of the spiritual life. What have we relied upon? We have relied upon "a cultured ministry", men who can talk about philosophy, who seem to be experts on science, men who can display knowledge. Never has the ministry been so cultured and cultivated as it has been in this century, yet look at the state of the church. "Except the LORD build the house, they labour in vain that build it." You can rise up early and sit up late; you can multiply your organizations (and how we have multiplied them!) but it will avail nothing. The life of the church has never been so complicated as it is today. We have organizations for children, we have organizations for youth, we have organizations for middle age, we have special organizations, each with its secretaries and secretaries to the secretaries. We have massed up these high organiz- ations until the church has become a mammoth organization. But it is all in vain. Man cannot build the church, for "ye are the body of Christ and members in particular". Unless the Lord is amongst us and building us up, all our efforts and endeavours and striving will lead to nothing but failure and disappointment and to ultimate disaster. It is as true of the church as it has been true of the state and of the world in this century of ours.

Lastly, it is **equally true of the individual**. Without God and His blessing all is vain. My friends, let us face facts on this first Sunday of 1950. If you set out to make life for yourself without God, you may think for a while you are succeeding, but I assure you will never be truly happy. If you are in business or in a profession, I do not care what it is, there will always be somebody else; you will need your watchman. But quite apart from all that, every moment you live is a moment in which you are just moving, gradually, certainly, surely to the end of it all and a day will come when you will be on your death-bed. Then you will ask, "What have I done? The energy I have put into it, the money I have spent! I have worked and sweated and toiled." Then you ask, "What have I got? Where is my durable edifice?" And you will find yourself with nothing, empty-handed. It will all be in vain. "Except the LORD build the house, they labour in vain that build it."

But there is another side to this matter! Thank God! "He giveth to his beloved even in sleep." How foolish is this human self-reliance apart from God. If we but turn to God we shall experience blessing. Who are these people that He blesses? Who is this "beloved one" to whom He gives in sleep? He is simply the man who acknowledges God; he is the man or woman who starts out by saying before anything else, "God. I owe my life to God. It is God's world; I must ever walk as under the eye of God." He is the person who acknowledges God; he is someone who humbles himself before God, someone who submits himself to God, someone who accepts God's way. And God's way for us is that we should believe on His Son whom He sent into this world, our Lord and Saviour Jesus Christ. "You are looking for happiness and peace and joy," says God to us. "It is all there for you. I provided it for you in My Son." That was what Paul discovered and what he expressed so eloquently in that third chapter of the epistle to the Philippians. There was a man who tried to build his house and found at the end that it came to nothing. Now he counts all as refuse. What does he want? He wants this righteousness of God in Christ Jesus. There is everything I want, he says, and my desire is "to know him and the power of his resurrection and the fellowship of his suffering being made conformable unto his death". The only thing I want, he says in effect, is more of Him. He did everything for me before I realized it, while I was asleep in sin. Now He has given it to me and I have begun to enjoy and possess it. I thank God that that is the message with which we can start this second half of this troubled, perplexed twentieth century. The salvation of God is His free gift in Jesus Christ. He offers us peace and happiness and joy and every satisfaction. He offers us a sense of security in life and in death and to all eternity. He enables us to say with the apostle Paul, "I am persuaded that neither death nor life, nor angels, nor principalities, nor powers, nor things present, nor things to come, nor height, nor depth nor any other creature shall be able to separate us from the love of God which is in Christ Jesus our Lord." If you are in the arms of Jesus you need not appoint your watchman. You have security; you are safe whatever may come to you. You are one with God and nothing can ever separate you. That is the security that can defy any war, any atomic bomb; it can defy man at his worst and hell let loose. Without that, all is vain. With that, come what may we can say with confidence that we fear nothing because His promise is, "I will never leave you nor forsake you." "Except the LORD build the house, they labour in vain that build it." But "He giveth to His beloved in sleep."